DESKTOP DIGITAL
VIDEO PRODUCTION

ISBN 0-13-795600-2

90000

9 780137 956005

Prentice Hall IMSC Press Multimedia Series
Bing Sheu, *Series Editor*

▶ **Desktop Digital Video Production**
Frederic Jones

DESKTOP DIGITAL VIDEO PRODUCTION

Frederic Jones

Prentice Hall PTR
Upper Saddle River, NJ 07458
www.phptr.com

Library of Congress Cataloging-in-Publication Data

Jones, Frederic H. (Frederic Hicks), 1944–
    Desktop digital video production / Frederic Jones.
        p.   cm.
    Includes index.
    ISBN 0-13-795600-2 (pbk.)
        1. Video tapes--Editing--Data processing.   2. Video recordings--
    Production and direction--Data processing.   3. Motion pictures--
    Editing--Data Processing.   I. Title.
    TR899.J66   1998
    778.5'235'0285--dc21   98-15956
                                         CIP

Editorial/production supervision: *Patti Guerrieri*
Cover design director: *Jerry Votta*
Cover designer: *Anthony Gemmellaro*
Manufacturing manager: *Alan Fischer*
Acquisitions editor: *Bernard Goodwin*
Editorial assistant: *Diane Spina*
Marketing manager: *Kaylie Smith*

© 1999 by Prentice Hall PTR
Prentice-Hall, Inc.
A Simon & Schuster Company
Upper Saddle River, NJ 07458

Prentice Hall books are widely used by corporations and government agencies
for training, marketing, and resale.

The publisher offers discounts on this book when ordered in bulk quantities.
For more information, contact: Corporate Sales Department, Phone: 800-382-3419;
Fax: 201-236-7141; E-mail: corpsales@prenhall.com; or write: Prentice Hall PTR,
Corp. Sales Dept., One Lake Street, Upper Saddle River, NJ 07458.

Adobe, the Adobe logo, After Effects, Photoshop and Premiere are trademarks of Adobe Systems
Incorporated. Kinetix is a division of Autodesk, Inc. Autodesk, Kinetix and 3D Studio Max are registered trademarks, and Character Studio is a trademark of Autodesk, Inc. in the USA and/or other
countries. DeBabelizer is a registered trademark of Equilibrium. ActionArrow, WatchMe, SuperPal-
ette, and the Art of Automation are trademarks of Equilibrium. All other products or services mentioned in this book are the trademarks or service marks of their respective companies or
organizations.

Printed in the United States of America

10 9 8 7 6 5 4 3 2 1

ISBN 0-13-795600-2

Prentice-Hall International (UK) Limited, *London*
Prentice-Hall of Australia Pty. Limited, *Sydney*
Prentice-Hall Canada Inc., *Toronto*
Prentice-Hall Hispanoamericana, S.A., *Mexico*
Prentice-Hall of India Private Limited, *New Delhi*
Prentice-Hall of Japan, Inc., *Tokyo*
Simon & Schuster Asia Pte. Ltd., *Singapore*
Editora Prentice-Hall do Brasil, Ltda., *Rio de Janeiro*

To Judith, Molly, Mary, Mom and Dad

TABLE OF CONTENTS

About the Author

Frederic Jones, attended Ph.D. programs at Florida State University and International College in Intellectual History and Cognitive and Developmental Psychology with an emphasis on Epistemology, Knowledge Based Information Systems and the Creative Process. He also holds bachelors and masters degrees in Theatre Design. He has spent twenty five years in the business of scenic, lighting and industrial design and architecture, ten years of which were focused on electronic publishing and multi-media information systems. He is the Chairman of Jones & Jones Multimedia, LLC, a multimedia producer and publisher with a string of major consumer CD-ROM and game titles. His latest title is *Beyond Time* (Dreamcatcher Interactive, Virgin & NEC), a major CD-ROM- based graphic adventure game that includes over 90 minutes of digital video. Prior to founding Jones & Jones, he founded Ebook, Inc., a seminal and influential CD-ROM publishing company. He also founded Eclat, Inc. an electronic publishing company specializing in multimedia electronic catalogs. At Eclat he was the chief business and marketing strategist as well as the Chief Technology Officer and principal designer and architect of a score of electronic information products and related software systems. He has produced industrial, training, multimedia and music videos. He is also the author of hundreds of magazine articles and fifteen books, including the best selling *The AutoCAD Database Book* (Ventana Press, 150,000+ worldwide sales), *Architectural Lighting Design* (Crisp Publications, Inc.) and *Interior Architecture and Design* (William Kaufmann, Inc.). He has taught and lectured widely on these subjects, and is recognized internationally as an authority in the areas of electronic database management, publishing and design.

e-mail: fjones@JonesSquare.com

Jones & Jones Multimedia Website:
www.JonesSquare.com

Book Website: www.JonesSquare.com/videobook

ACKNOWLEDGEMENTS

I would like to acknowledge the invaluable contributions of Phil Dein, who contributed a great deal of work to the writing, research and editing of several sections of the book and Ken Atchison and Judith Jones who edited the book at various stages. I would also like to thank the following companies who contributed a great deal of technical information, equipment and software for review and other technical assistance:

Intel Corporation, which provided information on CODECs and AVI.

Apple Computer for information on CODECs and Quicktime.

Adobe Corp., which provided Premiere and After Effects and technical support.

Sonic Foundry for Sonic Forge and technical information on their product and sound editing.

Sonic Solutions for assistance and training on DVD production and permission to include most of Chapter 18.

Progressive Networks for technical assistance, access to RealVideo server software and substantial help on Chapter 17.

HT Electronics for technical assistance and help with several illustrations.

Miro Corp. for providing equipment and technical information on FireWire and the Miro DV30Plus.

Image North Technologies for access to Inscriber Titling Software.

ABOUT THE CD-ROM

We have included a number of software products referred to or covered in this book on an accompanying CD-ROM. They include utilities, demonstration versions of software packages and other information. We have also included an Adobe Acrobat hypertext version of the entire book. This may prove useful as a reference or help text when learning or using your audio or video editing software. It is identical to the print book with the added advantage that many of the illustrations, in particular the screen captures, are in color. This will enable you to have a much clearer view of the effects illustrated. Please don't distribute this file to others who haven't purchased the book. We depend on royalties from these efforts to make a living and to be able to write more books. Thanks!

The software on the CD-ROM are Windows versions. The MAC version, when available, and more recent versions of the demos are also often available from the publisher's websites. You can also visit our website, www.videosquare.com for links and updates. The individual requirements to run the demos are contained in the readme files in their respective directories. Generally, however, a Pentium with 16 MB or more and a good amount of disk drive space is required. Check the aboutcd.txt file on the root directory of the CD-ROM for the final table of contents and last minute details.

INTRODUCTION

The new world of video, from acquisition through editing to final distribution is a contest with only one contestant, *digital*. Analog video at every level is obsolete, except for processing legacy content. The only practical question with regard to the inevitable is the timeframe for the transition from analog to digital video.

The first area of video to fall into the digital domain was that of effects, followed quickly by the entire editing process. Since most editing is now done on digital workstations rather than on analog tape, it followed naturally that the capture of the video content should evolve to digital as well. Finally, video has begun to be distributed in digital form. Computer video, delivered on CD-ROM was the first medium to utilize digital video. This has been followed by the Internet and currently by Digital Versatile/Video Discs. Eventually, all broadcast television will be HDTV digital. At that point the transition will be complete, but a change of that magnitude will not take place overnight. It began over two decades ago, and by most predictions, will not be fully realized for at least another decade.

This transition is not without precedent. In the audio world the shift from analog to digital dominance was completed in less than a decade, but it was much less complicated than it will be for video. There is still a real place in the audio production process for analog recorders and signal processors. Sound, particularly music, can be aesthetically enhanced by the analog process. A warmth caused by inherent distortion is imparted to the audio signal that is pleasing to the listener. This is not true in the world of video production. Similar distortion to a video signal imparts a degradation of the signal and is universally considered to be unwanted.

The change from analog to digital video must be addressed by everyone involved in shooting, editing, and distributing video product. Anyone interested in video equipment must consider the rapid obsolescence of analog equipment, and the increased requirement of clients and broadcasters for digital masters. Every videographer, amateur, industrial and professional, must learn new tools and techniques in digital editing and effects, and must come to grips with computer, DVD, Internet and HDTV's demand for digital video.

There is another revolution in addition to the technological one, taking place in digital production. Today, a $100 software package, running on a PC, can do many of the things that only a $100,000 dedicated workstation could do ten years ago. It is now possible, with $25,000 worth of digital video equipment, to exceed the quality and sophistication of effects of those earlier system which cost ten times more. This magnitude of reduction in production costs, combined with CD-ROM, DVD and the Internet, has the potential to create an independent production and distribution community that is exciting, compelling, and significantly more available to many aspiring and creative film-makers and producers. In the audio world "project studios" have become the focus of both amateur and professional production and have taken over a significant proportion of music recording, most of which used to take place in expensive rented studios. The same reduction of scale in the video process is rapidly occurring. Alternate distribution channels and independent record companies have emerged. We can expect the same to occur in the video world. In fact, the digital video and audio capabilities of DVD will revolutionize both the audio and video industries.

I hope this primer in digital video production will help you transition from the analog world or, if you are a newcomer, enter this exciting field. It is designed to help existing video amateurs and professionals confronted with the need to move from analog to digital. It is also a guide for the new video professionals in multimedia and the Internet as they learn to master the essential tools and technologies of video acquisition and editing in the digital domain. I have created a sampler tray from the entire video process to familiarize you with the range of issues. This includes shooting, or acquisition of both video and audio, lighting, software for editing, effects, digital compression and distribution. I have given enough "hands on" information for this book to be considered a basic manual for each of these areas. This includes coverage of the leading editing and effects software packages such as Sonic Forge, Adobe Premiere, and AfterEffects. I have not, however, attempted to provide an in-depth manual on any one of these packages. You are referred to other books and sources as you move beyond your transitional or start-up period. Remember, this is an introduction to digital video, not an advanced course. Visit my digital video website for up-to-date information on software and equipment, as well as to discover additional information and resources. Many of the video clips, created, edited and captured in my studio during the production of this book, and which serve as illustrations, as well as color versions of many other illustrations are available on the website. I hope this book will help open the door for you to this exciting field and its opportunities, and that you will enjoy it as much as I do.

Chapter 1
Video Acquisition

Introduction

Live Video, digital or analog, becomes video with a camera. The skilled use of video cameras is necessary to create program content. This chapter covers the basics of camera equipment and the primary issues of video shooting.

Our primary interest here is the technical aspects of video acquisition. There is a world of information and experience beyond what we cover here and it is suggested that you read books and take classes on the art of composition, lighting, directing and all the other aesthetic aspects of video. Ultimately, however, it is experience and experiment that will make you a professional videographer.

Even if your intention is not to become a videographer yourself, and you intend to work with skilled videographers, it is still important for the producer, director and editor to be familiar with the essentials and limitations of video cameras. By having at least a basic knowledge you can better direct or specify the kind of shot you need for your project and, if necessary, can be aware of the limitations and special technical needs demanded by CD-ROM and Internet distribution.

Equipment

The basic parts of the camera kit are: the camera or camcorder, lens and tripod or other means of mounting the camera such as Steadycams for stabilizing the camera during hand held shooting. There are also many other elements such as battery packs, microphones and other accessories that attach to the camera input connections. We will consider lighting and microphones in subsequent chapters and suggest the a browse in books, video equipment catalogs and supplier showrooms that specialize in the art of videography for many other ideas and gadgets.

Camera

All cameras being manufactured today are equipped with *CCD* technology, standing for "charged coupled device." The light coming from the lens strikes the light-sensitive CCD chip, which is aligned in a grid pattern of pixels, each of which creates part of the picture. The image is digitized as an optical image and converted or "encoded" into an electrical signal. Once an analog signal has been encoded by the camera, it can be broadcast, recorded to videotape, or recorded digitally onto a disk storage device.

Tip: Never point the camera directly into the sun or a bright light. Although, technically, this should not damage the chip, it is possible to desensitize it over time. When this happens, the damage appears as a small, white pixel on the screen. There is no way to remedy this, short of replacing the chip.

The more chips the camera has, the better, and the bigger the chips are, also the better. Low-end cameras have one chip to do all the work. Higher-end cameras have three chips for better color separation and detail. Low-end cameras have one-half inch chips, higher-end cameras have two-thirds inch chips. Bigger chips produce greater resolution. Actually, the gap between the low and high ends is smaller now than ever before. The electronics have become so precise and miniaturized that most cameras are able to take decent pictures.

Figure 1.1 Analog Camera

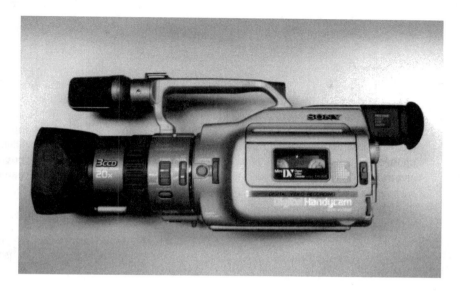

Figure 1.2 Digital Camera

Lens

The first link in the acquisition stage is the camera, and the very first "eye" on your artfully composed, beautifully lit image, is the camera lens. Remember, the quality of your final desk top product production can be no better than the quality of the raw material with which it begins.

While a great many words are spent in touting the technical specifications of various cameras on the market, far too little attention is given to how much difference a good lens can make. It is not uncommon, on high-end professional cameras, to spend 40% of the total cost on just the lens. A good piece of "glass" will precisely focus in good and poor lighting conditions and respond quickly during camera movements. When lenses are purchased separately from the camera, beware of the low-end lenses and their limitations. A too-small field of view, for example, will have the camera operator trying to back up for many shots. And when backing up enough is not possible, there will be extra cost for a wide angle lens or adapter.

Zoom

Zoom controls are also a part of the lens apparatus. These allow the operator to zoom out "wide" and see the entire scene, or zoom in "tight" to a small portion of the scene. Shots can be composed quickly without the need to physically move the camera. The zoom itself can be used (sparingly) as an effect, so check to see how smoothly the zoom controls work. Low-end cameras generally zoom at a constant speed and are either on or off.

Better lenses have variable speed control, allowing for smoother starts and stops or changing speeds during the zoom.

Filters

Lenses are also normally built to hold *filters*, pieces of glass which have been tinted, treated, or designed to hold some material between the subject and the camera. The effects may be subtle or stunning, and are more "organic" than post-production effects added later. Effects include polarization, diffusion, fog, star pattern, and gradated colors. At the very least, always use a skylight or UV filter. They are important for two reasons. They cut down on ultra violet light entering the camera, creating a bluish tinge in shadows. They also act as inexpensive protection for that very expensive lens, keeping dust, dirt, and fingerprints off of the main glass.

When cleaning a lens, never blow on it. That just gets more dirt stuck down past the seals. Always use proper lens cleaning fluid and paper. And never, ever use alcohol, which can remove the special coatings on many lenses.

White Balance

A variety of features and controls can add greatly to the cost of a camera, but ultimately make a significant difference in convenience of operation and quality of results. One example is *white balance*. This is the way the operator tells the camera what type of light it is shooting in and, therefore, how it should render colors.

The human eye and brain are able to adjust and compensate in a variety of lighting conditions. Cameras just see what is there, in a objective electronic fashion. Tungsten light is yellow while fluorescent light is blue. Daylight is blue during high noon on a cold November day, but orange at sunset in August. We refer to such different lights as being "cool" or "warm," these comparative terms having reference to variations in the light's actual Kelvin temperature.

The ability to control the white balance produces colors which seem natural and avoids the bluish look of much home video. Even consumer camcorders come with simple controls, often just "indoor" or "outdoor". High end cameras allow you to set the white balance for a particular lighting set-up. Focusing on a piece of white paper, the camera "reads" the Kelvin temperature and adjusts accordingly.

It is also possible, in this fashion, to "cheat" the camera into a different color scale for effect. For instance, by white balancing to a "cool" light source and then using tungsten lighting during the shoot, the video will be "warm"-rich in yellows and oranges. These settings can also be stored for future use in similar circumstances.

Camera Features

A basic feature of a good camera is that of *bars and tone*. A camera with this feature has a built-in color bar and 1 kHz tone generator. This is an electronic device that generates a 1kHz sound and a video image of color bars and writes them to the beginning of you video tape. The resulting signal is usually recorded for one minute at the beginning of a new tape, and the bars and tone provide a standard reference for proper setup during playback.

Another camera feature is *shutter control*, which allows the shooting of fast moving objects. For example, a car speeding by, or a waterfall would appear as blurs to the camera. With shutter control it is possible to see them clearly, even to the spokes of the wheels and individual drops of water. When it is necessary to shoot from a computer monitor, a *scan control* function allows "tuning in" or synchronizing the camera shutter to the same scan rate as the monitor, reducing the picture "roll" to a minimum.

Many cameras have additional controls and filters for dealing with fluorescent lighting, chroma balance, backlit subjects, and underlit subjects. All these features add to the flexibility and professional quality of the video.

Recording Formats

The advent of both professional and high end consumer or "prosumer" grade digital cameras made it possible to go directly to digital images in the camera. Further, it is possible to connect a camera directly to a computer and immediately begin editing the recorded images. Such systems are very important and we will cover them in a separate chapter, but their cost and limited recording capabilities make them prohibitive in many circumstances. The majority of existing equipment and most of the new equipment available are still analog cameras. We will deal with this mainstream equipment in this chapter.

When working in desktop video, you need to bring the cleanest, highest resolution picture possible into the computer. The computer cannot add detail. In fact, the reverse is true, and it looses detail. Therefore the quality and inherent characteristics of the recording format and tape are important considerations. VHS and 8mm are analog formats intended for consumer use, while S-VHS and Hi-8 are "prosumer" formats. Three-quarter-inch, one-inch, and Betacam are professional and broadcast analog formats. The Digital formats for "prosumer" and consumer cameras are: DVC, DVCAM from Sony and DVC Pro from Panasonic. The technical specification for both Sony and Panasonic are interchangeable but the physical tape formats are not. Both conform to the IEEE-1394 or Firewire transfer protocol so getting the signal into and out of digital edit suites is not a problem. These are compressed formats which rate between Hi-8 and Betacam in quality but allow a minimum of generational loss when transferred to and from digital edit suites. Digital formats such as D1, D2, D3 and D5 are used in high-end post production facilities, often for computer graphics and compositing.

A look at most spec sheets might lead one to believe that there is little difference between one recording format and another. However, there are two measurements which need to be studied carefully. *Bandwidth* measures how much information is available, often expressed in lines of horizontal resolution. But *signal to noise ratio* is the more important number to notice because it measures the quality of that information. Be aware that this ratio is logarithmic, not linear. A decrease of 3db in the S/N ratio means a 50% gain in the amount of "noise" in the picture.

DSR-80

Figure 1.3 DVCam digital record deck

Tape

For both digital and analog camcorders, tape is still the medium for acquisition and archiving. Videotape is similar to audio tape, consisting of a Mylar or other plastic film backing covered with a thin layer of either oxide or metal particles mixed with the binding agent. During the recording process, these coatings store the video and audio information in magnetized patterns which then can be read for playback.

The type of tape used and the way it is recorded can significantly effect performance. All analog tape is susceptible to *drop-out*, which occurs when the oxide or metal particles flake off the tape because of stretching or repeated wear. This is seen in the form of sporadic white horizontal streaks wherever there is a loss of picture information. Oxide tape is more likely to have drop-out than metal tape. Metal tape also provides higher quality video images, since it enhances recording sensitivity and increases the amount of recorded information.

A digital tape is inherently better than an analog tape because, technically, it cannot have dropout. The tape is recording the digital bits and bytes. The information is either there or it is not. This means that in an all-digital environment it should be possible to copy the tape any number of times without loss of quality from one generation to another. This ability to be copied without any loss over multiple generations of copies is one of the major advantages of digital recording over analog.

Signal Formats

There are three format types in which video signals are commonly encoded for recording and playback: *composite*, *S-video*, and *component*.

Composite means that all the video information is encoded in a single channel. Unfortunately, in a composite signal strong colors, such as red, tend to bleed. In the United States and Japan the standard composite format adopted by the television and video industries is known as the *NTSC* signal (for National Television Standards Committee).

S-video, also referred to as Y/C video, separates the luminance information from the chroma information. They are recorded separately and then put back together during playback.

Component video separates the video signal into three distinct elements—luminance, red minus luminance, and blue minus luminance—which are recorded in separate channels. Component video produces the best picture quality.

Keep in mind the capabilities of your capture board. Many dollars may be spent on a component system for very little gain if the capture card only accepts composite video input. You can't go up in quality. Along the video pipeline, image quality cannot be added, only maintained or lost. It is best to record at the highest level possible since a capture card could be upgraded at a future time, but the master footage is never going to improve. It is generally cheaper in the long run to shoot it right the first time! Here's how today's major recording formats stack up, ranked by S/N ratio.

Format	A/D	Sig	Tape	Hres	S/N
3/4"	A	C	OX	280	45
VHS	A	C	OX	240	46
8mm	A	C	OX	260	46
1"	A	C	OX	300	46
3/4" SP	A	C	MP	340	47
S-VHS	A	Y/C	OX	400	47
Hi-8	A	Y/C	OX	400	47
DVC	D	1394	500	54	
DVCAM	D	1394	500	54	
DVCPRO	D	1394	500	54	
Betacam	A	R-	OX	300	48
Betacam SP	A	R-	MP	340	51
Digital Betacam	D	R-	MP	450	54
D-2	D	R-	MP	450	54
D-3	D	R-	MP	450	54
D-1	D	R-	MP	460	56

A/D = Analog or Digital; Sig = Signal type: C= Composite, Y/C = S-video, R- = Component; Tape = Tape type: OX = Oxide, MP= Metal Particle; Hres = horizontal resolution; S/N = luminance signal-to-noise ratio, average

Signal Standards

There are several internationally recognized signal standards for broadcast video and video equipment. These standards allow equipment manufacturers, broadcasters and consumers to be assured of compatibility between the creation and distribution chain of broadcast and home video. In short it makes it possible for every TV set in North America to receive and display any TV signal broadcast in North America. The same applies to VCRs and video tapes. There are, unfortunately, more than one incompatible standard in various parts of the world. France and several Eastern European countries use the SECAM standard, England and most of Europe use the PAL and North America and Japan use NTSC. Other countries use one or the other of the standards.

Frame

As with other moving pictures, videotape records images as a series of still shots or frames. When played consecutively in rapid succession, the appearance is of continuous motion. A video frame is made up of two fields of scanned lines. Field 1 has the video data for all the odd-numbered scan lines, Field 2 the even-numbered scan lines. When interlaced, the two fields make up the entire image.

NTSC Standard

NTSC is the acronym for National Television Standards Committee. In 1953 this committee, composed of industry representatives, formulated a standard for the television broadcasting of color signals. Characteristics of this standard include 525 scanned lines with timing originally synchronized to the 60 Hz standard for AC power in North America, producing 30 frames per second (later redefined to 29.92 frames per second). The NTSC standard remains prevalent in North America, Japan, and many South American countries that have 60 Hz AC power.

PAL and SECAM

In Europe and much of the rest of the world the standard signal is PAL with 625 scanned lines and 25 frames per second. SECAM is a similar standard primarily utilized in France and a few other French influenced countries. The PAL standard is becoming the standard in Europe as a whole as a result of the European Economic Community (EEC). Most digital video edit systems can edit and output NTSC, PAL and SECAM if properly set. Analog monitors, recorders and cameras cannot be switched.

Control Track

A *control track* is recorded on each videotape for timing and synchronization purposes. VHS, S-VHS, 8mm, and Hi-8 cameras record timing pulses on this track to control the speed of the videotape upon playback. This timing has no relationship to the frame accuracy. Control-track timing pulses approximate frame locations by indexing a resettable counter, a process somewhat analogous to counting sprocket holes in motion picture film. This is a system for labeling video sequences and frames.

On many video capture boards it is important to have a smooth, continuous control track laid down on the tape. If there is a break in this track, the capture application may lose its reference and abort the capture. Breaks in the control track often are the result of repeated starting and stopping of the tape during recording. One strategy for ensuring a proper control track is to record at least five seconds of extra video before and after each shot. This way, even if there is a break in the control track, the capture application will have time to lock in and get all of the desired material.

Timecode

In the early 1970's a more precise labeling system was developed called *timecode*. Timecode specifically identifies video frames and audio signals by time. In the recorded timecode, each frame of visual and aural material has a unique identifier, or address. A timecode consists of four 2-digit numbers which represent hours, minutes, seconds and frames on a 24-hour clock. In this way, frame-accurate, repeatable edits are possible.

Timecode also has use in desktop video applications for controlling a video deck during capture, record, and batch digitizing operations. The most common standard in use was developed by SMPTE (Society of Motion Picture Engineers) and is commonly referred to as SMPTE timecode.

Drop Frame Timecode

Generally we consider NTSC timecode to run at 30 frames per second. In reality, for a number of technical reasons, it actually runs at 29.97 frames per second. *Drop-frame timecode* runs accurately at the 29.97 fps standard: one hour of indicated drop-frame timecode plays for exactly one hour. This is accomplished by skipping frame numbers 00 and 01 at the beginning of each minute, except at the ten minute mark. No actual video frames are dropped—only the respective frame numbers are omitted from the timecode sequence.

Non-Drop Frame Timecode

Drop-frame timecode is used when the exact length of a program is important, particularly for programs exceeding one minute in duration. Since non-drop-frame timecode is not time-accurate, one hour of indicated non-drop-frame timecode actually requires one hour and 3.6 seconds of play time. Non-drop-frame is typically used only for short programs of a few minutes duration, where the time difference is negligible, or in programs where the exact length is not important.

Composition

There is something special about a well composed picture, whether it be video, a photograph, or painting! The same rules of balance apply when shooting for desktop video, but there are a few extra technical considerations, especially if your final output is for CD-ROM or compressed video of any type. (More about compressed video later.)

Keep in mind that all video is eventually going to be represented, not by scan lines, but by pixels-square blocks of video. The bigger the blocks, the less detail can be recorded. It's the difference between looking at an original photograph with 2000 dots per square inch, and a newspaper photograph at 600 dpi. The computer does not distinguish between what is important in the image and what is not. Here's what can be done to help your computer.

Close-ups

Shoot tight. Get close to your subjects. Head shots do really well. Any extraneous action around your subject will only take away precious detail from what you really want to show. Just as in traditional video, do not expect to do major zoom-ins later during post-production. All you would accomplish is to increase the size of pixels. The image will be blocky and will not look sharp in comparison to the rest of the video.

Underscan vs. Overscan

There is a difference between what the camera sees and the image you see on a normal TV screen. If you have ever tried adjusting the vertical or horizontal holds on an old TV set, you may have noticed that there is video past the edge of the screen. This is called *overscan*. It is a built-in margin of error so that, even when a set is not perfectly adjusted, there will still be something on the screen. The white frame in the camera eyepiece shows what can reasonably be expected to appear on a normal TV screen. Some monitors have a switch allowing the viewer to go back and forth between overscan and underscan modes.

If your desktop video will eventually be reconverted to a videotape format, shoot in the normal way. But if it is only for use on a computer, remember that there is no overscan in the computer environment. The computer sees it all, every line and every edge. You may be able to shoot tighter than normal and maximize your screen space with what is important. Conversely, be extra careful about things which are not supposed to be seen, such as boom microphones and lighting equipment, or they will show up in the shot.

Tape Skewing

Depending upon equipment, it may be necessary to work around some shortcomings of the smaller tape formats. One such shortcoming is *skewing*, which appears as if the tape were rippling and tearing at either the top or bottom of the screen. In traditional video this is normally not a problem because it occurs in the overscan area. The other potential problem is a small horizontal green line appearing at the bottom of Hi-8 video playback as a result of signal weakness.

If you have either of these problems, there is probably not much you can do mechanically with your recorder to eliminate them. However, there are ways to crop the video to remove these artifacts, either as it is being digitized or during editing.

Movement

Digital video is sensitive to movements of the camera and subject, especially when used for CD-ROM or computer playback. When one frame after another looks pretty much like the frame preceding it, digitized video can look great. But when things start changing rapidly, sometimes the computer is not able to keep up and quality is sacrificed. This does not mean your video is limited to lock down shots of talking heads, but it does mean that you must be conscious of the effects of camera and subject motion. Use them sparingly, but use them effectively.

Camera Moves

Tripod

As morphing has been "The Effect" of the 90's, the use of the Steadicam may be considered "The Effect" of the 80's. Cameras moved high, swung low, crawled through the bushes and over the car; cinéma vérité was rampant.

If there is no good reason for walking or flying the camera, put it on a tripod! If you are trying to hand-hold long static shots, the little wiggles that do not seem so bad on video will look terrible on a computer screen. It is foolish not to invest in a good, sturdy tripod—something that will not fall over in the first substantial breeze. Ten percent of the camera's cost is not unreasonable for a good tripod. Think of it as cheap insurance.

Features to look for in a good tripod include fluid head control, smoothness of pans and tilts, and ease of set-up. Fluid heads will give smoother performance than friction heads and last much longer. Friction heads work just as you would suppose-the more you tighten down, the more friction there is, and the more pressure it takes to pan. They are also subject to abuse. When the same pressure points are constantly worn down, an unevenness is created which makes pans appear less than smooth as well as uneven in speed.

Also, do not neglect safety features. Does the tripod lock securely? Can you let go of the camera without fear? Are there "stops" to keep the camera from tilting more than 45 degrees at a time? Although ideally a camera should never be left alone, at some point, for some emergency, it may become necessary to leave it for a moment. Safety features can prevent disaster.

Pans & Zooms

Beware of long or fast pans and zooms. These stress many video compression schemes and can deteriorate otherwise good looking video. The zoom has long been called the "poor man's dolly", and it is also appropriate to call it the "lazy man's edit." Use two short shots instead on one long zoom (a recommendation which applies to traditional video as well).

Subject Movement

When the subject is a passing train, a galloping quarterback, or small child, there are few choices in controlling the motion. This would be an opportunity to experiment with a camera shutter so that everything does not blur. Otherwise, have move only what needs to move in the shot. Videotaping the company president standing in front of a big oak tree may sound like a great idea. If it is windy, however, the fluttering of the leaves will be motion that will distract the viewer, and will also take away vital detail from your primary subject. Generally, it is not the big move that causes trouble, but rather the host of little background movements that deteriorate quality the most.

Sets & Costumes

Such traditional video "thorns" as deep reds and thin vertical stripes are not problems to the same degree in desktop video. But since desktop video is still a hybrid technology—part computer, part video-the old rules generally apply, especially if the moving image is going to become videotape once again.

Color

Most quality video equipment has no problem making a good black and white picture. The addition of color, however, complicates everything. Remember to limit the use of highly saturated colors, especially the reds. It is better to have defined highlights of color instead of big washes of color covering the set. Digitized video tends to accentuate strong colors and lessen weak ones. All the fine tuning you did when balancing a shot may be lost if the one strong color on the set is magnified out of proportion. When in doubt, soften the colors; they can always be punched up a bit during editing.

Detail and Texture

Thin vertical stripes, polka dots, psychedelic patterns—all these things tend to make your screen dance and shimmer (it's called *moireing*). They also play havoc with desktop video. Like excessive movement, excessive detail and texture take away valuable compression capacity from the important parts of a picture, such as eyes and faces. Small items easily become swallowed up in a complex scene. To make sure that something is seen clearly and distinctly, get close and shoot tight.

Conclusion

This is just a taste of the subject. There are several sources of additional information listed in the Bibliography.

Bibliography

McQuillin, Lon. *The Video Production Guide*. Indianapolis: Howard W. Sams, 1983.

Millerson, Gerald. *Basic TV Staging*. 2d ed. London and Boston: Focal Press, 1982.

Millerson, Gerald. *Video Camera Tecniques*. London and Boston: Focal Press, 1983.

Rosen, Frederic W. *Shooting Video*. Boston: Focal Press, 1983.

Zettl, Herbert. *Television Production Handbook*. 5th ed. Belmont, CA: Wadsworth, 1992.

Chapter 2

Lighting

Introduction

Lighting is a highly developed craft and deserves more attention than can be given in this book. There are fine books and resources available on the subject of lighting for video production, but the best way to learn is through experience—moving the lights around yourself, making adjustments and seeing the results. I studied lighting design in college and discovered subsequently that all the theory came to life during the hundreds of hours spent in student and professional productions aiming the lighting equipment and seeing first hand what the results were. Ultimately the art of lighting depends on carefully looking at the results of your efforts, keeping the succesful techniques in your repertoire and avoiding the failures. A way to speed up the learning process is to work with an expert, if you can. You will learn the tips and tricks which will get results faster. For our purposes, here is a brief background on lighting concepts and techniques before we focus on issues of particular interest for desktop video.

Basic Lighting Principles

It can be helpful to think about lighting as having nothing to do with light, but rather to be about controlling shadows: where the shadows are and what type of shadows they are. Most people will pay little notice to lighting that adequately illuminates its subject, but will notice when the subject is underlit or if the lighting casts distracting shadows.

Direct/Indirect

There are two basic types of light in the natural world, sunlight and overcast. All artificial lighting sources and styles mimic these two. Sunlight is direct light. It comes from a single, identifiable source and creates clearly defined shadows. It tends to be harsher than indirect light, but more effectively shows texture and shape.

Overcast light is indirect light. It is diffused or reflected, coming from a larger source and casting softer shadows. It is flatter, more two-dimensional, but can smooth out a scene and make it more pleasing to the eye. Rarely will lighting set-ups be of only one type. Usually, a combination of set-ups is necessary, an interplay of types, to give the best effect.

Quality of Light

When we speak of the quality of the light, we generally mean the color of the light, most often measured by degrees Kelvin. Both a candle and an airplane searchlight are examples of direct light sources, but candlelight has much more orange and yellow in it. It appears warmer and, in fact, has a lower Kelvin rating. The searchlight appears whiter, brighter, and has a correspondingly higher Kelvin rating.

Even the same light source can have different color output depending upon various circumstances. For example, sunlight is warmer near sunrise and sunset than it is at high noon. (Remember, when we say a light is cool or warm, we are not referring to its temperature on a thermometer, but to the color of the light as it appears to the eye.) You can create the same kind of color changes in artificial light sources.

Candle Flame	**1,900 Kelvin**
100 Watt Light Bulb	**1,850 Kelvin**
Quartz Studio Light	**3,200 Kelvin**
Warm White Fluorescent	**4,500 Kelvin**
Average Daylight	**5,500 Kelvin**
Overcast Sky	**7,500 Kelvin**
Clear Northern Skylight	**25,000 Kelvin**

Figure 2.1 Kelvin Ratings

Lighting Instruments

Light sources can be distinguished by the type of light they create (direct/indirect) as well as the quality or color of the light. Examples of direct lighting instruments are open-faced lights with exposed bulbs, *fresnels* which have a focusing lens, and *ellipsoidals*, a compound lens spotlight, for spotlight effects. Indirect lighting sources include *scoops*, *softboxes*, lensless reflectors with diffuser filters, and direct light that is bounced off or diffused through something else. Warm lighting includes low-angle sunlight as well as tungsten bulb fixtures, which are the most common types of lighting instruments. Cool, whiter lights include direct, overhead sunlight, as well as fluorescent and special halogen lights known as HMIs.

Elipsiodal Reflector Spotlights

Fresnel Spotlights

Parabolic Reflectors

Strip Lights

Cyclorama Lighting

Figure 2.2 Lighting Instruments

Wattage

Portable lighting equipment ranges from 250 to 1000 watts, studio lights from 1000 to 10,000 watts. A good all-purpose starter kit might contain three 1000 watt lights, with stands and assorted grip equipment. Important: know the load your electrical circuits can handle. If you are limited by 15 amp household breakers, do not attempt to put more than one 1000 watt light into any single circuit. Although this may mean running extension cords, it is better than tripping breakers every few minutes.

Techniques

Three-Point Lighting

Three-point lighting is the most basic lighting set-up. Three-point lighting does not guarantee good lighting, and neither does it have to mean boring lighting. It is a point of departure. The following description will introduce many terms and concepts that can be applied to any set-up. When in doubt, go with the tried and true three-point set-up, and experiment from there.

The three-point set-up is a model for lighting an object or person in a way that provides definition and perspective. There are no dark spots; light is provided from all angles. Because the light is not even, there are differences which make the picture interesting and create a sense of depth and modeling. The following are generalizations from which any number of perfectly acceptable variations can be made.

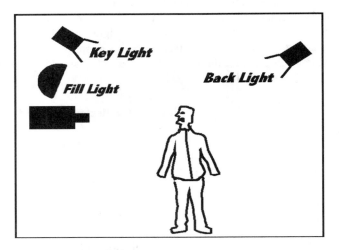

Figure 2.3 Three-Point Lighting

First and most important is the *key light*, which is the major source of light on the subject. It is often a direct light source, within 45% of the subject-to-camera axis, and slightly higher than the camera.

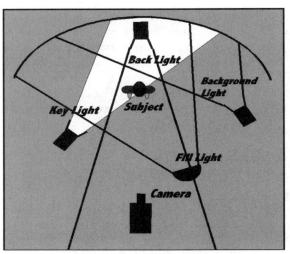

Figure 2.4 Key light

The *fill light* does what its name implies, fills in what the key light does not cover. It is placed on the opposite side of the camera from the key light. Usually it is a diffused source with 40% to 60% the intensity of the key light.

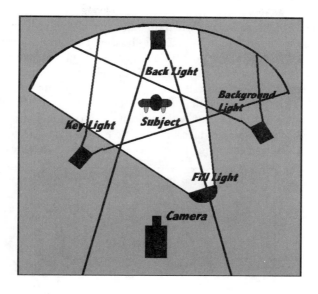

Figure 2.5 Fill light

The *back light* separates the subject from the background. It is a direct light source placed high and behind the subject. Make sure this light is tightly focused so that stray light does not reach the camera, causing lens flares. Other names and variations on the back light are *separation light*, *rim light*, *hair light*, and *kicker*.

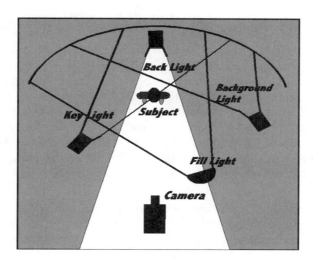

Figure 2.6 Back light

Bounce Lighting

Bounce lighting is a generic term that has multiple meanings within the field. For our purposes, bounce lighting refers to the use of diffused sources as the primary means of lighting a subject. The purpose of this type of lighting is to create a setting of soft shadows, with an even fall-off. Fall-off is the reduction of light or shadow receding from the center of the light source. It can be great for highly reflective items like watches and cars, and is particularly well suited for compressed video. The illuminated scene appears smoother, less blocky and without drastic contrasts between light and dark areas. Generally this technique produces a lower light level than direct light and therefore requires cameras sensitive enough to produce good results under those conditions.

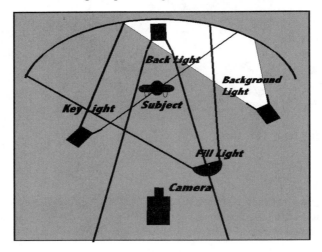

Figure 2.6 Bounce Lighting

The key light may come from a direct source bounced into a reflective umbrella, a large white board (foamcore works especially well), or even a wall. The key may also come from a light expanded to a wide beam and directed through a large piece of diffusion material (technically a direct source). Diffusion material is available in different styles and thickness, with corresponding differences in how much light is filtered and in what pattern it is spread. To work effectively, this technique requires a considerable distance between the light and the diffusion material. The distance between the source and the diffusion material can range from two or three feet in the case of an umbrella mounted on a light to several yards for a hand held white board.

There are special self-contained lighting devices called *softboxes* which house light, reflector, and diffusion material all in a single unit. The idea is to make the light source as large and uniform as possible. The bigger the reflective source and the closer that source is to the subject, the softer the light will be. Under these conditions, the fill light may be nothing more than white foamcore catching some of the spill from the key light and bouncing it back onto the subject. This method will work only if the fill board is fairly close to the subject and is best suited for close-ups with little movement.

By using a combination of large bounce lights it is possible to light an entire set with a minimum of harsh shadows and total freedom of movement for actors and camera alike.

Base Light

When lighting a scene, remember that there is a minimum amount of light required to properly expose your shot. This is called the *base light*. The amount of base light required depends to a degree upon the camera and lens you are using. Less expensive cameras tend to be less sensitive in low light conditions, or simply produce a very grainy picture in low light. There are two related concepts which you need to understand, *f-stop* and *depth of field*.

F-Stop

F-stop is a measure of how much light is being let through the lens. The actual aperture that controls this is called the *iris*. Most lenses have marked settings ranging from f 1.8 to f 16. For example, an iris setting of f 8 means that the lens is open to 1/8th of its total diameter. The smaller the f number, the more light is passed through to the lens.

Depth-of-Field

Depth-of-field is the range of distance within which objects in a scene are in focus. One of the factors in determining depth-of-field is the iris setting. Low f-stop numbers produce a short depth-of-field and larger f-stop numbers a greater depth-of-field. Another factor is *focal length*. When a lens is zoomed to a wider field of view, objects within the scene will be in focus over a greater depth of field. Similarly, when it is necessary to zoom-in on a scene (narrow the field of view), especially in low light where the iris must be set to a low f-stop value, it will be more difficult to achieve good focus.

Setting the Iris

A rough technique for determining when there is enough light on the set is to set the camera to *auto exposure* or *auto iris*. In this mode the camera adjusts the iris automatically. Auto exposure tracks only the brightest part of the scene, so zoom out wide and pan around a bit to find an "average" reading. The iris setting should read about f 5.6 or higher. An f-stop reading lower than f 3.2 means that the lens is almost totally open, taking in as much light as it can. This may result in a dark picture, loss of fine detail, colors not having rich saturation, and a reduced depth of field.

Signal Noise

For desktop video, it is important to have cleanly shot video. Most capture boards accept only composite or S-video signals, which inherently contain a certain amount of signal degradation. Given the compression and other electronic processing your video has to endure on its way through the computer to the hard drive, invariably there is some loss of video signal strength, even though slight.

Most capture software provides controls for adjusting the brightness and color saturation of the incoming video. Use these sparingly, since they tend to increase the amount of noise in the signal as well. (It's like setting up a microphone in the middle of a train station. If you turn up the microphone in order to hear the person speaking into it, you also turn up the level of all the background clamor.)

Having a good master tape in hand should give great confidence about the quality of the final product. Be sure every scene is adequately lit, which does not mean that every item in every shot has to have light on it. It does mean that every item which needs to be recognized must have adequate illumination.

Tip: While shooting, once you have found the "optimal" exposure setting for a shot, open up the lens another one-half *f*-stop. This will give your video a little extra boost without washing out the picture, and can always be adjusted down later if necessary.

Contrast Ratio

Contrast ratio is the difference in brightness between any selected objects in a shot. A sharply lit white ball in front of a black background would have a high contrast ratio; a gray ball in front of a gray background, a low contrast ratio.

In desktop video, because of the compression schemes used, there tends to be a smaller range of *gray scale* available. Gray scale, refers to the number of incremental steps available between pure black to pure white. On photographic film, the steps of the scale may be nearly imperceptible and therefore a transition through the scale is smooth and continuous. In video, fewer steps are available and transitions are somewhat more conspicuous. In compressed video, the differences between steps are even more obvious. For example a beautiful sunset—the bright yellow of the sun on the horizon melting into deep oranges, then reds, blues, purples and finally the blacks of a starry night—all may appear as eight discrete bands in a final compressed video for CD-ROM.

To sum it up, in video bright things tend to stay bright, dark things tend to stay dark. In between, contrast ratios need to be monitored carefully, depending on the type of video output intended. What looks wonderful on tape may prove overly drab or dramatic in its finished form.

Tip: If in doubt, remember that some contrast can be added later as an effect, but it is much harder to go the other way and smooth out a scene.

Color

Everything we have said about lighting up to this point has been in the context of brightness, that is, the black and white picture. The addition of color has always been tougher for traditional video, but for desktop video it is actually easier in many ways.

Hue

Hue is what we commonly think of as an actual color: red, blue, green, yellow, etc. Red has been the traditional bane of analog video production. It is the hardest color to reproduce and control. For a variety of technical reasons, video red tends to "bleed" and "bloom", which is to say, spread beyond its borders. Not only is the rose red, but also some of the space around the rose. For this reason, reds are carefully used or avoided altogether in video production.

Within its digital environment, desktop video can handle most hues without such problems. The problem comes when the digital images are converted to and reproduced as analog images. Therefore, you need to be careful when recording your master footage to tape and when your final output is to analog tape. If you like reds, component recording is strongly recommended. And remember that your computer may be able to handle all hues, but not your TV set. Some editing programs allow you to select and output TV-friendly colors.

Saturation

Saturation is a measure of quantity, how much color is present in a given hue and how far removed from a neutral gray. This is what makes the difference between pink and red. Heavily saturated colors tend to bloom in analog video, just as reds do. Digital desktop video generally handles saturated colors well, but again consideration must be given to the final output format. Is your finished product coming back out to tape for distribution? Then be careful with saturated colors.

Because of the lower gray scale range, compressed video does not have smooth *fall-off*. This means that a colored highlight of subtle shading could appear as no more than a solid block of a single color-another reason for cautious use of heavily saturated colors. Limited adjustments can be made during the editing process.

Conclusion

This introduction to lighting for video is only a taste of the subject. It is, however, one of the essential skills necessary to creating quality video for any purpose. I would suggest that both experimentation and additional reading is warranted. Listed below are a number of excellent texts and handbooks that are recommended.

Bibliography

Carlson, Verne, and Sylvia Carlson. *Professional Lighting Handbook*. Boston: Focal Press: 1985.

LeTorneau, Tom. *Lighting Techniques for Video Production: The Art of Casting Shadows*. White Plains, NY: Knowledge Industry Publications, 1986.

Millerson, Gerald. *The Techniques of Lighting for Television and Motion Pictures*. 2d ed. Boston: Focal Press, 1982.

Millerson, Gerald. *TV Lighting Methods*. 2d ed. Boston: Focal Press, 1982.

Sweet, Harvey. *Handbook of Scenery, Properties and Lighting*. Vol. 1. Scenery and Props. Boston: Allyn & Bacon, 1990.

Chapter 3
Chroma-Key

Introduction

It's the special effect that allows space ships to fly in front of planets, fantastic creatures to appear in your living room, and the weatherman to stand in front of a moving weather map. It's chroma-key, one of the most versatile techniques in video production. In this chapter we tell you how it works, and what's new in the way of software technologies that make it more accessible than ever before.

Creating the Virtual Set

We are fast approaching a time when it will be unnecessary to go on location for a shoot. Through the magic of digital compositing we can put actors anywhere, any time in the universe, all from the comfortable surroundings of a sound stage. Well, perhaps this is overstated a bit, but the creative freedoms of chroma-keying does open up the possibility of setting video in places where one could not possibly afford to take cast and crew, and even (through 3-D rendering) places that exist only in imagination.

This technique is essential for integration of actors and video action into video games. Compositing is also the principle technique underlying the new trend in live television's move toward virtual sets. The highest profile utilization of this technique, however, is in action movie special effects. It would be impossible to realize a *Jurassic Park* or any of the science fiction blockbusters without blue screen compositing.

Figure 3.1 Chroma-Key

Chroma Key and Compositing

Chroma-key shooting and compositing is the technique of replacing a specific color with another "keyed" source. You have seen it many times: the TV weather personality points out cold fronts and jet streams while standing in front of maps and satellite pictures which move and change on cue behind him. In reality he is just standing in front of a big blue board while, in the TV control room, all of the video that is blue is replaced by images from another source, in this case by maps and moving images. Or the actor appears to be flying through a primeval forest on a jet-propelled scooter, when actually he is on a stationary scooter in front of a blue screen, and the forest is composited in later. By this method it is possible to key out any color, so the "blue" screen may actually be some other color. Blue and green are the most commonly used colors for this purpose because they are the hues most distant from the skin tones.

It is most important to carefully prepare the set-up and lighting for a chroma-key shoot. The smoother and more consistent the background color appears to the camera, the easier it will be to key out and replace. Allow plenty of time for testing so as to avoid long frustrating sessions in front of a computer trying to fix problems which could have been prevented in the first place.

Techniques

Paper

A chroma-key set does not need to be large or even fill the entire screen. It only needs to be slightly larger than the object you are keying. All editing software allows for some kind of cropping, so only a small area needs to be treated. For many small objects and tight shots with little movement, a paper background works very well. It is inexpensive, it is mobile, and it can be set up anywhere.

Paper made specifically for chroma-key shooting is available through photography and video supply stores in rolls eight to ten feet wide and in blue or green. The most important thing to remember about working with paper is that it must be kept smooth. Wrinkles cause shadows and reflection of light which make the surface appear to be blotchy and irregular in color. The paper is thick and can be heavy when used to cover a large area. Secure it in several places using tape, clamps, and sandbags. One good thing about paper is that if an area is damaged or gets dirty, you can simply unroll more and start fresh.

Paint

Paint is used for chroma-keying large areas such as studio walls and props. Many production houses have permanent blue-screen stages. Others have a generic studio area which can be painted any color needed. For doing any wide, head-to-toe type shooting, get a stage equipped with a curved walled *cyc* (cyclorama), basically a stage without corners. About two feet from where the wall meets the floor a curved ramp is placed, making a seamless transition from wall to floor. It is a major benefit to have a perfectly smooth background, with a minimal number of lines and shadows.

Paint can also be used to make riggings disappear in the final picture, as well as some of the scenery itself. For example, perhaps an actor is to appear sitting on a park bench in the final composite. It is possible to place him on a blue box in front of a blue wall, and in the final composite replace everything but the actor, sitting in a natural position. The park bench would be added later. As with paper, special paint with a high level of saturation is available, made just for this purpose. Often it needs to be applied in two coats for even coverage.

Tip: Watch for scuff marks on large sets. Have everybody stepping onto the set work in socks until you're ready to roll tape. Keep a small can of paint around for touch-ups in between takes.

Basic Lighting Strategies

When lighting for chroma-key work it is necessary to light the background first and the subject matter second. The goal is an evenly lit set with as few variations in brightness as possible. Shadows are such a nuisance that they are generally avoided, sometimes difficult to achieve without the use of high-end lighting equipment with fine tuning controls. In any case, it is important to have the positions of everybody and every thing carefully planned.

It is also best to work with large, diffused light sources so that such shadows as cannot be avoided are very soft and have an even fall-off. Use as few lights as necessary. A few large wattage lights are easier to control than several small light sources. White reflector boards and diffusion *scrims* in front of lights are often used. These spread the light over a larger area, softening the impact.

The lighting on the subject matter, however need not be totally flat. Once the basic lighting for the set has been established, additional, carefully placed lights can still be used to produce dramatic colors and shadows. But be very aware of the effect that any light you add may have on the background. If the shot is a close-up and all the shadows fall out of screen range, there is no problem. If it is a wide, head to toe shot, you will need to be much more careful.

Reflection

Reflection of the chroma background back onto the subject is a major lighting problem. Fair skin, blond hair, and light colored clothing are common victims. This reflection, no matter how faint, is going to make it harder to get a clean edge around the subject when it is time to make the composite. The easiest prevention is to place the subject as far from the backdrop as possible. The greater the distance the reflected light must travel, the weaker it will be. If the shot is a close-up and the floor is painted blue, cover the floor temporarily.

It is also important to have a strong backlight or *kicker* coming from behind and to the side of the subject. A backlight focuses on the head and shoulders of an actor; a kicker emphasizes the arms and body. Both help to create a bright edge around the subject and make separation from the background easier. The effect can be further enhanced by using a colored gel on the backlight. A backlight will lighten the background chroma reflecting upon the subject, and the gel will also help change its hue. It need not be dramatic—a light amber or straw gel is usually all that is needed.

Working with large diffused light sources and subjects pulled away from the background requires a large working area. Allow plenty of stage area and work space, twice as much as for a normal shoot.

Using Ultimatte Technology

Benefits

Ultimatte is a brand name for a system of high-end chroma-keying. It is a total system, from special Ultimatte paint, to Ultimatte equipment run by trained Ultimatte operators. Ultimatte searches for something more specific than just a range of color to key out. It looks also for a specific hue and saturation. Unlike other systems, most blue and green clothing are acceptable in an Ultimatte shoot.

There are various configurations, depending on cost and the amount of fine control needed. Most of these systems are so expensive that they are rented out, with operators, at a daily rate. The production budget may increase by thousands of dollars per day, but the results are spectacular and can save hours of compositing time.

How it works

The product of an Ultimatte shoot is two master tapes. The first is the tape of the video just as it looks on the set, subject matter against a blue or green background. The second tape is exactly the same video, except it is black and white-black for the background, white for the subject. This becomes a matte with which to totally black out everything not to be seen in the original. Frame for frame, the two tapes are combined. White areas define the subject matter, black the areas to be replaced by new background material. The key is the combined master video, the mat and the video that replaces the mat in the new images.

A big benefit is that the key has been cut cleanly at the time of shooting. It is either on or off, and there are no surprises. Because the key can be clearly seen while on the set, it is easy to tweak the lighting and take care of problems before they ever go to tape.

There are new Ultimatte technologies arriving that are software, rather than hardware based. This means that you could shoot in a conventional blue-screen manner and then create the proper mattes once the video has been digitized into a computer system. This will be a huge money saver and allow for more detailed control over setting the keys.

Shooting

Movement

Remember the old rear screen projection effects used in movies of an earlier era? A shot over the dashboard of two people sitting in a car; outside the windows the passing scene bumps up and down while the car interior is perfectly still.

Today we have sophisticated equipment and software which makes it possible for the motion of the camera to match perfectly whatever happens in the background. With such systems a computer can record every zoom, tilt, pan, rack, dolly and focus change. This information can be fed directly to 3-D modeling programs and rendered as finished background. When the camera zooms, the background zooms; when the camera pans, the background pans, all in perfect sync. When composited, there is a seamless integration of the two, truly creating a virtual set.

Props

Chroma-key can be finicky at times and difficult to control. Beware of items that have tiny parts and lots of fine detail. For example, the long, thin antennae of a TV set in a wide shot may look fine on camera and on tape. But try keying it and see what happens! The antennae disappears altogether or reveals only rounded tips floating in mid-air.

This problem is compounded by motion, either of the camera or of the object. A close-up of a pencil may key well, but when it is waved in the air it disappears. When there is a possibility that important edge detail will be lost, either remove the offending pieces or make them thicker.

Costume

Know the limits of your keying capabilities. Sometimes faded blue jeans will work satisfactorily on a blue chroma-key set, but deep greens will not. That is because the software or system you are using may be weighted more towards saturation levels than towards exact hue. Try to use clothing materials thick enough not to transmit light.. A loosely woven shirt or dress may allow light from the background to penetrate, making it difficult to key correctly. Avoid using costumes or accessory pieces that are anywhere near the color of the chroma key. They may drop out—an unnerving effect!

Make-up and Hair

Suppose the script calls for shooting on a blue chroma-key set, but the star actress is wearing blue eye shadow and, even worse, has baby blue eyes. What to do? Either stay away from close-ups or redo the makeup and consider tinted contact lenses.

A close look at a performer's hair may reveal just how successful a chroma-key shoot has been. To avoid problems, minimize wispy strands, which may just disappear anyway, and keep hair close to the head, using hair spray as necessary. Beware of hairdos which are so inflated as to allow light to spill through, making a clean key nearly impossible.

Conclusion

This chapter only touches on the subtleties of the art of blue screen effects. The only teacher that will make you expert is experience. The best possible way to learn is to work with and observe experts in action, taking every opportunity to take notes. Then engage in careful experimentation. This technique and technology is extremely important to the future of digital video and cinema production.

Bibliography

Ultimatte Overview and Manuals. Ultimatte Corporation. Chatsworth, CA, 1997.

Chapter 4
Sound

Introduction

Video is really about "active" information or information in motion. This means animation/video and sound/music. Sound is THE element that gives a fourth dimension to information presentation. It is also the easiest element to create and add to any presentation or title. Wave files recorded by the user and within the scope of anyone who has used a computer and tape recorder and MIDI musical tracks created by the computer, are no more difficult to integrate than still photographs or blocks of copied text. This chapter addresses both the principles of sound recording and its application to video production.

Principles of Sound

Sound is the most basic means of human communication. It is the information "bottom line". Psychologists assert that deafness is a much more profound disability than blindness. This is not to argue against visual images, but to recognize the fundamental nature of auditory perception and the important part it plays in human communication.

In video and film, dialog, sound effects, ambient sound or foley and music are just as important as the video portion of the content. In many cases the sound track is much more important. In news, training, and documentary productions, for example, the audio track carries the majority of the information being imparted, with the visual components functioning primarily to illustrate the words.

Multimodal communication is the most effective form of communication. A classic demonstration of this is to turn off the sound accompanying any television program, and merely watch the pictures, and then turn on the sound and turn off picture. The amount of information present in the audio track is almost complete, versus the fraction obtained from the picture alone. A significant example of this is the effectiveness of San Francisco public radio station KQED's broadcast of the McNeil/Lehrer Report with virtually no degradation of content delivery as compared to the televised version with both sound and picture.

Sound Elements in Video

There are three primary elements of sound in multimedia production: dialog, sound effects and music. These elements are sometimes fully automated and sometimes they are mixed with live elements. An example of this is the use of recorded or computer generated music to enhance a live lecturer or presenter.

Dialog, Voice Over, and Lip Synch

There are several types of voice sound recording. Dialog, of course, refers to the words spoken by actors or presenters while they are visible on film. Voice-over is narration, where the voice of the narrator is heard while the viewer looks at pictures or text. Lip synch is the technique where actors or singers move their lips as if singing or speaking, but the actual sound of their voices is pre-recorded and played back, accompanying their "performance." Another type of lip synch is ADR or Automatic dialog replacement. This is the technique whereby actors re-record the dialog of a scene already filmed. The actor must perfectly match the new dialog with the lip movements already on film. This is done because it is generally impossible to record perfect sound during the actual filming of a scene. Where sound or voice-over are combined with text, as in a multimedia presentation, sound reinforces the content, even thrusts the information onto the reader who is inattentive or lacking in focus. Audio information combined with visual information provides information redundancy, one of the important elements in effective communication. It allows the user, in a multi-tasking environment, to attend to multiple elements simultaneously.

Sound Effects

Sound effects add depth and texture to a visual experience, increasing the effect of realism in a title or presentation. The snapped twig, the creaking door, footsteps on a dark street—these sound effects create a sense of suspense or menace in a way that often exceeds the impact of visual images. In the days of radio, sound effects were the primary tools of creating atmosphere, and how extremely well they worked! No one who listened to *Fibber McGee and Molly* will ever forget the "closet," the continuing "sound" gag of McGee forgetting and opening the door of the junk closet. The resulting cacophony of crashes and smashes as the unidentifiable avalanche of junk came cascading out of the closet was good for a laugh week in and week out. The sounds, plus the imagination of the viewer was more than enough. The animal sounds that enliven the *National Geographic Mammals* CD-ROM is a good example of the use of sound effects in an interactive presentation. Sound effects are an absolutely essential element in the sound designer's bag of tricks.

Music

Music increases psychological, sociological, emotional and cognitive effectiveness with an audience. The best example of this occurs within the first ten seconds of a movie. The viewer is able to predict the mood and to form content expectation based on the first few bars of the overture. Every composer who scores film and television knows how to create emotional effects and enhance the effectiveness of the experience for the audience. There have been several experiments by psychologists and sociologists pointing to a direct relationship between the music and the emotional effect of the film on the audience. One of these experiments is a study by Julian Thayer and Robert Levenson, of the effects of music on audience responses to a stressful film. This experiment supports the efficacy of musical scores for manipulating the mood of film audiences. There are also a number of experiments that suggest that cognitive ability, information transfer and understanding can also be enhanced by music. I have included a number of these studies on an accompanying bibliography.

Our experience of music in communication and psychological research supports the idea that it enhances both aesthetic experience and overall effectiveness of communication. There can be no doubt that skilled communicators in both business and the arts can improve their presentations with the use of high quality music. Music engages the listener in a way that visual information cannot. It allows the listener to think and integrate the information directly in the "rational" thinking process, a cognitive process that is an analog to speech and sound vs. images. In fact, words and sounds can create powerful images.

Sound Quality

We equate quality and "production value" with the seriousness and value of the message conveyed. There is a continuum between noise on one end, and high-quality sound on the other. People have the psychological ability in this era of audio information intrusion to "tune out" unpleasant or course sounds and noise, and to "come to attention" when presented with quality sound. The better the quality, the more likely the message will carry to the listener.

Communication Through Sound

Sound is the most basic means of human communication. In video, it is as important as the visual images in effectively presenting the message. Sound in a multimedia production must be carefully presented, designed to enhance and clarify, never to draw attention away from the main message.

Mood

As mentioned above, the mood of a multimedia project can be controlled by the intentional use of music. In Thayer's and Levenson's experiment on stress it was discovered that stress was increased by the use of diminished seventh chords, and that major seventh cords decreased the stress reactions. Researchers have no idea why this relationship between music and emotion exists.

Quality

As in any production, the quality of the elements of a presentation reflect the quality of the content. High quality text, graphics and music are all subject to this perception. The quality of any of the elements also increases the effectiveness of the information transfer to the audience. Misspelled words distract from the message, and low quality sound or poorly realized music also interfere with their purpose.

Timing, Pace, and Emphasis

Music in particular can set the pace of any production. Majestic fanfares create excitement and pride. They direct attention and focus on the information coming up, much as bullets do in text. Fast paced background music is often used at airports and subways during rush hour to subliminally "hurry along" the crowds. Richard Burris-Meyer, one of the pioneers in the use of industrial music, experimented with the use of music in the pacing of work in offices and factories.

Properties of Sound

A thorough knowledge of the properties of sound will form a basis for understanding how to record, edit and process the sound in digital form. This is because digital processing and editing manipulates directly the basic elements of the physical sound, amplitude and frequency.

The Sound Wave Form

Sound is physically created and transmitted as a wave within a medium. The primary medium of useable sound is air with secondary mediums being more solid objects in the environment. A vibration within a particular range of frequencies is set in motion by any number of causes including human vocal chords, musical instruments, etc. These vibrations are transmitted to the environment through a complex game of "tag" wherein the sound radiated away from the source and sets in motion one molecule after the next of whatever it encounters until the energy is absorbed and the molecules finally come to rest. The sound, when it set the medium in motion, creates waves that have a variety of strengths or amplitudes and vibrate at various rates or frequencies.

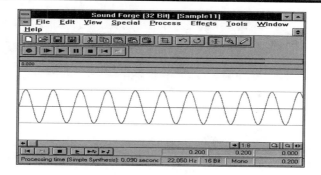

Figure 4.1 Illustration of Wave Forms

Amplitude

The amount of power that is present in a wave form, or in common terms, its volume level or loudness is expressed as amplitude. In a practical sense the amplitude is important at a number of levels in video production. The original amplitude of the sound must be loud enough to be distinguished by a microphone from the background or ambient noise. The amplitude must also be within an acceptable range for the limits of the transducer or microphone that is converting it to an electrical signal that can be recorded by the video or audio recorder. The electrical signal produced by the microphone must also be within the proper limitations of the recording and processing equipment. Care must be taken in the proper selection and placement of microphones and the use of either manual or automatic volume controls that process the electrical signal created by the microphones. The human ear can perceive and compensate for an extremely wide range of sound levels. Electronic equipment can't as easily and readily compensate for as diverse a range. It is important that the sound engineer or recordist pay close attention to sound levels, both low level and high levels during recording and editing to achieve proper signal to noise levels on the low side and prevent distortion on the high side.

Firure 4.2 is a chart giving several examples of typical levels for familiar sounds. The intensity of sound level is expressed in volume units or decibels (dB.) This is displayed on audio equipment panels as VU or Volume Unit meters. The higher decibel values are the louder sounds.

Typical Sound Levels in Decibels

Jet aircraft taking off	125 db
Niagara Falls	95 db
Heavy traffic	85 db
Normal conversation	60 db
Quite whisper	20 db
Outdoor silence	10 db

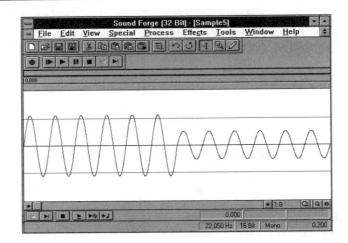

Figure 4.2 Illustration of Amplitude.
The First clip is at a higher amplitude than the second.

Frequency

The pitch, also called the frequency, means how high or low the sound is. Frequency is measured in Hertz (HZ). The audible frequency of sound is 20 to 20,000 hertz. This is the outside range of human hearing. Men with normal hearing can hear 16 to 16,000 hertz and women can generally hear higher pitches as well.

20 hertz is a very low frequency sound, such as the lowest notes of a pipe organ or the rumble of heavy machinery. In musical terms these sounds are *bass* tones. High pitched sounds include the chirping of birds or the highest notes on a violin. In musical terms these are *treble* tones.

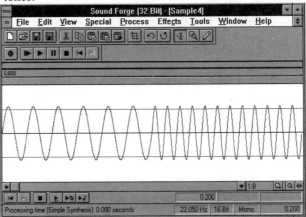

Figure 4.3 Illustration of Frequency.
The first clip is at a frequency of 60 HZ and the second is at 120 HZ.

Timbre

Sound wave forms rarely consist of a single, pure frequency. They usually consist of several primary frequencies and multiple overtones. This property of sound is referred to as *timbre*. Timbre is the characteristic of sound that is its "personality." The timbre of a violin is significantly different from the human voice even when they are producing a tone of the same pitch or frequency, and the same volume or amplitude. This characteristic allows us to identify sounds

The timbre of a wave form consists of primary tones and secondary tones called over-tones or harmonics. A harmonic is a tone that is a multiple of the primary tone (2x, 4x, etc.). A primary tone can have one or many harmonics. The presence of particular harmonics may not be immediately evident to the hearer but the perceived quality of the tone is effected by their presence. The presence and quality of harmonics in a wave form is effected by the frequency response of the microphone recording it, the electronic system storing or transmitting it. This effect is brought to mind by remembering the difference between listening to music over the telephone and over FM radio. The difference is entirely the result of many of the harmonics being lost due to the reduced bandwidth of the telephone versus FM. A telephone effectively transmits frequencies in a very narrow band while an FM radio station transmits frequencies over a much wider spectrum. There are many factors that effect timbre in similar ways. For example: bandwidth limitations of microphones, recording media, digital and analog processing equipment, quality of speaker systems and many more. We will consider these issues and how to make intelligent choices about sound quality when possible.

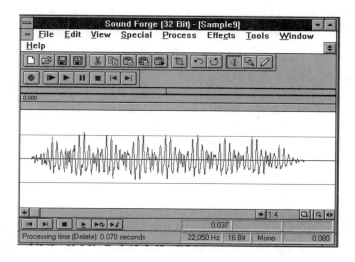

Figure 4.4 Illustration of Timbre

Amplitude/Frequency Relationship

Humans do not perceive all frequencies of sound equally. The ear is more highly attuned to the frequencies of speech. As a consequence, sound that is both higher and lower than these optimal frequencies need a boost, electronically, to compensate. Similarly, microphones don't translate all frequencies with exact fidelity. This is true of every stage of the sound processing. Both human and electronic idiosyncrasies are compensated for in a variety of ways. There are standard electronic circuits that balance recorded music for the normal human ear. An example of this kind of control is the Loudness control on an amplifier. This boosts the bass response as the volume is reduced to fool the ear into hearing the same volume relationships as at higher volume. There are also a variety of electronic tools, both analog and digital, that allow the sound person or engineer to customize the control of the signal. They range from the simple bass and treble controls on amplifiers and mixers to sophisticated software algorithms that process digital wave forms in an infinite variety of ways.

Shaping the Wave Form

The circuits mentioned above can be applied to a signal as it comes from the microphone or preamplifier and before it is recorded, or it can be applied to the wave forms that have been recorded in the post-production and/or editing process.

Bass and Treble

These simple analog or digital controls on amplifiers and mixer simply boost or attenuate the volume of the bass or treble frequencies of the signal or wave form. They offer only a coarse control because they act on a wide band of frequencies.

Graphic Equalizer

A graphic equalizer is just a series of bass and treble controls that act on much narrower bands of frequency. Instead of two controls for the entire bandwidth there may be 20 or 30 controls. Both analog and digital graphic equalizers are very useful to compensate for uneven or unexpected room acoustics both during recording and playback. They can also composite for idiosyncrasies of microphones.

Presence

The presence control boosts the mid-range frequencies from 6,000 to 10,000 HZ and attenuates tones under 100 HZ. This is used to emphasize speech and vocals.

Loudness

The Loudness control on an amplifier boosts the bass response as the volume is reduced to fool the ear into hearing or perceiving the same volume relationships as at higher volume. This control is generally found on amplifiers and consumer equipment and rarely found on professional equipment. This differs from the Amplitude control that does not compensate for the perceived difference in the sound level.

Amplitude Control

Simply put, amplitude is controlled by the Volume control on the amplifier or mixer. There is no compensation for the perceived sound level as in the Loudness control. The Volume control only works on the actual electrical signals strength or level.

Compressors

A compressor raises the average loudness of a signal. It increases the amplitude of low level sounds and decreases the amplitude of louder sounds. This means the average loudness is held closer to zero decibels or dB. The apparent loudness of the signal is increased.

Limiters

Limiters reduce and control the loud end of the dynamic range of the signal. This prevents loud noises from over driving electronic circuits and creating distortion in the signal.

AGC Circuits

Automatic Gain Control circuits are similar to limiters and compressors, in that they regulate the dynamic range of a signal. They automatically detect the low amplitude signals and increase their signal's strength. They also detect high level signals and lower their signal's strength. They are common on video production equipment but are rarely found in studio equipment. In the studio an engineer is usually monitoring the signal and manually adjusting it. There are significant problems with time response of AGC controls when a new signal, such as a burst of dialog suddenly interrupts a nearly silent period. AGC circuits take a brief time to engage and can clip the initial portion of the dialog. They can also increase the ambient noise of a scene by raising the volume of the signal and picking up unwanted noise. It is usually best, if given a choice, to manually regulate volume.

Expanders

Expanders can restore the dynamic range of signals that have been severely compressed and restore a more realistic quality. This process can also reduce the apparent noise, hum and hiss in a signal.

Meters

The Volume Unit (VU) is an important tool used to manage the proper recording level of a signal. These indicators or meters are sometime called peak level indicators or loudness indicators. The use of these indicators can help a recordist prevent weak recordings that contain excessive noise, and very loud signals that may create distortion in the recording system and the subsequent recorded signal. Either type of meter servers work well, with each having some advantages and disadvantages. It is also helpful to use headphones to monitor the quality and continuity of signals as they are being recorded. It is important for the recordist to pay attention to the indicators and adjust the volume or level controls accordingly. It is also important to listen to the sound that is being recorded during the process of recording. If you are working in a studio with an isolated sound room you can listen on speakers if you are in the field or in a studio with the cameras and artists you must use headphones. The best quality headphones you can afford should be selected.

Equipment

Microphones

Microphones are one of the most important video production tools and the primary way sound, dialog and music are recorded on the sound track. In case you are wondering how it could be done without a microphone, remember that MIDI or computer synthesizers don't require microphones.

Both the selection and use of microphones are essential skills. There are a variety of microphone types, both in the type of transducer or the manner in which they convert sound waves to electrical impulses and the directional characteristics of the individual microphones. We shall cover both aspects.

Types of Microphone Transducers

The transducer within the microphone is made up of the mechanical, electrical and electronic components that are involved in the process of converting sound energy to electrical energy in a form analogous to the original sound wave. The transducer types that dominate the current microphone market are: Ribbon, Dynamic and Condenser. Other types include: carbon and crystal. These types either are obsolete or have not been utilized in the manufacture of general purpose audio production microphones.

Ribbon

The ribbon microphone languished for many years but has recently enjoyed a resurgence of use. They have smooth and silky response and are used for vocals and voice over recording. They are very sensitive to air movement and sibilance and can be easily damaged in use. They are restricted to studio applications.

Dynamic

The dynamic or moving coil microphone is the most widely used in video production and audio field production. It produces a very high quality signal, particularly for voice and field recording , and is very rugged. The frequency response in a professional quality microphone is very good and it has good sensitivity. It comes in a wide variety of directional formats and physical packages. One of its strengths besides it rugged nature and sound quality is that it is the most inexpensive of the professional microphone types. The dynamic mic requires no power supply.

Condenser

The condenser microphone shows up in many forms, from high quality studio microphones that are very expensive, to extremely inexpensive electret microphones for amateur use. In general, professional condenser microphones are designed as omnidirectional microphones and are less rugged in field usage than dynamic mics. The frequency response and sensitivity makes them very important for musical recording in the studio as well as a variety of general purpose uses. Professional quality condenser microphones tend to be much more expensive than dynamic microphones. Condenser mics require a power source, either internal or external batteries or power supplies or in many cases they can be powered by the Phantom Power supplied by professional mixer boards and consoles directly over the microphone input cable.

Directional Quality of Microphones

Omnidirectional

The omnidirectional or non-directional microphone picks up sound equally well from all directions, in an ideal theoretical sense. In practice, they pick up sound from most directions. The omnidirectional microphone is useful for recording live musical performances, groups of actors or singers, ambient sound and similar applications. Video field recording situations seldom call for omnidirectional mics.

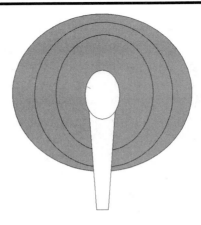

Figure 4.5 Omnidirectional Microphone

Bi-directional

Bi-directional mics are equally sensitive in two directions, along opposite poles. They are occasionally used in radio interviews with the subject and interviewer speaking into opposite sides of the mic, though two separate microphones are usually chosen for maximum control over volume.

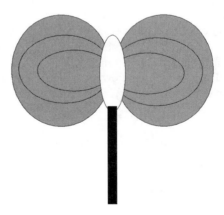

Figure 4.6 Bi-directional Microphone

Unidirectional

The unidirectional microphone is sensitive in only one direction. There are a variety of pickup patterns that range from wide angle cardiod to extremely narrow angle parabolic reflector microphones.

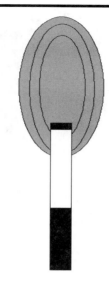

Figure 4.7 Unidirectional Microphone

Cardiod

The cardiod microphone, by far the most common type, has a sensitivity pattern that is heart shaped, hence the name "cardiod" or heart like.

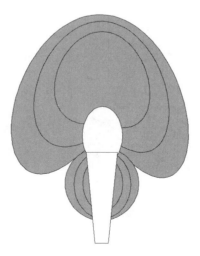

Figure 4.8 Cardiod Microphone

Supercardiod

A supercardiod is a cardiod with a more narrow angle of sensitivity. One version is the shotgun mic used on a boom or fishpole for tight recording of on-camera voice.

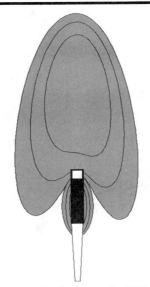

Figure 4.9 Supercardiod Microphone

Hypercardiod and Ultradirectional

Hypercardiod mics have an even more narrow sensitivity pattern. They are more specialized and also more difficult to use.

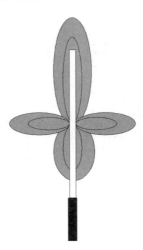

Figure 4.10 Hypercardiod and Ultradirectional Microphones

Parabolic

The parabolic is not technically a cardiod pattern mic but rather a microphone with the receptor mounted at the focal point of a parabolic reflector. This kind of microphone can retrieve sound from hundreds of yards away with high sensitivity. It is used in sports, in nature video and for applications requiring the acquisition of distant sounds.

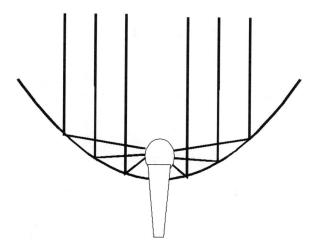

Figure 4.11 Parabolic Microphone

Proximity Effects

Supercardiod and Parabolic and other mics used at a distance suffer from a low frequency loss due to the loss of sound energy through the air, rather than limitations of the transducer or microphone itself. This generally doesn't effect voice recording but musical performances require post-production equalization to restore a more realistic sound balance. Microphones placed too close to the source of the sound can have exaggerated bass response. This is called proximity effect and is more difficult to adjust in post-production. The best remedy is proper mic placement. It is always best to audition the sound using headphones before shooting.

Impedance

A microphone's impedance must be properly matched to the equipment connected to it. This assures the integrity of the signal. Microphones are designed with two impedance types, High and Low. Impedance is expressed as Ohms. High impedance microphones are rated over 10,000 ohms and low impudence microphones are rated between 50 and 600 ohms. Some microphones have switches that can be set for either high or low impedance. If you are in doubt about the rating, it should be marked on the microphone or can be looked up in the technical documentation. Professional equipment is usually equipped with low impudence inputs, or with both high and low inputs. Amateur equipment is generally only high impedance.

Low impedance equipment is usually equipped with XLR microphone connectors, while high impedance equipment is usually equipped with ¼ inch or smaller phone jacks. Transformers that match impudence are inexpensive and should be installed between the microphone and the equipment if there is no matching option on either the mic or the gear.

Interference Problems

Electrical interference can be a problem if cables are not in good shape or ground wires are not intact. During shooting, you should be aware of electrical hums and pops and RF or radio interference, and remedy it on the spot. It is virtually impossible to remove in post production.

Microphone Application and Placement

The selection and placement of microphones is an important skill. A microphone placed too close to a source can pick up breath noise and distortion. A microphone placed too far from the source can pick up ambient sound or reflected sound that makes it hard to distinguish the intended focus of the recording from the background noise. The type of microphone selected can work for or against your intentions. The use of an omnidirectional microphone in a street-side interview can pick up too much street noise and drown out the subject, where a directional or cardioid microphone might eliminate this problem.

Room Acoustics

Often the acoustics of a room can negatively effect sound quality. The most common problem is that of sound reflections from hard surfaces. The use of absorptive materials such as packing blankets can reduce this problem. It can also be reduced by moving mics closer to the subjects. This is a greater problem with fixed placement of microphones.

Personal Mics

Personal microphones are those that are attached to a subject. They are generally either clipped on to the subject's clothing (clip-on microphone), or suspended on a cord around the subject's neck (lavaliere or lav microphone). These can be either wired or wireless and are primary tools for the videographer. Personal mics are designed to be placed within about a foot of the subject's mouth. Pay attention to jewelry or clothing that might brush against the mic or produce sound that might be picked up by the mic. As always, listen to the signal to check the results of the placement.

Hand-held Mics

Hand held microphones are used by on-camera talent, particularly in high noise situations. They are also good for news-style interviews. Be sure to select a cardiod pickup pattern. Hold the mic at about a 30 degree angle and at a distance of 8 to 16 inches to eliminate sibilance or popping from the subject's breath. The use of windscreens over the mic pickup area can reduce this problem, as well as noise from wind. Some mics have proximity effects settings that may be used to eliminate this problem.

PZ Mics

PZ or Pressure Zone microphones are omnidirectional and rely on reflected sound. They are placed on table tops or stage floors, and serve as pickups for group interviews or musical recording. They can provide a high quality signal, but their omnidirectional pickup pattern means that they are not selective in the sound they acquire.

Headset Mics

Microphones mounted on headsets are useful for sports and off camera narration. Be sure that the microphone is designed for video production and is equipped with wind screens.

Contact Mics

These microphones are usually placed on musical instruments and are seldom used in video production.

Wireless Mics

Wireless microphones may have self-contained transmitters or may require the use of a standard microphone plugged into an independent transmitter. They can be used on any type of microphone desired. The receivers may be mounted on a camera or attached to a mixer or console. Their range is generally from 50 to 500 feet depending on conditions. Interference from commercial radio and television transmitters can be a problem. The selection of transmitter frequency and their use can be complex. Be sure to follow the manufacturer's instructions in use.

Off-Camera Mics

Up to this point we have been discussing the use of on-camera microphones. The use of off-camera microphones is of equal importance. They eliminate the problem of seeing the microphone in dramatic works and allow more unrestricted movement of the talent. Their use can also reduce the number of microphones required when there are multiple sub-jects.

Hanging and Slung Mics

Microphones can be hung on cords suspended over the set or recording area. Be sure that mics suspended from lighting equipment or grids don't pick up electrical interference or filament hum. The fixed placement is good for static productions but can cost time if they need much movement or adjustment.

Fishpoles

Microphone "fishpoles," or microphones attached to the end of metal or Fiberglas rods and held by an operator, are an excellent solution to recording a single subject or interview. This method requires the operator to use headphones in order to assure that the pickup and direction of the microphone is correct. This is also a standard news gathering technique where proximity to the subject is difficult.

Booms

Booms serve the same purpose as fishpoles but are mounted on either fixed or moveable stands. Small one can be managed by a single operator while larger ones require two.

Hidden Mics

Microphones may be incorporated into set elements. This is useful in news sets or similar fixed productions. Be sure to turn down unused mics to eliminate phase cancellation of signals.

Line Mics

Line mics are hypercardiod or shotgun mics that are usually contained in a rubber or fur windscreen. They are usually condenser mics that are very sensitive. They are commonly used on location for recording at distances up to 20 feet. They are normally mounted on fishpoles. Line mics can also be mounted on cameras but this is a less than optimal compromise used only when crews are short-handed.

Stereo

People hear in stereo. The stereo sound track allows a sound designer to simulate space, realistic ambiance and to have more control of the emphasis in complex soundscapes. Surround Sound utilizes four or five tracks with speaker locations in front and behind the listener/viewer. It is common on broadcasdt, laser and DVD disc programming. Most of the stereo and surround effect is created in post-production.

Stereo and Surround Sound are the normal ways to create sound tracks for commercial distribution. Mics and mic placement are important for ambient sound, musical recording and subject location. When stereo or surround is critical to a production it is usually created in post production. If location or studio production requires special attention to stereo sound, it is best to simultaneously record it, with a time code track, to a multitrack recorder. When clips of small groups or individuals are being recorded standard mic placement is usually all that is needed. Most sound effects and foley are added in post-production.

Stereo Mics

For simple stereo recording, quality stereo microphones can be used. They give little separation, however. This is particularly useful in creating a stereo signal from an interview.

X-Y Micing Technique

Two microphones can be arranged across each other at a 45 degree angle, forming an "X". This is a very good arrangement when stereo recording is necessary. It does not translate as well into mono.

Maintaining Stereo Perspective

A literally realistic audio perspective is impossible in video and film because of shifting camera angles and quick edits. The objective is to create an aesthetically pleasing one. One of the quickest ways to annoy your viewer is to include too much movement in the sound. It should be rich and complex but not confusing.

Using Pan Pots

Using pan pots on a mixing console to position the apparent location of voices and sound elements is the primary technique for assembling a stereo sound track. A pan pot simultaneously mixes a portion of a mono signal into the right and left track on the recording. The control, indicated as left or right on the panel, can range from all of the signal to left to all of the signal to right or any degree in between. This gives the illusion of changing the apparent location of the sound source in the stereo mix. Digital audio edition software allows this to be done very easily and can be adjusted graphically. It is more difficult to keep track of the stereo position of elements in analog/linear editing. Generally it is best to hold dialog to the center of the stereo mix.

Recording

Much of audio for video recording is done directly to the audio tracks in the camcorder or VCR. This is called single system recording and requires little more than the mics, a mixer and the camcorder. Professional equipment can often record from 2 to 8 tracks while non-pro gear records two, and in more expensive consumer gear there is a third time code track. When more complex recording is necessary, the choice becomes double system recording. This requires the use of a device which generates a common time code signal, such as SMTE time code, which is recorded on a track in the camcorder or in the tape recorder along with a mono reference track, and is also simultaneously recorded to an external multitrack recorder for later synchronization with the video and as many audio tracks as required. This time code, analogous to an electronic clock tick allows the later re-synchronization of multiples tapes to restore lip sync and sound continuity. Commonly audio is stored on 8 to 24 tracks.

Recorders

There is a wide variety of portable and studio audio recording equipment in both analog and digital formats. The traditional professional recording systems were reel-to-reel analog tape recorders with from 2 to 24 tracks. The 2 track systems are still commonly used but are rapidly being replaced by digital tape and disk recording systems. The most common today is the DAT or Digital Audio Tape recorder. This system records on a cassette and stores two track plus, in more expensive gear, a SMPTE time code track. There are also multitrack DAT recorders that store from six to 8 tracks per module and can be linked together to create almost limitless numbers of tracks. The two most common multitrack formats are Alesis ADAT and TEAC's DA-88. These systems are licensed to other manufacturers. The TEAC system, which records on special editions of Hi-8 video tapes, is the more common in video and film because it can record an uninterrupted 100+ minutes of audio. The ADAT system, which uses S-VHS video tapes, is limited to about 60 minutes. They both produce high quality professional recordings. The recorded audio tracks can be transferred to non-linear hard-disc based editing systems while maintaining their digital format. It is also possible to record directly to hard-disc with many available systems. This is usually not the best choice because of the fragility of hard-disc systems in the field, and the cost and unreliability of them in the studio. The usual procedure is to record to digital tape, transfer it to hard disc for editing and mixing the final audio track to stereo and multitrack tape (audio and/or video) for distribution and archiving.

Analog multitrack recording is still widely used in musical production and post-production because of the "musical" quality that it imparts to the program content. The ultimate format for almost all editing and much professional distribution is, however, digital. The cost of professional digital format audio equipment is much lower than similar analog equipment. The choice is based on the aesthetic and logistical problems that the producer is trying to solve. Multitrack recording can be from four to 48 or more tracks, the most common being 8, 16 and 24 tracks.

Time Codes

Time codes consist of a regular series of pulses combined with timing information that are generated by an electronic circuit and recorded on one or more video and/or audio recorders so that subsequent editors can synchronize multiple playback machines to each other during editing and can locate audio and video clips with single frame accuracy. There are a number of proprietary time code schemes that have been developed by individual manufacturers, principally for consumer grade equipment. Sony has several such schemes. The primary system used by professionals is the SMPTE (Society of Motion Picture and Television Engineers) scheme that is either included in professional equipment or can be added by the use of external modules. SMPTE code capability is also included as a feature in all professional non-linear video editing software, MIDI software and many audio editing systems.

The Society of Motion Picture and Television Engineers (SMPTE) time code may be one of the most misunderstood concepts among individuals within the music industry. After working with SMPTE time code for years, many people are still confused by the concept, so don't feel bad if you haven't got it all figured out. Hopefully this discussion will clear the mud.

The biggest problem with SMPTE time code is that, depending on whether you sit on the video or audio side of the fence, SMPTE time codes may mean different things to you. When dealing with SMPTE you will probably see five, perhaps six, different types of time codes formats (six is for the people who are really confused).

Here is a description of each SMPTE time code format:

SMPTE 25 EBU

This SMPTE code runs at 25 frames per second and is also know as SMPTE EBU (European Broadcasting Union). The reason for having this rate is that European television systems run at exactly 25 frames per second.

SMPTE 24 Film Sync

This SMPTE code runs at 24 frames per second and is also know as SMPTE Film Sync. This rate matches a nominal film rate of 24 frames per second (the slowest speed possible for apparent continuous motion).

OK, those two are easy. Now things start to get a little crazy.

SMPTE 30 Non-Drop (as used in the audio world)

In the US, the 60 Hz power system makes it easy to generate a time code rate of 30 frames per second. This rate is commonly used in audio environments and is typically known as 30 Non-Drop. You will probably use this rate when synchronizing audio applications like a multi-track recorder or your MIDI sequencer.

If all you care about is working with audio and not dealing with video, stop reading right here. We mean it! All you really need to know is that there are three different SMPTE rates you might want to use: SMPTE 24, SMPTE 25, and SMPTE 30 Non-Drop. However, be aware that SMPTE 30 Non-Drop in the video world runs at 29.97 frames per second.

True SMPTE 30 Drop and SMPTE 30 Non-Drop (as used in the video world)

If you are planning to work with video, the frame rate of exactly 30 frames per second is never used. When NTSC color systems were developed, the frame rate was changed by a tiny amount to eliminate the possibility of crosstalk between the audio and color information. Even though it is still referred to as SMPTE 30 Drop or Non-Drop, the actual frame rate that is used is exactly 29.97 frames per second. This poses a problem since this small difference will cause SMPTE time and real time (what your clock reads) to be different over long periods. Because of this, two methods are used to generate SMPTE time code in the video world: Drop and Non-Drop.

In SMPTE Non-Drop, the time code frames are always incremented by one in exact synchronization to the frames of your video. However, since the video actually plays at only 29.97 frames per second (rather than 30 frames per second), SMPTE time will increment at a slower rate than real world time. This will lead to a SMPTE time versus real time discrepancy. Thus, after a while, we could look at the clock on the wall and notice it is farther ahead than the SMPTE time displayed in our application.

SMPTE Drop time code (which also runs at 29.97 frames per second) attempts to compensate for the discrepancy between real world time and SMPTE time by dropping frames from the sequence of SMPTE frames in order to catch up with real world time. What this means is that occasionally in the SMPTE sequence of time, the SMPTE time will jump forward by more than one frame. The time is adjusted forward by two frames on every minute boundary except 00, 10, 20, 30, 40 , and 50. Thus when SMPTE Drop time increments from 00:00:59:29, the next value will be 00:01:00:02 in SMPTE Drop rather than 00:01:00:00 in SMPTE Non-Drop. In SMPTE Drop, it must be remembered that certain codes no longer exist. For instance, there is no such time as 00:01:00:00 in SMPTE Drop. The time code is actually 00:01:00:02.

When synchronizing audio to video, it is crucial that the SMPTE time code (30 Drop or Non-Drop) used in your sequencer or digital audio workstation is the same as the SMPTE time code striped onto the video. Only then will the SMPTE times on the video screen and computer monitor match exactly during playback.

In the audio world, people have started to call 30 Non-Drop (which runs at 29.97 frames per second) 29.97-Non-Drop to distinguish it from the 30 Non-Drop used between audio applications (which runs at a true 30 frames per second). SMPTE 30 Drop (as used in video) may also be referred to as SMPTE 29.97 Drop just to reiterate that the frame rate is actually 29.97 frames per second. It just depends on who you talk to.

However, you must remember that there is no difference between 30 Drop and 29.97 Drop time code. There are those who have tried to say that there is such a thing as a SMPTE time code which actually runs at 30 frames per second and generates drop frames. This practice would be silly, as the whole point of a SMPTE Drop time code is to make up for the discrepancy between the 29.97 frames per second "video" rate and the 30 frames per second "real time" rate.

Mixers and Consoles

The mixer is the central control of the recording system. It can be as simple as a mono portable mixer with three or four inputs, each with a volume fader, or as complex as automated fader computerized multitrack consoles with scores of inputs and outputs. In spite of the range of differences, they serve the same purpose, the connection, control, mixing and signal processing of multiple microphones and other signal sources and their ultimate connection to recording or sound reproduction equipment. In general, the requirement of video production is less complex than in the audio recording studio, the difference being not in quality but in the necessary number of input and output channels required. Traditionally, mixers are a collection of mechanical faders and analog signal control and processing circuits. These boards, while by no means obsolete, are being challenged by systems that manage much or all of the control and processing digitally. There are even systems that present the entire fader panel and cable patches as mouse controlled windows on a computer screen. Certainly all non-linear audio and video editing software have at least simple software mixer controls built in to them.

Input

Mixer inputs are generally divided into four basic categories: high and low impedance and high and low level signal strength. The impedance setting are in sync with the impedance of microphones and other gear. As with microphones, most professional gear is low impedance. Low level signal strength is standard for most microphones. The only exception will be if there is a preamplifier in between the microphone and the mixer board. High level signals come from preamplifiers, equalizers and other signal control and processing circuits. These circuits are also referred to as Line Level inputs.

There are three common connector types encountered on professional mixers. Low impedance microphone inputs are always XLR connectors. High impedance microphone inputs and line inputs are usually ¼ inch phone connectors. Low impedance line inputs are often XLR connectors but also can be ¼ inch phone connectors. There are often switches that allow the selection of the impedance or signal strength of the input circuit.

The number of inputs common on mixers used for video commonly range from three inputs on a battery powered portable mixer to 48 or more in a studio console. These are a combination of microphone and line inputs. Portable mixers are dominated by microphone inputs while studio consoles often have more line inputs to accommodate video recorder playback, CD and DAT players for sound effects, etc. The number and type of inputs required is determined by the primary use of the system. Many mixers can be expanded with additional input circuits.

Output

Mixer output circuits range from monaural systems, though these are rarely used except in simple portable mixers for news collection, to 16 or 32 outputs. The most common for portable and simple studio mixers is 2 channel stereo or 8 channel (or bus) studio consoles. These mixers generally have, in addition to the primary outputs, monitor and other secondary outputs that can be put into service in a pinch. These generally accommodate all but the most demanding situations.

Output connectors include: XLR, ¼ inch phone connectors, RCA connectors and special analog and digital connectors.

Controls

All mixers have input faders. These are the primary volume controls that regulate the level of the individual input. There are usually output faders that regulate the output level of each channel. In addition there can be sub-channel faders that mix a small selection of inputs together and then feed them to individual channels prior to the final mix.

Stereo and multi-channel mixers also have Pan (for panorama) controls on each input. The controls allow some or all of the signal to be distributed between the Left and Right stereo channels.

Mixers usually have some kind of tone controls. These range from simple bass and treble controls on each channel to either multi-channel graphic equalizers or multiple frequency equalizers on each channel.

More complex mixers also have a variety of other switches and controls on the input circuits and output circuits. Consult you user manual for more information about your particular piece of gear.

Foldback

These specialized input/output connectors and their related controls allow the editor to send a piece of a signal to an outboard signal processor and to mix that processed signal back into the mixer board. One of the most common uses for this is the addition of reverberation to a vocal track.

Outboard Equipment

Outboard equipment, generally preamplifiers and signal processors, are external circuits that work in conjunction with the recorders, microphones and mixers. These commonly include reverberation units and other signal enhancers, compressors, limiters, preamplifiers and equalizers.

Monitoring

Monitoring is an extremely important part of both the recording and editing processes. In field recording high quality headphones are the primary tool. In the studio both headphones and specialized studio monitor speaker systems are utilized. Speaker systems need to be properly placed and adjusted to the acoustical environment of the studio itself. Monitor circuits and controls are a part of every professional mixer board and console.

Sound Effects and Music

Source

Perhaps the ideal solution for music and sound effects for a multimedia presentation is to have an in-house composer/sound engineer who can produce the required audio materials. Unfortunately, this is not practical for many producers. On the other hand, there are alternatives. This section considers the use and sources of pre-recorded sound and music, as well as the procedures for capturing original material.

Music and Effects Libraries

Commercial sound effects and music libraries are essential tools in the sound designer's palette. There are a wide variety of products available with widely varying quality. While libraries, in the past, were distributed on LP records, the current formats are CD-Audio and CD-ROM discs. CD-Audio discs are the highest quality and are the most expensive. Most libraries are available, for at least a portion of their collections, in both formats.

Sound Effects libraries include collections developed especially for commercial distribution and developed by major movie studios for their own internal use in general or for specific movies. The movie studio collections are then selectively licensed for commercial use. Virtually all the major studios have licensed collections for distribution. The effects libraries may be general purpose collections with ambient sounds, crowd scenes, airplane and animal noises and more. They may also be special applications, like trains or military sounds or collections for use in cartoons or dramatic productions. Some of the sound effects publishers will make custom collections from their libraries and can be persuaded to provide special custom effects for a particular production. This custom development can be expensive.

Licensing

The licensing restrictions for sound effects libraries are generally such that once the collection has been purchased, they may be used in an unlimited way in video or other productions with no additional fees to be paid. They may not, however, be re-sold as sound effects libraries. In general terms this is call "Buy Out" licensing.

Live Capture/Sampling

Often a production requires at least some custom or live sound effects recording. This may be because the director is concerned about stock sounds sounding "canned" or being identified because of over use. There are several rules for quality sound effect capture.

1. Always use the highest quality microphones and recording equipment.
2. Record as "hot" or at the highest signal level possible without creating distortions in the recording. This creates the best signal to noise ratio and assures a clear sound with a minimum of background noise.
3. A realistic sound effect is not as simple as placing a microphone over a particular sound and recording. Mic placement and room acoustics or wind can change the expected quality of the sound and the end result may sound nothing like expected. Also, the actual sound of a particular object or event may not, when recorded, sound like the real thing at all. Many times the recording of something unrelated to the desired sound sounds more like the effect required. In other words, the real, recorded roar of a lion may not sound nearly as impressive and "lion-like" as a composed sound effect made up of sounds from entirely different sources. In this case, art may surpass nature. Listen to the recorded result, and if the sound does not come across as expected, try again or try something else.
4. Sometimes an effect needs to be modified in post-production to change the quality of a sound, or extend or contract its duration or pitch. Anything that works is correct.

Stock Music

Stock music libraries, with music for every possible situation, are widely available with varying quality. The musical clips may be long form compositions designed for background tracks for dramatic productions or documentaries, or may be 10, 15, 30 or 45 second clips for commercials. The biggest reason to use stock music is production cost. Stock music can be very inexpensive. The down sides include: difficulty of timing clips to editing, over use of the tracks in the market place and difficulty finding "just the right" composition. Almost any style of music can be found from a country jingle to classical music of the masters.

Licensing may be the "buy out" system described in the sound effects section above, or may be "needle drop" licenses. The needle drop system requires that a license be paid for each use of a musical clip. If you are using a great deal of stock music you may wish to obtain one or more "buy out" collections. This will assure that you have a piece of music for a last minute production need and can be cost effective. Buy out collections need not be expensive. They are, however, much more ubiquitous. If you are concerned about hearing the same music in someone else's production this may not be the best choice. Needle drop collections may be purchased and maintained in-house with the license fees paid before actual use of a clip in a production, or can be auditioned at the time of need from submissions by the publisher. Needle drop collections that are retained in house are less expensive to purchase but have higher use fees when incorporated into a video. Needle drop collections also tend to be more unique and up to date. Stock music producers and publishers will generally compose special music for a score under contract. If you use performances from a library, copyright and publishing clearances are generally covered. If you license musical performances from record companies you will probably need to obtain permission separately from the publisher of the musical composition and perhaps the artist performing the work. If you are recording live performances of a musical work, use fees and permissions must be obtained from the artist and publishers. There are very stiff fines and penalties for even minor copyright violations. These permissions should be planned in your production budget and should be obtained early in the process due to time lags in the permission process, or in case of turn downs.

MIDI

MIDI or Musical Instrument Digital Interface, is a command system that allows computers and electronic synthesizers to talk to each other and to record virtual performances of sound or musical compositions in a form that can be replicated without creating an actual sound recording. The term MIDI is used in a general, though not entirely accurate, sense to refer to synthesized music and sound effects generated by a computer or synthesizer device. The actual sound generation may be from a recorded collection of live or acoustic music, musical tones or sound clips called "samples" stored in a computer or other device, or may be synthesized using a series of oscillators and sound processors entirely electronically.

MIDI Sequence vs. Wave Form

MIDI is an important music source when:

* Timing is critical. MIDI files can be easily time adjusted to fit and exact spot in a presentation. Wave files are much less editable by the casual user in this respect.

  Disc space is critical. MIDI files are much more compact, per minute of content, than the equivalent wave form files.

* Computer processing resources are critical. Typical DOS and MAC multimedia systems require much less of the CPU to process MIDI information than wave files.

Wave form files are important when:

Voice recording, acoustical music or sound effects are essential and "sampled" MIDI instruments do not fulfill the sound need.

MIDI or Synthesized music and sound effects, particularly those controlled by MIDI software or sequencers, give maximum editing control. They may be minutely adjusted and linked to audio and/or video editing software for complete control. The major problem with MIDI controlled samplers or synthesizers is the inevitable synthetic quality of the sound. This can be an aesthetic limitation if the object is to achieve the sound of acoustic music. If contemporary sounds are required, there is no better solution. There are large libraries of MIDI sequences of custom, popular, traditional, ethnic and classical music available as well as libraries of samples of every conceivable kind of musical instrument and sound effect. The licensing terms are usually on the buy out plan as with sound effects. If MIDI sequences of popular or current music is used, copyrights must be honored and permissions from publishers must be obtained.

MIDI integration with the Sound Forge Audio Editing Software

The Musical Instrument Digital Interface (MIDI) is a set of commands used by many pieces of music software and hardware to speak to each other. MIDI is most often used for sending commands such as Play Middle C Now, but can also be used to send information like Current Time is: 00:00:01:23 SMPTE, or even digital sound data.

The most common way to use MIDI is to have a Master device (such as a MIDI sequencer) to generate MIDI commands to a Slave device (such as a synthesizer which plays a note when instructed). If both were in separate hardware boxes, you would run a MIDI cable from the sequencer's MIDI OUT port to the synthesizer's MIDI IN port.

MIDI Time Code (MTC) is a way to transmit SMPTE timing signals between devices for synchronization. Although MIDI Time Code is most often used to sync audio tracks to visual action on video, it can also be used to synchronize other playback devices, like a MIDI sequencer.

Playing regions using MIDI Time Code from a software MIDI sequencer

It is possible to specify start times for each region in your Regions List for synchronizing digital sounds with other timed events. For example, if your MIDI sequencer or other device generates SMPTE Time Code, Sound Forge can make its SMPTE time accurately follow the device's SMPTE time and play the regions at the specified times. Synchronizing to MTC is very similar to synchronizing to other MIDI events. However, if you just want to trigger a few sounds in Sound Forge from your sequencer, it might be easier to use

Note-On MIDI Triggering and not worry about MTC or SMPTE synchronization (refer to the section on Triggering from internal sequencers). MTC synchronization uses up more of your computer's processing power, yet its the only way to go if you don't want to (or can't) generate MIDI triggers. Also, MTC synchronization allows you to specify accurate SMPTE start times in Sound Forge instead of in other software or hardware devices.

Playing regions using MIDI Time Code from an external device

If you have a hardware device (i.e. SMPTE Time Code to MTC card) that generates MTC, the procedure is basically the same as outlined above. In Sound Forge's MIDI/Sync Preferences folder, you should be able to directly select the device's MTC output driver as Sound Forge's MIDI input port.

Using Sound Forge to generate MTC for an external device

If you want Sound Forge to send MTC to an external device, follow the previous instructions for sending MTC to a sequencer with a few changes. Instead of sending to the VMR, have Sound Forge's MIDI output port send directly to the device's MIDI driver. Check the device's manual for more detailed information on using MTC.

Conclusion

The technology and art of sound recording, editing and sound design can be a life-time activity. If you practice, experiment and above all else, listen to video and movie sound tracks, and carefully listen to the work you create, you can quickly become competent and skilled. Don't minimize the importance of the sound, or take it for granted. Ultimately, in a video, cinema or multimedia production, there is no single element as important to the communication of ideas and emotion as the sound track.

Bibliography

Alkin, Glyn. *Sound Techniques for Video and TV*. 2d ed. Boston: Focal Press, 1989.

Atlen, Stanley R. *Audio in Media*. 2d ed. Belmont, CA: Wadsworth, 1986.

Clifford, Martin. *Microphones.* 3d ed. Blue Ridge Summit, PA.: TAB Books, 1986.

Campbel, Ivy G. "Basal Emotional Patterns Expressible in Music." *American Journal of Psychology* 55 (1942):1–17.

Davis, Hallowell. "Psychophysiology of Hearing and Deafness." In *Handbook of Experimental Psychology*, edited by S.S. Stevens. New York: John Wiley and Sons, Inc., 1951.

Gurney, Edmund. *The Power of Sound*. London: Smith, Elder and Co., 1880.

Hodges, D.A. *Handbook of Music Psychology*. Lawrence, Kansas: National Association of Music Therapy (1980).

Huber, David Miles. *Audio Production Techniques for Video*. Indianapolis: Howard W. Sams, 1987.

Huber, David Miles. *Microphone Manual: Design and Application*. Indianapolis: Howard W. Sams, 1988.

Hunter, H. "An Investigation of Psychological and Physiological Changes Apparently Elicited by Musical Stimuli." *Psychology of Music*, 2, (1973): 53–68.

Irvine, Demar B. *Expression of Ideas and Emotion in Music*. PhD dissertation, Harvard University, 1937.

Jacobs, Robert L. "A Gestalt Psychologist on Music." *Music Review* 17 (1956): 185–88.

Koriat, A., Melkman, R., Averil, J.R., & Lazarus, R.S. "A Laboratory Study of Psychological Stress Produced by a Motion Picture Film", *Psychological Monographs*, 76, (1972), (34, Whole No. 553).

Martin, F. David. "The Power of Music and Whitehead's Theory of Perception." *Journal of Aesthetics and Art Criticism* 25 (1967): 313–22.

Markey, Brian D. "Business Opportunities in Multimedia." *MIX*, January 1992: 101–104.

Meyer, Chris. "General MIDI—Growth and Myth." *Keyboard*, February 1992: 130.

_____ "The Next Big Thing." *Keyboard*, March 1992: 99.

Meyer, Leonard B. *Emotion and Meaning in Music*. Chicago: University of Chicago Press, 1956.

_____ "Meaning in Music and Information Theory." *Journal of Aesthetics and Art Criticism* 15 (1957): 412–25.

Moles, Abraham. *Information Theory and Esthetic Perception*. Translated by Joel E. Cohen. Urbana: Universtiy of Illinois Press, 1966.

Nesbett, Alec. *The Techniques of the Sound Studio: For Radio, Recording Studio, Television and Film.* 4th ed. London: Focal Press, 1979.

Nesbett, Alec. *The Use of Microphones.* 2d ed. London and Boston: Focal Press, 1983.

Oringel, Robert S. *Audio Control Handbook: For Radio and Television Broadcasting.* 6th ed. Boston: Focal Press, 1989.

Payne, Elsie. "Emotion in Music and in Music Appreciation." *Music Review* 22 (1961): 39–50.

Peretti, P.O., & Swenson, K. "Effects of Music on Anxiety as Determined by Physiological Skin Responses." *Journal of Research in Music Education,* 22, (1974): 278–283.

Pierce, John R. *Symbols, Signals and Noise.* New York: Harper and Brothers, 1961.

Pike, Alfred. "Perception and Meaning in Serial Music." *Journal of Aesthetics and Art Criticism* 22 (1963): 55–61.

Pohlmann, Ken C. *Principles of Digital Audio.* 2d ed. Indianapolis: Howard W. Sams, 1989.

Rohner, Stephen J. "Cognitive-Emotional Response to Music as a Function of Music and Cognitive Complexity". *Psychomusicology,* 1985, Vol 5, Numbers 1-2, 25–38.

Savill, Agnes. "Physical Effects of Music." *Music and Letters* 39 (1958): 16–28.

Schaub, S. "Study of the Interaction Between Mood and Music Experience Under its Musical and Clinical Psychological Aspects." *ZKBEA,* 28:2 (1980): 134–142.

Schoen, Max, ed. *The Effects of Music.* New York: Harcourt, Brace and Co., Inc., 1927.

Sherburne, Donald W. "Meaning and Music." *Journal of Aesthetics and Art Criticism* 24 (1966): 579–83.

Skiles, M. *Music Scoring for T.V. and Motion Pictures.* Blue Ridge Summit, PA: TAB Books, (1976).

Smith, C.A., & Morris, L.W. "Effects of Stimulative and Sedative Music on Cognitive and Emotional Components of Anxiety". *Psychological Reports,* 38, (1976) 1187–1193.

Stechow, Wolfgang. "Problems of Structure in Some Relations Between the Visual Arts and Music." *Journal of Aesthetics and Art Criticism,* 11 (1953): 324–33.

Sweeney, Daniel. *Demystifying Compact Discs: A Guide to Digital Audio.* Blue Ridge Summit, PA: TAB Books, 1986.

Thayer, Julian F. and Levinson, Robert W., "Effects of Music on Psychopysiological Responses to a Stressful Film," *Psychomusicology,* 1983 Vol. 3, No. 1, 44-52

Watkinson, John. *The Art of Digital Audio.* London and Boston: Focal Press, 1988.

Winold, C.A. *The Effects of Changes in Harmonic Tension Upon Listener Response.* Ann Arbor: University Microfilms, 1963.

Youngblood, Joseph E. "Style as Information." *Journal of Music Theory* 2 (1958): 24–35

Zink, Sidney. "Is the Music Really Sad?" *Journal of Aesthetics and Art Criticism* 19 (1960): 197–207.

Zuckerkandle, Victor. *The Sense of Music.* Princeton: Princeton University Press, 1959.

_____ *Sound and Symbol.* Translated by Willard R. Trask. New York: Pantheon Books, Inc., 1956.

Chapter 5
Sound Editing

Introduction

Video is really about "active" information or information in motion. This means animation/video and sound/music. Sound is THE element that gives a fourth dimension to information presentation. It is also the easiest element to create and add to any presentation or title. Wave files recorded by the user are within the scope of anyone who has used a computer and tape recorder and MIDI musical tracks created by the computer are no more difficult to integrate than still photographs or blocks of copied text. This chapter addresses both the principles of sound recording and its application to video production. The necessary skills for successful sound editing include some musical ability or at least sensibility and the patience to carefully listen to the source audio and the subsequent recorded and edited audio and musical tracks. Professionalism is the result, just as in lighting and videography, of assessment of one's work and learning from one's mistakes and successes.

This chapter focuses on the editing of the primary audio and musical elements and clips that will be finally assembled into the video project. This process is similar to reviewing and selecting the clips or scenes of video that will be assembled into a final production. This part of the production process is also the place that special sound effects, the editing of mistakes and the adjustment of timing takes place. Once the list of sound elements is complete the next step is the video assembly and final editing process.

Editing

In the past, where analog electronics and reel to reel tape recorders dominated, editing audio was a combination of mixing and re-mixing signals from one recorder to another, combined with the physical cutting and pasting of pieces of audio tape together into a final mix.

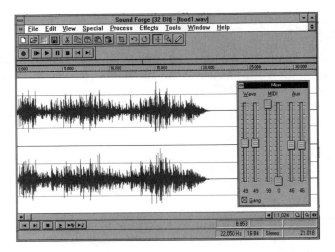

Figure 5.1 Sound Forge Audio Editing Screen with Mixer

This, like linear video editing, was a tedious and time consuming process and the mixing and re-mixing process ultimately reduced the quality of the audio signals. Today almost all audio editing in professional studio productions is done with computer based non-linear editing systems.

Common Editing Operations

The edit operations used most often include cut, copy, paste, delete, mix, and trim/crop. Most of these make use of the Clipboard, which is a temporary storage area which can also be used to move data from one window to another. The following list provides a brief description of each operation:

Cut Deletes a selected portion of data and copies it on to the Clipboard.
Copy Copies a selected portion of data on to the Clipboard.
Clear Deletes a selected portion of data but doesn't copy it on to the Clipboard.
Trim Deletes all data in a window except the selected section.
Paste Inserts the contents of the Clipboard into a Data Window at the current cursor position.
Mix Mixes the contents of the Clipboard with the current data in a window starting at the current cursor position.

Trimming

Trimming (also called Cropping) allows you to single out a section of data and cut everything else out of the window except that section. This is a handy feature since you can keep using the Play button to hear selections until you have just the right amount and then get rid of everything else with the Trim/Crop command in the Edit menu.

Mixing

Mixing is a powerful and useful edit operation which you will use often. Mixing allows you to combine two sounds together into one window so you can create complex sound effects.

Status Formats

When editing sound files, the ruler, total length status field, and Playbar Selection Status fields can be set to different formats so you can coordinate sound files with other events, or edit to a timing base that you feel most comfortable with.

Lengths and positions can be displayed in a variety of formats including Samples, Time (seconds and milliseconds), Frames, SMPTE, and Measures and Beats.

Selecting a Status Format

To select a format choose the Status Format option from the View menu. This shows the nine different formats available. Choosing one of these options sets the status format for the current data window.

The available formats are:

Samples	Number of samples.
Seconds	Seconds and fractions there of.
Milliseconds	Milliseconds and fractions there of.
Frames	Frames and fractions there of.
Beats	Measures: beats, tenths of a beat.
SMPTE Non-Drop	SMPTE at 30 or 29.97 fps non-drop.
SMPTE Drop	SMPTE at 29.97 fps with drop.
SMPTE EBU	SMPTE at 25 fps.
SMPTE Film Sync	SMPTE at 24 fps.

Configuring Frames and Beats

When setting the status format to Frames or Beats there is additional information you can provide to Sound Forge to customize how these values are displayed. The Edit Frames dialog in the Special menu allows you to change the frames per second. In the Edit Tempo dialog, also in the Special menu, you can specify the beats per minute and beats per measure values used to calculate measures and beats. The default values for Frames and Beats are set in the Status Preferences folder (File menu).

Editing Stereo Files

When editing stereo files you have two channels of data on which to work. The upper channel is the left channel and the lower channel is the right channel. We will refer to them in both ways left (upper), and right (lower).

Selecting Data in Stereo Files

When selecting data in stereo files, Sound Forge allows you to select either the left channel, right channel or both channels for playing, editing, and effects processing.

When editing a stereo file, the Waveform Display showing the two channels is split into three logical sections for selection with the mouse. The upper quarter of the Waveform Display is the left channel "hit" section, the lower quarter is the right channel "hit" section, and the middle half is for both channels. When selecting data with the mouse, which area you are in determines what channel(s) will be selected.

Toggling Channel Selections

Once you have made a selection in a stereo file you can switch between channel selections by pressing the Tab key. The Tab key will cycle between selections of left channel, right channel, and both channels. You can also set the channel selection by using the Channel drop-down list in the Set Selection dialog.

Previewing Channels

Selecting a single channel allows you to hear a preview of a single channel in the stereo file. For example double-click in the opened files active window to select all the data (or use Select All from the Edit menu). Press the Play button and listen to the clip. Next press the Tab key to toggle the channel selection into a single channel and press the Play button again. Do this one more time to hear the other channel.

Single Channel Editing

Stereo data files are "tied" together by their nature and other cosmic forces. In other words, they always play together. This means that there are some edit operations, such as Cut and Paste, which you can't use on a single channel. It would leave one channel shorter or longer than the other. This is usually not a problem in real world editing situations.

You can copy a selection from a single channel to the Clipboard by selecting the data in either the left of right channel and using the Copy command. This will place a mono clip on the Clipboard. You can then paste the mono clip to a mono file, both channels of a stereo file, or you can mix it into a single channel or both channels of a stereo file. When mixing mono Clipboard data to a stereo file you will be asked with a dialog whether you wish to mix to a single channel or both channels.

Recording

Recording Basics

To start a record session you can either select Record from the Special menu or press the record button on the Transport toolbar. The record button is the first button on the Transport with the red circle on it.

After pressing the Record Transport button or selecting Record from the menu, you will be presented with the Record dialog. Notice that the window into which you will be recording has its title displayed in the dialog title.

In the upper left of the dialog are the recording attributes. These are the record sample rate, sample size, and number of channels which will be used when recording. These are the same as the attributes of the Data Window into which you will be recording. If you want to change these attributes you either need to exit the Record dialog and change them in the Data Window, record to a new window, or pick another window to record to.

Recording to a New Window

If you want to record to a new window rather than the currently selected record window, select the New button found at the upper right of the Record dialog. This brings up the New Window dialog where you can specify the Sample Rate, Sample Size, and number of channels for the new Data Window, which will also be used while recording.

Selecting an Alternate Record Window

If you wish to record to a window other than the one currently displayed in the Record dialog title, you can do so by selecting the Window button. Pick the window into which you would like to record from the drop down list box in the Record Window dialog and select OK. The title of the window you select will now appear in the Record dialog title.

Available Recording Time

Near the bottom of the dialog you will see the Time recorded and Time left on drive fields. These two boxes show how much time you have recorded and how much time is available on your hard drive for additional recording. If your Time left on drive field is displaying a limited amount of available time you may want to free up some space on your hard drive or pick an alternate drive where Sound Forge stores its temporary files. You can get more information on temporary file usage by referring to the Reference section on Temporary Storage.

Checking Record Levels

Sound Forge allows you to check the level of your input source before recording begins. To check your levels check the Monitor check box. The meters will light up relating to the volume of the recording input. For best results, the level should be somewhere in the yellow range with an occasional red. Once your levels are checked you can immediately begin recording by selecting the Record button. If you do not see the meters light up, you may have your mixer levels or input source set incorrectly. You can refer to the Questions and Answers section for more information on these problems.

Adjusting Levels Using the Peak and Margin Values

The Peak and Margin values displayed next to the level meters are useful for maximizing your input level without clipping. When recording you almost always want your input signal to be as hot as possible without clipping. By this we mean you want your input levels to be as high as possible without exceeding the range of values which can be stored digitally when recording. When you clip, the peaks of your waveform become clipped off and you will hear noise. The Peak values show you the percentage of the total range which input levels have reached since you selected the Test button. The Margin values show you the percentage of level you have left until you will reach the clipping state. You never want your Margin to reach 0% or your Peak to reach 100%. If they do then clipping has occurred.

To adjust your levels check the Monitor check box so that Sound Forge begins to listen to your recording device. This is just like recording except that Sound Forge doesn't store any of the data it receives. Apply an input signal by speaking in your microphone, or playing your CD, or whatever it is you're trying to record. If the Peak value stays at a low value you should increase the levels of sound you are supplying so that the Peak value is somewhere in the 90% range and the Margin value is somewhere between 0 and 10%. If the Margin reaches 0% (or the Peak 100%) then you have clipped and need to lower your input levels. Once you lower your input levels select the Reset button to clear the current peak and margin values. Sound Forge always keeps the maximum peak and minimum threshold value since the last time you selected the Reset button.

Once you have adjusted your levels you can immediately begin recording by selecting the Record button or end monitoring the levels by un-checking the Monitor button below the Meters.

It is particularly important to record sounds with the hottest levels possible when you plan to later convert 16-bit data to 8-bit. This assures that you will use the greatest dynamic range possible in an 8-bit file which has less values with which to represent the waveform.

Previewing Recorded Sounds

After recording your material, you can listen to what you have recorded by selecting the Play button. You can also listen to the section over which you plan to record in Punch In mode. To stop playing select the Stop button at any time.

Using the Prepare Button

The Prepare button is used when you need Sound Forge to begin recording as soon as possible after selecting the Record button. The Prepare button opens the wave device and loads all recording buffers in order to minimize the time between selecting the Record button and sound actually beginning to be recorded.

The Prepare button is optional. It is not necessary to select this button prior to recording, however it does allow for more accurate takes in the Punch In mode.

Recording Modes

Sound Forge has four different modes of recording. These are Automatic Retake, Multiple Takes with Regions, Multiple Takes (no Regions) and Punch In. Each mode is described below.

Automatic Retake

The Automatic Retake mode is the easiest method of recording. Recording starts at the position shown in the Start field when you select the Record button and continues until you select the Stop button. Any data which is currently after the position in the Start field will be replaced. When recording is stopped, the start position is reset to the beginning of the take allowing an immediate review and retake if desired.

Automatic Retake is the default mode when recording into an empty Data Window or when you select the record button with no data selected in the current Data Window.

Multiple Takes with Regions

The Multiple Takes with Regions mode allows for the recording of multiple takes, with each take automatically having a Region defined in the Regions List. Recording starts at the position shown in the Start field when you select the Record button and continues until you select the Stop button. Any data which is currently after the position in the Start field will be replaced. When recording is stopped, the start position remains at the end of the next take allowing the take to be recorded immediately.

Multiple Takes (no Regions)

The Multiple Takes (no Regions) mode allows multiple takes to be recorded, but no Regions are defined in the Regions List. Recording starts at the position shown in the Start field when you select the Record button and continues until you select the Stop button. Any data which is currently after the position in the Start field will be replaced. When recording is stopped, the start position remains at the end of the take allowing the next take to be recorded immediately.

Punch In

Punch In mode is used when you want to record over a region of data in an existing Data Window. Recording starts at the position shown in the Start field when you select the Record button and continues until you select the Stop button, or the length of the data recorded is equal to the length in the Length field. This makes it easy to record over a section of audio without effecting the rest of the file. You can use the Play button to hear the selected Punch In region at any time.

You may adjust the Punch In region by changing the values in the Start, End, or Length edit fields. You may also adjust the format of these fields to a variety of different display status formats by selecting a format from the Input format drop down list box.

Punch In mode is the default mode when you select the Record option while you have a region of data selected in the current Data Window.

Using Pre/Post-Roll with Punch In Mode

At the bottom of the Record dialog are two edit fields which contain the Pre-Roll and Post-Roll times. These can be used when listening to a region in Punch In mode. These times define the amount of audio you will hear prior to (Pre-Roll), and after (Post-Roll), the selected region when using the Play button. This allows you to hear the transitions between the Punch In region and sound before and after the region. If you wish to use the Pre/Post-Roll option you must check the Review check box at the bottom of the dialog. To disable Pre/Post-Roll un-check this box.

Recording Status

While you are recording, the amount of time recorded will increase and the Time left on drive will decrease. Make sure and keep an eye on your Time left on drive if your available record time is limited. It's never fun running out of recording time!

Finishing Recording

When you have finished recording select the Close button to exit the Record dialog and return to normal editing mode.

Processing

Applying an Effect to a Portion of a Sound File

To apply an effect you may first select a section of data on which you wish to operate. To select the entire file, double-click on the Waveform Display.

If you do not have a selection when you perform an effect which requires one, Sound Forge will apply the effect to the entire file.

Canceling a Function in Progress

While applying an effect, the progress meter at the lower left hand side of the main screen shows what percentage of a selection has been processed while running a function. You can select the Cancel button to stop processing the file. When you cancel an operation in progress, the affected data remains in the sound file. Undoing the operation will return the file to its original state.

Delay/Echo

The Delay/Echo function creates copies of the original sound which are then mixed with the sound file to create simple echo effects.

Reverberation

Reverberation is the result of sound reflecting off of room surfaces. Having traveled different distances and bounced off different materials, these sound reflections do not reach the listener at the same time and have a different frequency content than the original sound source. When blended together, these reflections become what we recognize as reverberation. To the listener, reverberation gives aural cues about the sound source location, such as room size and wall material.

Simulation of these sound reflections is accomplished using delay taps and feedback along with other processing functions like pitch modulation and filtering. A delay-tap is a time-delayed copy of the sound which, depending on the feedback setting, gets repeated over time. Delay-taps are used to generate the early reflections which are heard as echoes. Using feedback generates decaying copies of the early-reflection. This simulates sound bouncing around in a room to generate reverberation.

In Sound Forge, the Reverb function allows you to specify up to eight delay-taps spaced anywhere within one-half second of the original sound. For normal reverberation, the delay taps decrease over time. However, the Reverb function in Sound Forge is not limited to reverb simulation. With different tap arrangements, many non-reverb effects are possible.

Chorus

The Chorus function is used to simulate multiple sound sources from a single sound. This is achieved by mixing a delayed, pitch modulated copy of itself to the sound source.

Flange

The Flange function is used to create the sweeping effects often heard in 60's guitar recordings and techno-sounds of today.

Noise Gate

When recording a sound, there is often an audible noise floor during silent breaks. Noise is generated by many different things, including electrical equipment, machinery, and traffic outside your window. When your sound source is much louder than this background noise, it is simple to remove the noise during silent breaks, where the noise is most noticeable, with a noise gate.

Compression and Limiting

Compressing and Limiting are terms used to indicate effects that lower the dynamic range of a sound. When you compress a sound, you lower the volume of loud sections and raise the volume of soft sections in the sound file. This is done to keep the volume level from fluctuating too much over time. Limiting works exactly like compression, but to a higher degree. Limiting is often used to keep signals from going above a certain level, but can also be applied to create heavily-compressed effects.

Expansion

Dynamic Expansion is the opposite of compression and limiting. Sound above the Center Level gets boosted and sound below gets attenuated. The most common effect of expansion is to attenuate low-level noise, such as a noise gate. However, you can also use expansion to add more dynamic range to a sound.

Changing Pitch and Time Duration

Altering pitch by changing playback rate

You are probably familiar with how changing the playback rate of a recording affects its pitch. For example, playing a 33 1/3 RPM vinyl record at 78 RPM makes the Beatles sound like the Chipmunks. Likewise, playing a 78 RPM record at 33 1/3 makes a trumpet sound like a tuba. This concept is used by most sampler units to make a single sample achieve different pitches.

Changing time duration without changing the pitch of a sound

Another Sound Forge process unique to digital processing is the ability to stretch or compress the time duration of a sound without altering the pitch. This is useful for lengthening or shortening sounds to meet a specific time length.

Other ways of using Time-Compression/Expansion and Pitch Change

When using the Preserve Duration algorithm, the Pitch Change function is very computationally intensive and can take a long time to process a sound. Also, when making large pitch changes it can add unwanted artifacts to your sound. Likewise, the Time Compression/Expansion algorithm can also degrade the sound of your file in some circumstances. Here are some suggestions for you to try when trying to change the pitch or duration of a sound:

Small and accurate changes in time duration

If you have a sound file that is one minute and three seconds long, but you need it to be exactly one minute, there are two ways to go about it. If a very small change in pitch is acceptable, you might try using the Pitch Change with no Preserve Duration. Keep the Semitones at 0 and adjust the Cents until the required Final Length is reached. It is sometimes possible for this method to give better sounding results than if you used the Time Compression algorithm.

Changing pitch and then compensating for a change in duration

Let's say that your singer hit a few flat notes. Of course, you can use the Pitch Change with Preserve Duration to change the pitch without changing how long the voice lasts. Another possibility is to change the pitch with Preserve Duration off, and then compensate for the change in duration using the Time Compress/Expand algorithm. This method is much quicker, and in some cases provides better results. If the amount of time that you are pitch correcting is small, you may not even need to correct for time as the time difference in this case is small as well.

FM and Simple Synthesis

Simple Synthesis

The Simple Synthesis tool can be used to generate a simple waveform of a given shape, pitch, and length. More complex waveforms can be generated with the FM Synthesis tool.

Example

Create a new window by selecting the New item from the File menu and set the data format for the window to be 16-bit, 22,050 Hz, mono. Next select Simple Synthesis from the Tools menu.

Select the Middle C Reference (3 Secs.) Preset and press OK to generate a Sine wave in the window that is 3 seconds long and has a pitch of 261.52 Hz (Middle C). Press the Play button to hear your reference tone.

FM Synthesis

Sound Forge's FM Synthesis tool allows you to use frequency modulation (FM) and additive synthesis to create complex sounds from simple waveforms.

In frequency modulation, the frequency of a waveform (the carrier) is modulated by the output of another waveform (the modulator) to create a new waveform. If the frequency of the modulator is low, the carrier will be slowly detuned over time. However, if the frequency of the modulator is high, the carrier will be modulated so fast that many additional frequencies, or sidebands, are created.

Sound Forge allows up to four waveforms (operators) to be generated in a variety of configurations. Depending on the configuration, an operator can be a carrier, a modulator, or a simple un-modulated waveform. Waveforms can also be added together (additive synthesis) to add more complexity to the sound.

The best way to become familiar with this module is to start with a single operator configuration and try out all the different waveforms by themselves. Experiment using feedback on each waveform to hear the different effects of self-modulation. Feedback adds overtones to the sound by modulating the sound with itself. Zero feedback indicates simple synthesis.

In the second configuration, two un-modulated operators are mixed together (horizontal connection) and heard simultaneously (additive synthesis).

Now change the configuration to two stacked operators (vertical connection) and again experiment using different waveforms and frequencies on the carrier (bottom operator) and the modulator (top operator). With the modulator frequency set low (1–5 Hz), lower the modulator amplitude to create slight detuning. Raising it creates big pitch bends. If the modulator frequency is set high, many unusual FM sounds can be achieved. Make sure that the modulator amplitude is not too high, otherwise the result will be harsh noise-like sounds.

Setting the modulator frequency to 0.00 allows absolute control of the carrier's pitch by using the modulator's envelope, which you can use for detuning over time.

Adding more operators increases the complexity of the waveform. When both FM and additive synthesis are combined, an almost endless variety of sounds can be generated.

Filtering and Equalization

What can you do when you have a sound that is not quite perfect, but not bad enough to throw away? Sometimes, judicious use of filtering can keep a favorite sound bite from losing favor. Filtering is not a cure-all for bad sound, but slight alterations of a sound can bring it back to life.

Sounds are composed of varying amounts of one or more frequencies. For example, a sound with a rich timbre will contain many different frequencies. A sine wave sound has only one frequency in it, like 60 or 440 Hz.

Filters allow the tailoring of the frequency spectrum of a sound. A spectrum is nothing more than a representation of how much of each frequency component (from 20 Hz up to one-half the sample rate) is present in a signal. Less of any given component means that the given frequency component is not as prevalent aurally as another component. Filters pass or reduce (attenuate) frequency components in response to your inputs through Sound Forge. Note that other factors such as the frequency response characteristic of your computer's speakers and sound card can also affect which frequencies are more prominent during the playback of a sound.

Graphic EQ

The Graphic EQ divides all the possible frequencies into ten bands which you can boost or attenuate (cut). Each band has a center frequency related to it. The 125 Hz band, for example, affects frequencies between 90 and 190 Hz. The Gain value above each band indicates the amount of cut or boost applied to the band. When a band is set to zero, it means that the frequencies in the band will not be modified. Positive Gain values indicate a boost and negative values indicate a cut in amplitude.

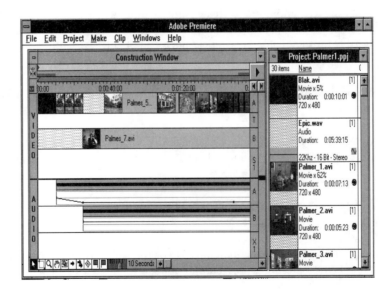

Figure 5.2 Adobe Premiere Audio Editing Window

Conclusion

The technology and art of sound recording, editing and sound design can be a life-time activity. If you practice, experiment and above all else, listen to video and movie sound tracks, and carefully listen to the work you create, you can quickly become competent and skilled. Don't minimize the importance of the sound, or take it for granted. Ultimately, in a video, cinema or multimedia production, there is no single element as important to the communication of ideas and emotion as the sound track.

Chapter 6
Capture Hardware

Introduction

In order to edit video digitally it is necessary to have a computer with the proper configuration, an audio and video capture or interface card and lots and lots of hard drive space. We will consider the proper hardware needs in this chapter and introduce you to some of the issues involved in selecting and assembling a system.

Computer Platforms

The Silicon Graphic Workstation

Silicon Graphic workstations, like the Indy and Indigo, have found a niche in high-end graphics, animation, and compositing work. They're relatively more expensive, but extremely fast. Most often, they're used as a final composite and render station, with prepared source material being fed into them from less powerful personal computers over a network. However, Avid Technology has a version of their popular video editing system, Media Suite Pro, available for the Silicon Graphics platform.

The Video Toaster

Some hardy souls are still plugging along with the Video Toaster, based on the now defunct Commodore Amiga computer. There was a time when the Toaster could do things no other personal computer in the world could. The Toaster still has a loyal following in some circles; effects created on these systems still pop up regularly on network television. Due to the limited availability of hardware and software, however, and the boom in comparable products for Macs and PCs, the Toaster is not covered in this book.

Windows vs. the Mac

In the desktop video world, nearly all video production is being created on Apple Macintoshes and Microsoft Windows PCs. Early in the evolution of multimedia and desktop video production, the Macintosh had an advantage due primarily to Apple's development of Quicktime, and that the nucleus of software applications and hardware development in multimedia and video focused on primary development on the Mac. During that period it was virtually imperative that video producers who wished to use desktop video adopt the MAC as their primary platform. This is no longer the case. Virtually all of the publishers of multimedia and video software, and manufacturers of related hardware have Windows versions of their products. Further, while once the initial release of virtually all multimedia and video software was for the Mac, now the Windows PC version is released first or simultaneously with the Mac version. The interfaces and features of the products are generally identical. It now comes down to personal choice rather than necessity in choosing between the Mac and Windows PC.

CPUs

The CPU (Central Processing Unit) is the heart of any personal computer. It is the primary determinant of how fast certain basic functions can take place. The CPU is often referred to as the computer's "engine," and for good reason. As with a car, the bigger the engine, the faster it can go. A CPU is measured by clock speed in megahertz per second. This speed has huge implications for desktop video. Because of the vast amount of data through put required, the CPU can make the difference between an application running smoothly, or slowing to the point where it's just not feasible to do the project at all. Certain functions, like creating video with multiple layers of effects, can literally take hours for just a few seconds of video. Consequently, a CPU with half the clock speed will take about twice as long to create the same movie. Extend this out to an hour's worth of video, and now you're talking weeks of extra time involved.

A whole new generation of RISC-based processors for personal computers are arriving on the market. RISC (Reduced Instruction Set Code) processors work differently than the chips of old that have to read, interpret, and carry out each line of programming code for any given application. RISC chips work by using a form of programming shorthand. In simple everyday terms, instead of having to say, "I want you to walk out to the car, open the door, turn on the ignition, drive to the store, get out of the car, walk to the dairy case, and buy a quart of milk", a RISC processor would be able see the command "Use car, get milk" and know what you mean. The speed gains are especially noticeable with repetitive, commonly used functions, like those used in rendering 3-D animation. Silicon Graphic computers and Power Macintoshes are RISC-based.

Multiple processor systems utilizing both Intel and RISC processors have become available. These systems, depending on the operating system and the application software, can significantly increase image processing speed and, in many cases, can handle multiple rendering and signal processing tasks simultaneously. Real time processing of digital video for the Internet generally requires multi-processor systems to handle the necessary through put.

Operating Systems

The operating system is more than just a collection of windows, menus, and trash can/recycle bin icons. It is the basic set of instructions that tells the CPU how to perform all of its functions, like how to open a file, access a hard drive, or display the video. And yes, this also includes the user interface. Of primary concern for desktop video applications is the data bit rate. This measures the data flow between the CPU, operating system and applications. 8-bit computers, like the original Apple IIe, send data in "packets" 8 bits wide and 8 bits high. A 16-bit system, like most PCs on the market today, send out data in a 16 bit by 16 bit packet. The increase is exponential; data flow in a 16-bit system is 4 times as great as an 8-bit system. Applications are written and programmed to work with a specific operating system, or, more specifically, to work through an operating system. The operating system is the middle man, shuttling instructions from the application, sending it off the CPU, taking the results, sending them back to the application, and so on, while also managing all the other computer's functions. The bottleneck is rarely the CPU. CPUs have traditionally been improved to a higher performance level, so fast that operating systems can not keep up with them. The reason is simple. To replace a chip for a few hundred dollars is a fairly simple thing. To replace your operating system and *every program you're using* is a much more complex, time-consuming and risky undertaking. Obviously, this can also be an expensive proposition.

Bus Platforms

Buses are the actual hardware used to connect peripherals and add-on cards to the brains of the computer. These buses are often used for hard drives, video capture boards and graphic accelerators. The speed of a bus will limit its capability to access the main processor and the amount of information that can flow between the two. The CPU is rarely the bottleneck, it's more likely the bus that can't keep up with the flow of data. This is important for real-time functions like video capture. The faster the bus, the more data that can be shoved through the system, resulting in a higher quality image.

IDE (Integrated Drive Electronics)

IDE buses are relatively slow and are most often used for internal hard drives. This is where the system and application software resides and once a program is loaded into memory, the hard drive is rarely accessed. On occasion, it's been proven the best bus for certain capture hardware. Because there's generally less hardware and routing involved, it can capture video data faster, coming directly from the CPU. There are new Enhanced

IDE hard drives designed for high speed audio and video capture that promise very low cost and high quality systems.

ISA (Industry Standard Architecture)

ISA buses have a very low data rate and are mostly used for low-end capture boards. In addition, an ISA bus machine will not be able to make use of Fast SCSI-2 or Fast-Wide SCSI-2 drives. Even standard SCSI is limited by the ISA bus data transfer rate. ISA has essentially been replaced by PCI in new systems.

SCSI (Small Computer System Interface)

SCSI (pronounced "scuzzy") buses are the industry standard for connecting hard drives and other external peripherals. The first format, SCSI-1, is now rarely found. Much more common is SCSI-2 and it comes in a variety of "flavors." In order of data through put from lowest to highest, there's SCSI-2, Fast SCSI-2, and Fast-Wide SCSI-2 . A hard drive that is SCSI-2 compatible will work with any of the SCSI-2 bus controllers.

EISA

EISA buses used to be the fastest available on the PC, but are being phased out with the introduction of PCI systems.

NuBus

NuBus has been the Mac standard for buses for years. In order to get around the bus bottleneck, some video capture systems used up to 3 or 4 NuBus slots at a single time. Their established market usage and long-term future are for less demanding applications, like sound and graphics. This system is now obsolete in new systems.

PCI

PCI buses are the wave of the future. Not only are they super-fast, they will work well with all the new CPU chips being developed, and they're platform independent. That is, the same board will work on both a PCI-compatible Mac or PC, with just a different version of software installed. Older video capture systems that peaked out 4.5 MB per second, are now getting through put rates over 9 MB per second. And it's only going to get better, as more development and faster multi-processor computers come onto the market. PCI bus systems currently dominate the personal computer world for virtually all hardware and operating systems.

Firewire

At the top level IEEE 1394 or Firewire interface is a potential replacement for SCSI and PCI both. It is a very high speed high bandwidth technology of transferring data from one device to another. It's seminal use is in connecting digital video equipment, camcorders and decks to each other and to computers. At this time most consumer and prosumer and some professional video equipment have these connectors. An add-on board is required for the computer. The advantage to these over the usual capture boards are that there is no quality loss when transferring the video data from device to device.

Mass Storage

When it comes to talking about desktop video, there's plenty of discussion about new compression algorithms and improved software, but you hear very little about hard drives. Let's face it, they're not inherently exciting. It's like talking about the gas tank in your car; you need it, but it's not something you drool about in your dreams. So eventually, all your beautiful video has to be stored somewhere and it's off to the hard drives. Take notice! Hard drives are often the single biggest determinant in maximizing the quality of video captured. They are also often the single most expensive component of a desktop video system. Yes, hard drive prices are coming down dramatically. Just as the capability to capture huge amounts of video data are increasing. Many systems are measured in the tens of gigabytes of storage for basic desktop video. Can terrabytes be far away?

Capturing to Memory

Before we consider hard drive capture, make note of an important alternative. With many boards it's possible to capture directly to memory, rather than to a hard drive. RAM (Random Access Memory) is the resident memory available when the computer is turned on. This memory is used by the operating system and any other applications that have been opened. It is also used for storing data, such as an open word processing document. This data can be an audio/video data stream. Capturing video to memory has both advantages and disadvantages.

On the plus side, capturing to memory can often provide the best possible video quality for a given capture board. It's best used to increase the frame rate of video captured. The flow of data coming from the capture board may be so overwhelming that a hard drive can't keep up with all of it. In order to stay in synch, the hard drive will record as much as it can, but bypass certain data. This results in dropped frames. Instead of getting 15 frames-per-second, you may end up with a random selection of 12 fps. The playback will seem uneven, stuttering. Because all RAM is immediately available, there is very little chance of creating any dropped frames. Capturing to RAM works best with a very fast CPU, so that some kind of compression may be applied to the video data stream. This makes the file size smaller, and consequently, longer movies may be captured.

The downside of capturing video to memory is that it takes a lot of available RAM to do this, even for short captures. It's not unreasonable to use 50 MB of RAM for a minute of

320 x 240, 15 fps video. Remember, this is available RAM, above and beyond what the operating system and capture application need in order to run. To maximize the available RAM, close down any unnecessary applications and TSRs. TSR (Terminate and Stay Resident) programs are often opened by the system upon start-up and include screen savers, system utilities, and the like. You'll also need to allow more time for the capture session. It's a two-step process: the first, capturing to RAM; the second, recording the RAM data to a hard drive.

Beware! Don't think of this as a panacea for all your video capture problems. RAM is much more expensive than fast hard drives. It may maximize the capability of your board and if you can scrounge together enough RAM chips to get you through a project, great. But it's not always the answer. Generally, the boards that allow this process capture at less than full-screen resolution, using bulky software compression techniques. If you're really serious about desktop video, it may be cheaper to get a better capture board that assists in compressing and managing the data rate, coupled with a really fast SCSI controller and hard drive. Oh, and your video will be full-frame size, 30 fps, with much higher quality.

Capturing to Hard Drives

Hard drives are like paper clips–you can never have enough of them. Just when you think you've got a lifetime supply, you'll be scrounging around for an extra one. There are a number of factors that determine whether a hard drive is suitable for desktop video production. But remember, just because a drive's raw specs are good, doesn't mean it's going to work well with a particular capture system. Always check with the capture board's manufacturer first. They often have lists of recommended hard drives and have tested them for performance.

AV Rated Hard Drives

One of the primary requirements for any desktop video hard drive is that it be A/V (Audio/ Video) rated. Regular hard drives allow for re-calibration during a long data write sequence. Obviously, any interruption to the hard drive during a real-time video capture could result in lost data and dropped frames. With A/V hard drives, this re-calibration feature is turned off.

Average Access and Seek Times

Measured in milliseconds, average access and seek times are defined as the time it takes to find and retrieve data from the disk. A digital video drive should have numbers below 15ms and preferably under 10ms.

Average Latency

The delay, in milliseconds, for the drive platter to spin to the correct position is the average latency. A drive with an average latency under 6ms is acceptable.

Spin Rate

The spin rate is the revolutions per minute (rpm) that the drive performs. A digital video drive should have a spin rate of at least 5400 rpm. 7200 rpm is better and sometimes required for high-end systems.

Average Throughput

The average throughput is the consistent data rate, in megabytes per second, that the drive can sustain. This is a mechanical rating of the hard drive only. It doesn't take into account for system management of data transfers. Data from a video capture card can't be written directly to a hard drive. It must first be transferred to a "holding area" in system memory. From here, data is accessible to peripherals and hard drives. As data is fed into this holding area, data can't be written to a hard drive. And while data is being written to a hard drive, data can't flow into the holding area. Therefore, part of each second is spent copying data to the system memory, while another part is performing data output to disk. So a drive that may be capable of an average throughput of 5MB/sec, in reality, will only be able to capture 2.4 MB of data per second.

Mean Time Between Failures (MTBF)

Mean time between failures is the average number of usage hours between failures. Drives for digital video production have a hard life. They are constantly reading and writing large amounts of data in a sustained transfer. Average MTBF is about 300,000 hours. Don't be afraid to invest in a more rugged drive. Just think how you're going to feel if all your precious video is gone when the hard drive crashes.

Capturing to Arrays

Think of arrays as hard drives with an attitude. They are really individual hard drives, linked together using special hardware and software. To the computer an array looks like a single big hard drive, and a very fast one too. Instead of having to wait for a single hard drive to finish writing its data to disk, the computer can continue sending data to another waiting hard drive. In this way, the data for a single piece of video can be spread over several hard drives. For example, Drive A may record Field 1 Video, Drive B will record Field 2 Video, and Drive C records Audio. When it's time for playback, each drive plays its own piece of the data sequence, in perfect synch with the others.

Termination and Cabling

An often overlooked but common source of problems is the proper termination and cabling of SCSI devices such as hard drives.

Caution: Always turn off the computer and all peripherals before attaching or detaching any cables, terminators, or devices. Doing otherwise could cause permanent physical damage to the computer or SCSI devices as well as the loss of important data.

SCSI devices chained together form an electronic signal path. At the end of the path, signals tend to "reflect" and "bounce" back up the SCSI path causing interference. This interference can cause problems with the host computer and/or one or more of the SCSI devices. Terminating a SCSI bus preserves high transmission speeds, and can clean up the signal along the entire length of the line. In most cases, termination needs to occur only at the first and last device in the chain. Since nearly all systems have some sort of internal termination, either through an internal hard drive or other SCSI device, it is generally necessary to terminate the last SCSI device in a chain. A standard method of terminating is to place a plug-in terminator at the end of the last section of cable, or on the second connector of the last drive in the chain.

Another potential problem area when working with hard drives is the cabling. It's important to always use high quality, double-shielded cables. Poor quality cables are often the cause of seemingly mysterious SCSI problems. Cables that are small in diameter and very flexible are likely to be poor SCSI cables. Also, avoid mixing brands, types, or styles of cables. Each cable has a different type of construction, impedance, and wire placement, which can result in bus reflections. In mixed cabled configurations some devices simply may not work even if all other guidelines are followed.

The total length of all cables used, (all devices and cables added together), must not be greater than 19.6 feet. Don't forget to consider the internal cabinet wiring, which is generally about 18 inches on most SCSI devices. The total length allowable is also a function of the number of devices distributed along the chain. The more devices, the shorter the aggregate length should be.

Keep cables between devices as short and even in length as possible. Generally, 18 to 24 inches is best, but never exceed 6 feet or you will most likely have problems.

Capture Boards

The equipment to transfer analog video to a computer and convert it to digital information that can be processed by a computer is called a Video Capture Board. These are not an inherent part of most personal computers. The technical specifications for capture boards range as widely as do their prices. Simple boards designed for home and limited multimedia use cost a few hundred dollars and professional systems with component analog or digital input and output are several thousand. The cost and complexity of the peripheral equipment such as AV rated hard drives and software also range widely. Some boards capture only video and some capture both video and audio. The analog capture boards convert analog video signals to digital information and save it to a hard drive. Digital boards, such as the Firewire prosumer systems, transfer digital video signals from camcorders and decks to and from the computer but don't digitize the signal since they are already in the digital domain. We will consider here typical desktop capture boards that are capable of professional broadcast quality editing but are within the budget of the desktop producer.

Video Only Cards

There are a number of video capture cards that only capture video. One example is the Personal Video Recorder (PVR) manufactured by Digital Processing Systems, Inc. These systems have their origins with video producers and animation artists who focus on the capture and playback of animation. The PVR and similar boards are being upgraded to on-board audio capture or are being combined with associated cards that synchronize with them.

Video and Audio Cards

The majority of digital video capture boards being produced now integrate synchronized audio capture into the boards themselves. This assures a high quality audio track and helps eliminate the synchronization problems that can occur with separate boards.

Audio Only Cards

These boards, essential to the audio editor and sound designer, can be utilized to capture audio for video or audio only. They range from add-on or integrated sound capture and playback associated with the basic computer, to high-quality professional analog and/or digital capture systems with multiple tracks and on-board effects. The highest quality system available should be used for audio capture and processing.

Analog

Most audio and video boards capture from analog input and output connections. The consumer grade systems utilize mini audio connections and RCA composite connections. The mid-level systems add DIN connector S-Video connections. The high end industrial and professional systems add component video and balanced analog audio (XLR) connections and might also include digital audio connections.

Digital

The simplest digital inputs for audio are the SPDIF system that uses RCA connections. Optical connections also utilize the SPDIF standard. Professional digital audio connections utilize XLR connectors and conform to the AES/EBU standard. Both systems produce high quality signals. The simplest digital video standard is the IEEE 1394 or Firewire bus connection. This system is utilized by the new consumer and prosumer digital video camcorders and record decks. Professional systems utilize serial connectors and proprietary connections.

Beware of the Hype!

As new products come onto the market, it's easy to get caught up in the excitement of all this great technology, especially, if it's accompanied by some slick color advertising. Here are some catch-phrases that sound impressive until they are really explained.

Digital

When a capture board manufacturer says you can "digitally" capture and store video with their product, what they mean is that your analog video is being analyzed, compressed, and converted in bits and bytes that the computer can understand. What was formerly on tape is now a data file on a hard drive. This is different from a true digital transfer, where the bits and bytes outputted by a digital tape deck or disk recorder are transferred into the computer system, one for one, with no change or loss in quality. The exploitation of the word "digital" has been going on for quite some time. In the mid-70's, at the height of the "Pong" craze, a few hand-held games were marketed as being "digital." Why? Because you had to use your fingers (digits) to work the mechanical buttons to run the thing!

Non-linear

Well, that's sort of the whole point of doing anything on a computer, isn't it? With tape, you began at the beginning. Start with the first scene, first shot and just keep on going until you get to the end. If a scene is to be deleted or inserted, it's necessary to pick it up at that point and re-edit everything that follows. In the computer realm, that's all changed. Now it's possible to make wholesale changes, quickly and simply, without drastically affecting the time it takes to complete the project. It's the difference between working with a typewriter and a word processing application. So what's so special about being non-linear? On the grand scale of things, it's a monumental improvement over tape-based editing systems. But for a computer, that's just what they do.

Broadcast Quality

This used to be an easy one. In the old days, when video cameras were only slightly smaller than refrigerators, and there were only four televisions channels to pick up (with the rabbit ears adjusted just so), broadcast quality meant just one thing–it was worth putting on network TV. In the 1950's that could mean it was black & white and run through a grainy Kinescope. As the first consumer video products hit the market, broadcast quality could be measured objectively, through waveform and vectorscope readings. The gap in technical standards between consumer and broadcast level equipment was so huge it was easy to see the difference. Then everything went crazy. The electronics got miniaturized, the costs came down, and everybody was running around with a home camcorder. Some of the new equipment had just as good quality raw specs as the broadcast equipment, if not better. Worse yet, video shot with this consumer brand equipment actually got on the air. The line between broadcast and consumer quality didn't just get fuzzy, it got wiped out of existence. So now what's broadcast quality? Basically, anything you want it to be. The phrase has been so over-used, maligned and misinterpreted it doesn't hold much value in today's marketplace. However, from a video professional's point of view, broadcast quality today is generally reserved for video and audio that matches the subjective and objective qualities of professional Betacam.

Input/Output

The types of input and output that video capture cards support are in order of video signal quality: composite, S-Video, component analog, component digital, serial digital and Firewire. At this time desktop and prosumer systems are not commonly equipped with component or serial digital interfaces. The minimum professional interface is the S-Video and component analog and Firewire are the minimum for broadcast quality.

Cables and Connections

The connections between hardware components will vary with the equipment used. You will need to connect the video out ports of the video source to the video capture card. S-Video is better than Composite connections. Component is better than S-Video.

Your audio source, normally the audio out port of the video source, must be connected to either the video capture card, an external digitizer, or built-in sound digitizer, as applicable. Use balanced, line-level audio input if possible. Balanced audio uses professional XLR-type connections and is less susceptible to electronic distortion or background "hum." Line-level audio is at a signal strength of +4dB, as compared to Mic level which is at -10dB. Line level audio also minimizes the amount of electronic noise and distortion in an audio signal.

Be sure to use the highest quality connections available with your capture board. Use short cables and as few adapters as necessary. Signal strength can be sapped through distance and poor connections.

Remote Control

If you have a controllable tape deck, a device controller, and the proper software and connections, it may be possible to remotely control playback deck through the capture application. This is necessary for timecode operations, such as batch digitizing. There are a variety of remote control protocols. "Professional" video decks use a 9-pin, RS-422 connector. "Prosumer" grade equipment commonly employs VISCA, Control L or Control S protocols. You'll need to check your equipment and system's capabilities to see if it supports remote control.

Timecode

If you have a controllable video playback device, you can capture video clips automatically by making reference to their timecode. Clips may be viewed, logged and then batch digitized. With timecode it's also possible to capture a large amount of material at a low resolution, and then re-capture the final selected clips at a high resolution. This maximizes disk storage space. To capture using timecode you need a device controller such as the Pipeline Digital Pro VTR, or the Diaquest DQ Timecorder, to control the source remotely. Some video capture cards come with timecode support built into them.

Monitors, Mixers, and Test Equipment

In order to maintain as high a quality signal as possible, it may be desirable to have traditional monitoring and test equipment available.

Video monitors are used for looking at any video going into or out of the desktop video system. They are especially helpful for comparing captured video with how it appears off tape or seeing how the desktop video will appear on a real-world TV set.

TBCs (Time Base Correctors) make sure that the video plays back at the proper NTSC 30 frame, 60 field per second rate. They also provide control for adjusting the video signal. This can be important for making sure the tape plays back the same way it was recorded. Some tape decks come equipped with a TBC. These TBCs often provide additional features, such as a drop-out compensator. This means that video information that has been lost due to absence of oxide on the tape, is replaced with video from a preceding frame, giving the illusion of a complete image. These drop-out compensators can work miracles, especially on older, more heavily damaged videotapes.

Some capture systems will accept any level of audio input. Other high-end systems, like the Media 100, accept only line level input. -10 dB (decibal) is mic level and often used with prosumer grade equipment. +4 dB is line level and used with professional equipment. It's important not to mix the audio signal output of your deck with the input of the capture system. Putting line level audio in a mic level input or mic level audio into a line level input can cause serious audio distortion or deterioration of quality. If needed, a small audio mixer, like the Mackie 1202, may be used to convert one signal strength to another.

More and more capture systems come equipped with internal waveform/vectorscope monitors. These are used to measure the luminance, hue, and saturation levels of the incoming video signal. Waveform/vectorscope monitors are mainstays of traditional video production for ensuring quality control so that each piece of video plays back to a specific standard. Remember, waveform/vectorscope monitors just look at the video, they can't change it themselves. You'll need a TBC or other video signal controls for that.

Conclusion

The technology and suppliers change frequently, though the principles of video capture will remain the same. Select the boards with the best technical specifications that you can afford. Pay particular attention to the type of inputs and outputs. S-video is the minimum for multimedia and corporate editing, and component analog is essential for broadcast quality. The other major quality consideration is the lowest compression ratio. The primary performance issue is rendering speed of output. The latest boards feature hardware effects acceleration. This feature, if it accelerates effects that you use often, can make a considerable difference in the time it takes to render an edit and send it out to the final tape. The primary difference between high quality desktop video and the high end systems is in the speed to render and review the edited video. If you have time to wait, you can produce competitive video.

Chapter 7
Project and Data Management

Introduction

Often the difference between success and failure in creating projects is governed by coming in on time and on budget. Unless money and time are no object, the only way to assure conformance is to plan and control the project. Video and multimedia projects often have hundreds and thousands of audio and video clips and graphic elements. Misplacing or accidentally erasing key elements can waste valuable time, and creating and capturing unnecessary video and audio clips can likewise waste time and money. This chapter includes an example of a technical specification for a multimedia project, and the structure of a database that was created to manage its elements. A similar database can be created using any standard database package such as Access, dBase, Excel or in smaller projects, even a template in a word processing file. The extra time it takes to set up and maintain such a system will be repaid many times over as a project progresses and becomes more complex. In addition to asset management, it is also important to perform regular maintenance on your equipment and undertake organized backup procedures. The stories of lost data and destroyed projects due to hard disk crashes, power outages and improperly aligned recorders and software are legion; don't let your project be added to the lore.

Managing Your Assets

The following asset specification was used for a major CD-ROM game title. Most of the technical specifications would serve for industrial or broadcast quality video and would serve as the basis for creating web delivered video. There is also an example of a simple computer database that was created to manage the large library of video, graphic and audio clips required for the project. There were over 60,000 individual graphic clips generated for the interactive game navigation and animation clips. Without a robust database the process of keeping track of assets is hopeless. A small project can be managed with a carefully updated word processing file or a notebook.

Acquisition Format for Assets

Independent of the final distribution format for assets (graphics, audio, video, etc.) we will create and archive all the assets at "broadcast" quality.

Still Graphics

640 x 460 x 24bit (16 million colors) Targa files. When the images are composited with text they will be archived in Adobe Premier or Micrografix Picture Publisher object files so they can be manipulated for localization.

Video

Live video will usually be shot with Betacam SP though in some cases we will use HI-8. These tapes will be archived. Final edited masters will be archived on BetacamSP for future use.

Animation will be created with 640 x 480 x 24bit Targa or AVI files and archived on DAT tapes.

All Adobe Premier edit and project files will be maintained so that any video and animation that is edited for the final project will be able to be easily localized by replacing the English voice-over with whatever language required. These files will also allow upgrading of the digital video to any required format (eg: MPEG).

Audio

Original music and sound will be recorded on ADAT digital multitrack tapes and/or RDAT digital two track tapes. A 44KH, 16bit sample rate will be used.

MIDI files will be General MIDI compatible when possible.

3D Models

The majority of the 3D models are built or are being built using *Caligari Truespace*. The scenes and objects will be created and archived in the native Caligari SCN and OBJ formats. They can be translated into AutoDesk DXF or 3DS formats for exchange to 3D

Studio or other modeling and rendering packages. We may use 3D Studio or other packages for special effects. All the packages import and export DXF files.

We are developing and maintaining hard copy maps of each scene as well as detailed descriptors of them. Each scene contains lighting, texture map information and cameras for still and animated picture generation. They are well documented. A detailed explanation of the use and integration of every camera view and animation into the game will be kept in a "continuity" database.

Image File Naming Convention

Every master background file in the game, those images that are derived from the 3D models will have file names that make them easy to track within the game and the assets library. The convention is as follows.

Scene
Camera
Frame
Subframe
Version
File Type

OA2003_A.BMP

Scene	The Caligari .SCN file the image derives from
Camera	The camera in the Caligari scene
Frame	The sequence of the image in the game.
Subframe	Used if the image is subordinate to the master frame
Version	The version of the rendering (eg: progress, sizing or palette work, etc)
File Type	The type of file (eg: BMP, JPG, AVI, etc.)

Any files that are composited from multiple images will be done in Micrografx Picture Publisher or Adobe Photoshop with "floating" objects so that any modifications can be accessed. This will be particularly important for those files that include text. This will enable alternative text (eg: German) to be floated onto the image easily without completely reworking the composite image. In most cases these files are self-documenting. Sound recordings and MIDI files will be maintained as multitrack files with all music and sound FX and voice-over on separate tracks for the same purpose. Premier project files will allow foreign voice-over track to be substituted for the English tracks without reediting the entire files.

These databases combined with the scripts, maps of the worlds, flow charts of the game elements, Caligari scene files, Adobe Premier files will give us and our partners a detailed map to the construction and localization of the complete game.

Project Asset Database

Besides the image naming convention, if time permits, we plan to create a detailed Project Asset database in FoxBase Pro (or similar package) to record and link all the screens, sub-screens, video, audio, animation, etc. The database will have data entry screens for each asset type (eg: animation, sound, etc.), There will also be a master SCREEN data input screen that will allow the game screens to be tested for elements and navigation. This is essentially a "pre-authoring" screen. The database tables created and linked to this screen can be exported to the game engine script to "pre-build" much of the script. The main screen is shown below.

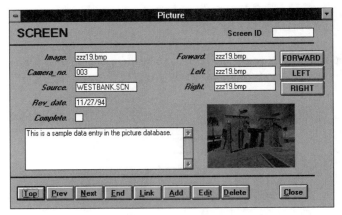

Figure 7.1 Game Screen Database Entry Screen

SCREEN.dbf

Screen_ID	C	8	Composite game screen ID
Image	C	12	Master image file
Source	C	12	The Caligari .SCN file the image derives from
Camera_no	C	3	The camera in the Caligari scene
Forward	C	12	Next screen Forward in game
Left	C	12	Next screen Left in game
Right	C	12	Next screen Right in game
Icon	C	12	Postage stamp icon for data screen
Rev_date	Date	8	Last revision date
Complete	L	1	"T" if final verson for release
Comment	Memo		Any comments

EXTURE.dbf

Image	C	12	Image file
Icon	C	12	Postage stamp icon for data screen
Rev_date	Date	8	Last revision date
Complete	L	1	"T" if final version for release
Comment	Memo		Any comments

ANIMATION.dbf

Image	C	12	AVI, Quicktime or MPEG file
Source	C	12	The Caligari .SCN file the image derives from
Camera_no	C	3	The camera in the Caligari scene
Sound	C	12	Sound file linked
Edit_file	C	12	Adobe Premier edit file
Icon	C	12	Postage stamp icon for data screen
Rev_date	Date	8	Last revision date
Complete	L	1	"T" if final version for release
Comment	Memo		Any comments

SOUND.dbf

File	C	12	
Source	Memo		
Rev_date	Date	8	Last revision date
Complete	L	1	"T" if final version for release
Comment	Memo	'	Any comments

TEXT.dbf

File	C	12	
Rev_date	Date	8	Last revision date
Complete	L	1	"T" if final version for release
Comment	Memo		Any comments

LINK.dbf

Screen_ID   C   8

Link_ID   C   12

Sound Design Overview

We expect all the sound and music to be Wave files rather than MIDI. We are looking at MIDI as a possibility but are concerned with technical support of the MIDI side of sound cards and the lack of uniformity on the MAC.

Overture (22KH, 16 bit, stereo if possible)

These musical elements will underscore the opening (Prolog) and closing (Postlog) video sequences.

Ambient Sound Loops and Transitional Loops (Generally 11 or 22KH, 8bit, Mono)

Each world and ancillary areas within the world will have motivated ambient sound loops that establish an auditory presence. These will include wind sounds, birds, etc. Some of the loops will serve as transitions, sound to cover the loading of game segments. The transitional loops might be loaded onto the player's hard drive to minimize impact on RAM usage and to allow them to play during CD-ROM access. Transitional loops will be limited to 2 to 3 Megabytes of audio.

Incidental Score Loops (Generally 11 or 22KH, 8bit, Mono)

Modular musical building blocks of a measure or two of music to be used to underscore interesting and dramatic elements of the game play. There will be motifs for: Egypt, Atlantis, Maya city, Tibet and the space station. We may also have motifs for some of the characters. These modules will be strung together with ambient loops to create the feeling of a complete cinematic musical score.

FX (Generally 11 or 22KH, 8bit, Mono)

We will provide motivated sound effects to go with animated action and games and puzzles. Examples would include: fire, falling rocks, water, mechanical and electronic noises associated with puzzle action and buttons, opening doors, etc.

Video Tracks (Generally 11 or 22KH, 8bit, Mono)

Beyond voice-over ambient noise and music may be included in video tracks and animation.

System Management

There are several settings that can be made to optimize a desktop video system for capture. In general, the purpose of these settings is to stream-line the system, so that all available power and resources are focused on just one thing—capturing video and moving the data to a hard drive as fast as possible.

Smartdrive

On PCs there is a commonly used utility called Smartdrive. Smartdrive creates a temporary buffer storage area on hard drives for application programs that may not be loaded in their entirety into resident RAM. This is done automatically by the computer to optimize memory for current operations. Parts of the program that aren't immediately needed are shuffled off through Smartdrive to the buffer area. Meanwhile, the extra RAM can be used for memory hungry tasks, like computations.

Unfortunately, Smartdrive interferes with continuous, unobstructed flow of video data to the selected hard drive and must be turned off. This can be done be using the REM command in the AUTOEXEC.BAT file where Smartdrive is listed. For example: rem Smartdrive

Another way to turn off Smartdrive on the drive where video is to be stored is with the DOS command "smartdrv (drive letter)-." For example, if video is to be stored on the "C:" drive, the command would look as follows: C:\>smartdrv c-

TSRs

Terminate and Stay Resident programs are applications that are always on and in memory. They are often opened by the system upon start-up. TSRs include screen savers, virus checkers, and the like. TSRs take up memory and CPU time and should be disabled.

On PCs, this can be done by using the REM command in the AUTOEXEC.BAT file. Microsoft Window programs running in the background (i.e. simultaneously with the video capture application) should also be turned off.

On the Mac, TSRs are usually found as extensions. These can be disabled by going to the Extension Manager under Control Panels in the System Folder. Be sure to turn off any other unneeded extensions, as these only take up valuable RAM. Just like for PCs, any programs running in the background should also be turned off.

Networks

Network applications and drivers should be disabled. It's obvious when you think about someone on another computer trying to access data on the drive you're trying to store captured video. But even if the network is not in active use, network software interrupts current operations on a regular basis to check the network for possible commands. This interruption can interfere with the flow of video data to a hard drive.

On PCs this can be done by using the REM command in the CONFIG.SYS and AUTOEXEC.BAT files.

On Macs, this can be done by turning off network extensions in the Extensions Manager, under Control Panels, in the System Folder.

Peripherals

Make sure that all peripherals on your system are turned off or are loaded with the proper media. This includes floppy drives, tape drives, and CD-ROMs. This way the CPU won't be continually checking the empty drives, taking away from the capture process.

Memory Management

The general philosophy of memory management is free up as much random-access memory (RAM) as possible. This allows the CPU to dedicate itself entirely to the capture process. A certain minimum amount of RAM is necessary to run the system and capture application software. Systems at the minimum level may not perform optimally. Additional RAM, up to a point, may improve the quality and quantity of capture possible.

Memory controls on the Macintosh may be found under System Folder/Control Panel/Memory. Under Windows 3.1 for the PC, check under Main/Control Panel/Enhanced/Virtual Memory/Change. The following suggested settings may not be found on all systems. Check your computer manual or capture board manual for additional information.

Disk Cache

A disk cache improves computer performance by using a portion of RAM to store frequently used information from disk. For video capture purposes this merely ties up valuable RAM. Set the disk cache to as low as possible—32K on the Mac, 128K on the PC.

On the Mac, there is a control called the Memory Manager. This is used to allocate and manage the on-board memory. The Memory Manager should be On.

Virtual Memory

Virtual Memory allows your computer to use space on an attached hard drive as RAM. This can be quite useful when running multiple applications, or large applications, that might not normally work with the available RAM. This should not be used with capture software, as the access time to a hard drive is much slower than RAM itself. Turn Virtual Memory Off.

A RAM disk is the opposite of Virtual Memory. It allows you to use a part of RAM as a high-speed disk. This is used for quick retrieval of frequently used data or images. Once again, this only ties up the RAM from full use by the capture software. The RAM disk should be Off.

32-Bit Access

32-bit File Access allows for greater performance in reading and writing data to hard drives. Turn 32-File Access On.

Allocating Memory

On the Macintosh, it's possible to allocate memory to specific programs. If you're not capturing to RAM, this should be as high as possible. Find the capture program icon, and select Get Info from the File Menu. A window will appear with info about the application. At the bottom, in a box labeled Memory Requirements, you will find a Suggested memory size, a Minimum size, and a Preferred size. In the Preferred size box, type in the number of megabytes you will be able to allocate to the program. Make sure you allow for the memory already being used by system software. The application must be closed to make these memory changes and will take effect the next time it's opened.

Drive Management

Defragmentation

The hard disk where you are planning to store video should be defragmented. A fragmented hard drive has data blocks interspersed with empty blocks. This can happen over time by alternately writing new data files and erasing old ones. When the hard drive goes to write new data it will start at the first available empty block. It will then continue to the next block. When it finds one that is already full, it has to skip to a different part of the drive to the find an empty block. This can interrupt the hard drive enough to cause a loss of data and skipped frames. It can also slow playback because the drive head has to jump around the hard drive so much.

On PCs with DOS 6.0 or greater, type DEFRAG at the DOS prompt and follow the instructions on the screen. Some disk utility programs include defragmenting features that work faster than DEFRAG. On the other hand, they may not be able to handle a full 2GB DOS limit hard drive or partition.

On the Mac, there are several utilities for defragmenting hard drives. One of the best is Disk Tools Pro. It not only defragments hard drives, but also checks and fixes them of viruses and other system errors.

Scratch Disk

Some capture systems require or recommend the use of a scratch disk. A scratch disk is a dedicated disk, or portion of a disk, used just for storing captured video and audio data. When data is written to a hard drive, certain basic drive "housekeeping" functions take valuable time away from the continuous flow of data streaming through the system. Imagine an assembly line with product (data) flowing down a chute. In the conventional manner, a new box (data blocks on a hard drive) must first be created before the chute is opened. With a scratch disk, the boxes are already made, in order, ready to receive product. By creating a pre-determined file, the disk can spend all of its effort in storing data as quickly as possible.

The scratch disk is designated and created with the specific capture software in use. It needs to be bigger than the largest movie expected to be captured. If the capture extends beyond the size of the scratch file, the hard drive will continue writing data, but in the slower, conventional manner. This may result in loss of image quality or cause the system to abort the capture altogether.

Once the capture is finished, the data is transferred to another drive or part of the same drive for permanent storage. Be sure to factor this time into your schedule. The capture itself may be "real-time", but the transfer of data may take five times as long, depending on the size of the files.

In addition to these basic system settings, be sure to check your capture board's instruction manual for other important set-up information. Every board is different and the way it works may require more adjustments than listed here.

Conclusion

In addition to the topics included above there will be many project management needs that are specific to your project and to your particular combination of hardware, software and other equipment. It is necessary to be completely familiar with all of the technical requirements and maintenance and set-up procedures, and to think through as carefully as possible as many of the acquisition and editing issues as you can. Vigilance and attention to detail is the key to project management success.

Bibliography

Aldridge, Henry B., and Lucy A. Liggett. *Audio/Video Production: Theory and Practice.* Englewood Cliffs, NJ: Prentice Hall, 1990.

Armer, Alan A. *Directing Television and Film.* Belmont, CA: Wadsworth, 1986.

Burrows, Thomas D., et al. *Television Production: Disciplines and Techniques.* 4th ed. Dubuque, IA: Wm. C. Brown, 1989.

Chapter 8
Capturing to Disk

Introduction

Before we begin the capture process, it is assumed that the entire system has been properly configured: hardware and software installation; proper formatting of hard drives; the creation of scratch disks as necessary; appropriate memory and system settings; and all video, audio, remote control and other connections completed. Although there are a variety of capture application interfaces and options, we will be following the capture process as used in Adobe Premiere 4.2 for the Mac. The functions available in the MAC version of Premiere are common to the Windows version and other video edit programs. Many video capture boards, even if they come with their own software, allow Adobe Premiere to be used as the capture interface. When using Premier of other full-featured edit packages, there are utilities and add-on software and cables that allow you to create an automated capture list to ease the process and alow efficient recaptures if necessary. This is a work saving feature.

Video Capture

For the capturing process either your editing software or the dedicated capture software that came with your capture board will work fine depending on your choice of work process. Video may be captured in two ways: in real time or non-real time.

Real Time Capture

In real time capture, hardware or software compression is used as the video is fed into the system. It's the easiest and fastest method of capturing.

Non-Real Time Capture

Non-real time capture works by grabbing a single frame of video at a time, or making multiple passes until the computer has captured all the needed frames. These methods require a frame-accurate tape deck, timecode on the source tape, and a third-party utility, such as DiaQuest QuickPass, for controlled capture of the video data. Non-real time capture can provide for a very high level of capture quality, since each frame is analyzed and compressed individually. The downside is that it is very time consuming and requires a tape and deck that can stand up under the strenuous mechanical demands of being in freeze-frame playback/pause mode for long periods of time.

Settings

Here is a run through of the procedures involved for a full audio/video capture using Adobe Premiere. The steps listed are in a logical, preferred order, but certainly not the only order possible. Some of these steps may not even be necessary, depending upon the type of capture being done. See the Adobe Premiere Users Guide or your specific capture software owner's manual for more information.

Source Controls

The first task is to tell Premiere where the source video is coming from and what signal format it's in.

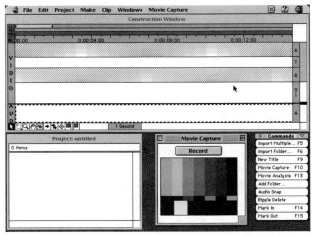

Figure 8.1 Movie Capture Window

1.   From the File menu choose Capture/Movie Capture. The Movie Capture window appears and the Movie Capture menu appears in the menu bar. The Movie Capture Window will contain a sample of the digitized video and a Record button. We'll come back to this window when we're ready to record later.

2.   From the Movie Capture menu select Video Input. The Video Input dialog box appears.

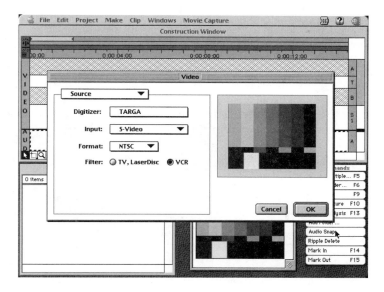

Figure 8.2 Video Input Dialog Box

A sample of the image you are digitizing will appear in the upper right half of the dialog box. At the top left is a pop-up menu containing at least three choices for Video Input control panels: Compression, Image, and Source. The choices and options available will be determined by the video capture board you are using. Some options may be dimmed out and unavailable or chosen automatically by the capture card.

3.   Choose Source from the pop-up menu. The Source panel appears.

4.   Select the digitizing board you want to use.

5.   Select the type of source video you are capturing. This is based on the connections used between the playback deck and video capture board. The choice may be component, S-video, or composite.

6.   Select the format in which you want to capture the images–NTSC, PAL, or SECAM. Unless

you're creating material for international broadcast and know exactly which video format to use, always choose NTSC.

7.   Select a the video synchronization filter that matches your source video—TV/Laserdisc or VCR.

Frame Rate and Compression

Now select the compression and frame rate to be used for the captured video.

1.   Choose Compression from the pop-up menu at the top of Video dialog box. The Compression control panel appears.

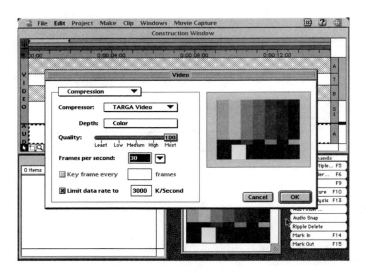

Figure 8.3 Compression Control Panel

2.   Select a compressor. For more information on software compression, see "Survey of Codecs", in Chapter 15. For video capture boards with hardware compression, select the compressor recommended by the manufacturer.

3.   Select a depth from the Depth pop-up menu. Select Best Depth to capture at the depth preferred by your digitizer.

4.   Set a quality level by using the Quality slider control. Generally, a default setting will appear based upon the compression chosen and type of capture board used. It is best to start with this default setting. The quality may be increased if all other capture targets (compression, size, frame rate) can be achieved with no difficulty.

5. Select a frame rate from the Frames per Second pop-up menu. It is best to have Adobe Premiere automatically capture at the highest frame rate possible with your system.

6. It is possible to crop the video to be captured by drag-and-drawing a highlighted window inside the sample area in the Movie Capture window. Only the portion of the image inside the highlighted area will be captured. Be very careful using this option. Some boards will capture at a decreased frame rate if the aspect ratio is set to anything other than 4:3. If you are capturing at a size larger than the target output, there are other cropping tools available during editing that provide for greater control and flexibility.

Video Levels

Before capturing it's important to always adjust the levels of the incoming video signal. This can be done through this same Video Input Dialog box by selecting Image from the pop-up menu. However, these slider controls are purely subjective, with only a sample screen of the digitized video available to show what changes these make. A much better way is to use Premiere's Waveform Monitor and Vector Scope controls.

1. Select OK on the Video Input Dialog Box.

2. Press the Play button on your tape deck. Use the pre-recorded color bar portion of the tape if possible. If not, then play a representative portion of the video.

3. From the File menu choose Capture/Waveform Monitor. The Waveform Scope dialog box appears.

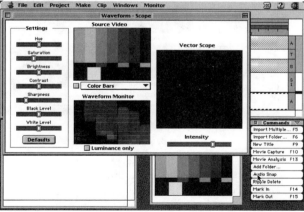

Figure 8.4 Waveform Scope dialog box

The Waveform Scope dialog box can be broken down into four areas.

The Source Video window displays a sample of the digitized footage and the effect of any video settings. This is also where the standard color bars recorded on your videotape will appear. A pop-up menu is available to select an Adobe Premiere reference image, such as standard color bars. This can be used for visual comparison and help in getting a better match to the bars on your videotape.

The Waveform Monitor window displays the luminance and color saturation values in the video as a series of vertical lines. Black (0 IRE) is at the bottom and white (100 IRE) is at the top. Saturation is represented by the height of the lines. Luminance is at the mid-point of each line. Click the Luminance Only option to read just the luminance levels.

You'll notice a thinner line between 0 and 10 on the waveform scale. This is set at 7.5 IRE and represents "true" video black, since all NTSC video, even black, contains some chroma information. You'll also notice that during playback of standard color bars, yellow creates the highest levels on the waveform monitor, even higher than pure white. This is because of the additional chroma information encoded with NTSC video.

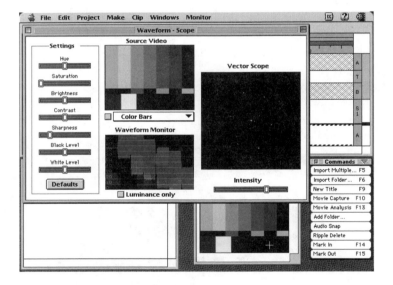

Figure 8.5 Close-up Waveform scale

The Vector Scope displays hue and saturation values of the source video. The hue is represented by the angle it appears on the scope. The saturation is represented by its distance from the center of the scope. The optimum range of values for each primary color in the standard color bar pattern is enclosed by a small box. The primary colors represented are magenta, blue, cyan, green, yellow, and red.

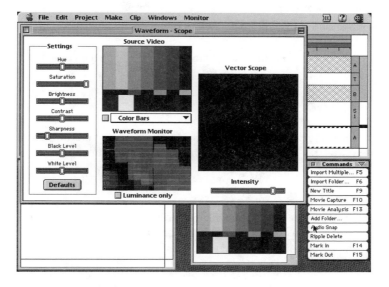

Figure 8.6 Close-up Vector Scope

The Settings window contains all the controls for adjusting the incoming video. This includes: hue, saturation, brightness, contrast, sharpness, black level, and white level. There is also a Default button that returns all controls back to a standard setting.

4.   Adjust the Settings. These suggestions are all made under the assumption that you are using standard color bars for reference. If not, then you'll have to search through your video for representative shots.

Start by clicking on the Luminance Only option below the Waveform Monitor and adjust the Black Level and White Level so the readings match the black and white swatches on the color bars.

De-select the Luminance Only option and adjust the Brightness and Contrast so that the saturation and luminance readings are as close as possible for all areas of the Waveform Monitor.

Adjust the Hue and Saturation to match the Vector Scope targets. The most important target to hit is red, since it's the color closest to most flesh tones and the color most likely to "bleed" through over-saturation.

Sharpness may be adjusted, but is best used in moderation.

It may be necessary to go through the process a couple of times in order to find a best overall setting. Also be sure to look at footage besides color bars and observe the effects of your adjustments. Color bars provide a standard reference, with every extreme that could possibly show up in a piece of video, but don't be a slave to them. Your video may have been lit in a special way that isn't truly represented by the color bars. Pay special attention to flesh tones. Continue making adjustments as needed.

5.   Close the Waveform Scope dialog box by clicking the upper left window close button.

Audio Input

Hopefully, you were able to record a 1k Hz audio tone along with your color bars. Since you're still in that portion of the tape, let's go ahead and adjust the settings for audio input.

1.   Choose Sound Input from the Movie Capture menu. The Sound dialog box appears. The left side of the box varies with the hardware in use and the panel selected from the pop-up menu at the top of the dialog box: Compression, Sample, or Source. The right side of the dialog box contains a meter and controls for audio input and speaker set-up.

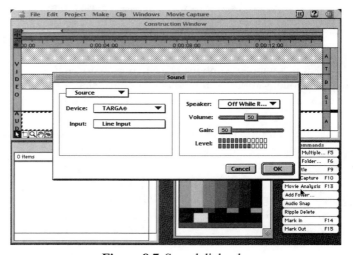

Figure 8.7 Sound dialog box

2.   Choose Source from the pop-up menu at the top of the dialog box. The Source panel appears.

From the Device pop-up menu, select the audio digitizer to use. From the Input pop-up menu, select the proper audio input connection.

3.   Choose Sample from the pop-up menu. The Sample panel appears.

Select an audio sampling rate. Choose 44kHZ if your audio board is capable of sampling at that rate. Select a sampling depth, either 8 or 16 bit. Use 16-bit sampling if possible.

Select mono or stereo recording. Remember, stereo doubles the size of the audio file and should only be used for true stereo applications.

4. To apply compression, choose Compression from the pop-up menu. In most cases, compressing audio is not advisable and should be left at None.

5. Select the Speaker On option and start playback of your videotape.

6. Use the Volume slider control to adjust the speaker volume. This control does not affect the levels of the input audio signal

7. Adjust the Gain slider control so that the input audio levels do not extend into the red zone of the meter below.

8. Choose Off or Off While Recording from the Speaker pop-up window unless you need to hear sound as you record. Capturing performance improves with the speaker turned off.

9. Click OK to return to the Movie Capture Window.

Recording Settings

The final part of setting up is selecting the Recording Options.

1. From the Movie Capture menu, choose Recording Settings. The Recording Settings dialog box appears.

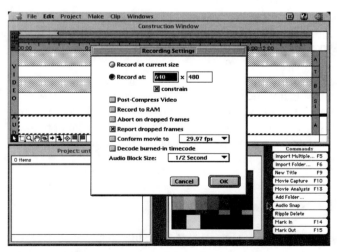

Figure 8.8 Recording Settings Dialog box

2. Set the Size of the video to be captured. The basic strategy is to capture at a resolution equal to or greater than the target output. For example, if your final output is to a CD-ROM

with a 320 x 240 screen size at 15 frames per second, that should be the minimum parameters of capture. If the output is tape, then full-screen, 640 x 480, 30 frames per second capture should be striven for.

Note that this is not always the case. With low-end capture boards it may be acceptable to capture at quarter-screen resolution (320 x 240). The video is then zoomed up to full screen size during playback out to videotape. In many cases, image quality with zooming is the same as if the video were captured at full-frame. This is because these boards can generally capture all of the video data at quarter-screen size but only half of the video data at full-screen. This method uses one-fourth of the disk space for data storage and improves editing speed.

If the video is to be used in any chroma-keying or compositing effects, then capture at the greatest resolution possible, regardless of target output. The extra detail and resolution will be necessary to create clean keys and sharp edges. The video can always be scaled down later to the target size.

With many high-end capture boards, the screen size resolution is pre-determined at 640 x 480. This is because these boards have been designed and maximized for full-screen video production. In this case, no other capture size options are available.

Select the Record at Current Size option to capture video at the dimensions currently displayed in the Movie Capture window. Select the Record At button to type in different dimensions. Remember, some boards will capture at a decreased frame rate if the aspect ratio is set to anything other than 4:3.

3.   Set the following options:

Post Compress Video

Selecting this option means that the video will be captured uncompressed. When the capture is finished, then compression will be applied and a new file on the hard drive is created. Compressing after capture may allow for a higher frame rate because the compression process itself takes CPU time. However, compressing during capture allows for longer and larger movies. You should not select this option if your capture board provides hardware compression.

Record to RAM

Select this option to record to RAM rather than to disk. Recording to RAM can allow for very high quality and size settings, but requires a great deal of memory.

Abort on Dropped Frames

Select this option if you want Adobe Premiere to stop capturing automatically in the event that a frame is dropped during capturing. This is the default setting. In some cases, it will be impossible to capture video without dropping at least a few frames and you will need to de-select this option.

Report Dropped Frames

Select this option if you want Adobe Premiere to automatically analyze the movie for dropped frames after it has been captured. The Movie Analysis window will appear after capturing only if frames have been dropped.

Conform Movie To

This acts like a built-in time base corrector. Use this option to ensure that all captured frames have exactly the same duration. This is important for precise editing. With this option selected, Premiere will adjust each captured frame to match exactly the frame rate you select from the pop-up menu. If you'll be outputting your movie to videotape, you should set the conform frame rate to 29.97.

The rest of the options in this window refer to remote device control and timecode features. Consult the Adobe Premiere Owners Manual for information about these options.

4.   When you are finished, select OK to close the Recording Settings dialog box.

Saving Settings

Save your Settings. This is important if you are going to digitize footage over several sessions or have to re-digitize at a later date. It is also quite possible you will have different settings for different tapes or subject matter.

1.   From the Movie Capture menu, choose the Save Settings command.

2.   A standard Save dialog box will appear. Type in a file name, select a target directory, and select Save. All recording, compression, video input, and sound input settings will be saved in a single file.

You can load these settings at a later time by using the Load Settings command from the Movie Capture menu.

Capture and Review

Starting the Capture

Believe it or not, now you're ready to start capturing.

1.   From the File menu, select Capture/Movie Capture. The Movie Capture window will appear.

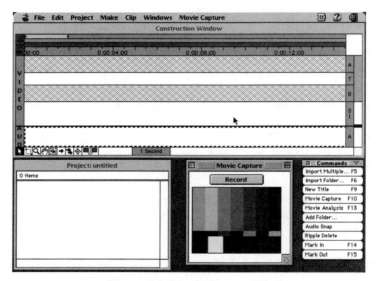

Figure 8.9 Movie Capture Window

2.   Press the Play button on the tape deck to start the tape. A preview of the image will appear in the sample area of the Movie Capture window.

3.   Click the Record button to start recording. Begin recording a couple of seconds before the first frame you want in the clip, to ensure that the video capture board is digitizing at full speed. The cursor will disappear during recording. To stop recording, hold down the mouse button. When recording is finished, the clip appears in an untitled Clip window.

4.   It is a good idea to check the video before saving. This way you can be sure of the quality

of the capture and that the clip is of the desired footage. This is also a good time to analyze the clip for important details like dropped frames. (More information on this next.) It may be necessary to re-digitize the clip using different settings. Checking capture is especially important with the first couple of clips, as it will determine the quality level for all of the video captured during the session. Take your time and experiment with different recording settings and options. Once you are satisfied with the captured video, use the Save command to save the clip.

Analysis Tools

Adobe Premiere is equipped with a Movie Analysis feature that can be used to get detailed information about video clips. This includes the file size, number of video and audio tracks, duration, average frame rate, audio rate, compression settings, and a report on dropped frames.

To analyze a clip that is in the active Clip window (such as a piece of newly captured video) hold down the Option key while choosing the Movie Analysis command. The Movie Analysis window will appear with information about the current clip. The contents may be printed or saved in a file.

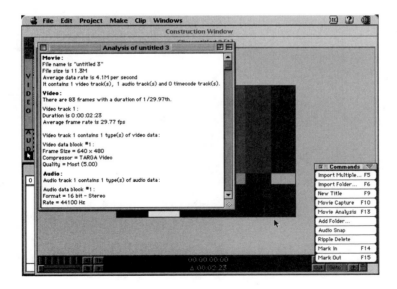

Figure 8.10 Movie Analysis Window

An alternate way of opening up the Movie Analyzer is to choose Tools/Movie Analysis from the File Menu. Use the standard Open File dialog box to choose the desired clip.

Conclusion

The proper and high quality capture of video assets is the foundation upon which the entire editing process is built. Attention to detail and carefully following the process assures that, in the long run, you will save time and money getting the set-up right. Once the clips are captured and logged on your edit sheets and into your asset management database, it is time to move to the editing process.

Chapter 9
Preparing to Edit

Introduction

Here is where it happens! Editing is a highly technical skill without a doubt, but what differentiates technically good editing from artful editing are a clear vision and style. A clear vision is derived from two sources: familiarity with the subject matter and audience, and a strong foundation based on looking at the work of others. Skill is then layered on top through practice, practice and practice. It is important that the audio and video assets to be edited for the project are of the highest technical and aesthetic quality. It is impossible, contrary to rumor, to fix serious problems during the edit. It is even less possible to conjure up a clip or a scene that was overlooked during the shoot. Ideally, the editing process begins during the pre-production period and carries on through post-production. This chapter covers the organization of an edit project from the asset database to the script. It focuses on the internal project management issues of editing software.

Organization

In preparing to edit, it's often in the organization that the battle is won or lost. There are two major areas of concern: file management and project management.

File Management

File management deals with how the data files are organized on the hard drives. This is physical management, making sure that the files are readily accessible for use. It defeats all the time advantages of non-linear editing if you don't know where your source material is, or have to hook up three or four hard drives to find it all. An easy system is to divide material into common elements, using a series of folders. This is especially important with large productions that may extend over several hard drives. For example, all video clips may be stored in one folder, music clips in another, and graphics in a third. This can be subdivided even further, so that all Scene 1 material is in its own folder, and all Scene 2 material is in a different folder. The organization format you use will depend a lot on personal style and the amount of material. The most important thing is to have a file management strategy before you start and to be consistent with its use. It's better to have a poor plan than no plan at all.

Project Management

Project management deals with how the material is organized through the editing application. This is software organization, or how the files appear for use in editing. Each program has its own terms for each level of organization, but the basic concepts are nearly identical.

The first level is the project. This encompasses everything in use from source material to the edit list to how the windows on the screen are laid out. The actual source files are not saved as part of the project. The size of these files makes this unfeasible. Instead, the project contains pointers to the original source on the hard disk. Clips behave in the same way as the original source audio or video, but really are just samples of the original.

Inside each project are bins, or folders, where references to all source material are imported. The source material may include any combination of video, audio, or graphics. These bins may be organized in any number of ways—by scene, source type, or however you wish.

Also part of each project is the actual edit list. This contains all the information about the finished program edits, transitions, effects, audio mix, etc. In addition, the project saves all settings for the layout of windows, input/output controls, and other project management preferences.

Making Backups

The most critical part of working with project files is to establish a plan for backing them up on a regular and timely basis. Backing up the original source data is important and should be done as soon as feasible. Accidental loss of source data happens, but it's much more likely that the editing application will crash sometime during an edit session. The chances of this happening rise with the complexity of the program (lots of filters, keys, and effects) which strains the memory capacity of the application and computer system. When this happens all information for that project will be lost. So back up early and often. Some programs will create these backup program files automatically at specified intervals. Be sure to save a copy to another hard drive or floppy disk. In the unfortunate (and rare) event of a total hard drive crash and all source data is lost, something can be salvaged by recapturing the video using the same file names and using the original project file as a basis for a re-edit.

Creating a Project File

The following steps are for creating a project file using Adobe Premiere 4.2 on the Mac.

1. Start a new project by choosing New/Project from the File menu. The New Project Presets Dialog box will appear.

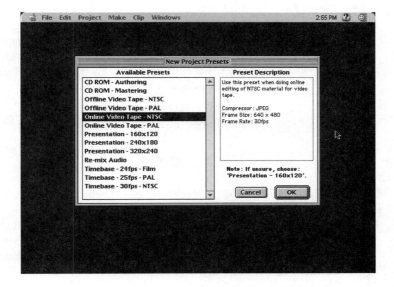

Figure 9.1 New Project Preset Window

Presets specify the project time base, movie frame rate, compression scheme, preview options and output options for a project. Premiere comes with several optimized presets, such as on-line editing or outputting to CD-ROM.

2. Select an appropriate project preset and click OK.

You may edit or add presets of your own to this list. All settings can be changed once the project is created. The one setting that can't be changed, without serious consequences, is the project time base.

The time base determines how many frames make up a one-second movie. It is expressed as a rate, such as 30 fps, but has nothing to do with the actual playback rate of your movie. It also affects how clips are imported and represented in various edit windows. Therefore, it is important to properly set the time base before importing any clips. The time base should match the rate at which the clips were captured. Also consider the frame rate of your final movie. If the final output is at 15 fps, then set the time base to 30 fps, since it's a multiple of 15. Otherwise, data could be lost through interpolation of differing frame rates, resulting in unpredictable playback.

Importing and Opening Clips

When a new project is created, Premiere opens a new, untitled Project window. Clips must be imported before they can be edited into a program.

Method

All imported clips are placed in the Project window. It's possible to import clips in a variety of ways. It may be done as a single clip, multiple clips, or an entire folder of clips.

To import a single clip into the Project Window:

1.   From the File menu, choose Import/File. The Import dialog box appears.

2.   Locate and select the clip to be imported.

3.   Click Import to import the clip into the Project Window.

This technique works for all source material—video, audio, and still images. Still images may be given a default duration upon importation. From the File Menu, choose Preferences/Still Image. In the dialog box that will appear, enter a frame duration and click OK.

Project Window

Let's take a closer look at the Project Window. Proper management here can make a huge impact on how easy it is to find selected material and speed the editing process.

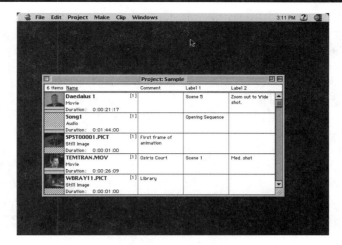

Figure 9.2 Project Window

Notice that clips are arranged in alphabetical order. For each clip, the default Project window displays the name, a small sample (or thumbnail), the general type, and duration. The window also displays a Comment box and two Label boxes. These allow you to attach notes to a clip. The Project window may be enlarged by dragging the Size box control in the lower right hand corner. To search through the clips, use the scroll bar at the right side of the window. Clips can be located or sorted by any column heading: Name, Comment, Label 1 or Label 2.

To change the Project Window display:

1. Make the Project Window active by clicking anywhere on the window. From the Windows menu, choose Project Window Options. The Project Window Options dialog box appears.

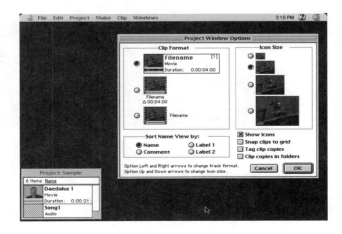

Figure 9.3 Project Window Options window

2.   Select a clip format and icon size by clicking the appropriate buttons. If you want to turn off the display of thumbnails in the Project window, deselect the Show Icons check box. The thumbnails will then appear as gray boxes. Not displaying thumbnails speeds up access time when working in the Project window.

It is very useful to organize clips in folders. Elements may be grouped together by type or scene. This can reduce search time dramatically. To add a folder to a project:

1.   Make the Project window active by clicking anywhere on it.

2.   From the Project menu, choose Add Folder. The Folder Name dialog box appears.

3.   Type a name and click on the OK button. The new folder will appear in the Project Folder.

To open a folder and add clips:

1.   Double-click on the folder you want open. The Folder window appears, displaying the clips in the folder.

2.   Drag clips or other folders from the Project window to the Folder window. It is also possible to add clips to a closed folder by using standard drag-and-drop techniques.

Figure 9.4 Folders in Project Window

To delete a clip or folder from the Project Window:

1.   Select the clip or folder. Hold down the Shift key to select more than one clip   or folder.

2.   Press Delete on the keyboard, or choose Clear or Cut from the Edit menu.

Converting Source Material

Material other than captured video can be imported into a project. Graphics, audio, and video created in other programs may all be used, as long as they are in a compatible file format. If not, the source material will need to be converted before importing into the editing application. Your user's manual will list which formats are readily accepted. Here are three likely scenarios for converting files for use between Mac and PC.

Graphics

Graphics are often created on PCs because of their cost efficiency as render stations. These may be 2-D or 3-D modeled graphics, individual frames or an animation sequence. An animation sequence may contain thousands of individual pictures that, when played in sequence, will create the illusion of motion.

Graphics on the PC may be saved in any number of different file formats. Two of the most common are Bitmap and Targa. Bitmap files have a .BMP extension, Targa files a .TGA extension. Neither of these formats are compatible with Premiere for the Mac. The most common file format for graphics on the Mac is the PICT format. PICT files are not compatible with Premiere on the PC and must be converted to a compatible format. To make this conversion, an application like Debabilizer must be used.

Debabilizer is one of the great all-purpose tools for graphic production. Previously only available on the Mac, it is now available for use on the PC as well. It not only converts file formats, but also performs a variety of other graphic processing functions, including cropping, scaling, and dithering. Debabilizer is the most popular application for creating color palettes. One of its main strengths is its power in working with batches. A batch is a group of images, that may or may not be part of a sequence, and that are to be processed exactly alike. Animation and video can make for notoriously large batches. With Debabilizer, the computer can process for hours or days at a time without the need for constant supervision. Obviously this is a huge time and money saver, as well as a convenience.

The following is a typical example for converting a PC animation sequence of BMP files for use in Adobe Premiere on the Mac using Debabilizer.

1. Make the BMP files available to the Mac. The easiest way to do this is to connect the Mac to the PC that contains the image, via a network. The files will be readily accessible. Processing over a network, however, is relatively slow and ties up the PC from doing other work. It is better to transfer the BMP files to the Macintosh using one of the following methods.

    If there are only a few images, floppies are a convenient transfer medium. BMP images transferred to a DOS formatted floppy can be used in conjunction with Mac utilities like Apple File Exchange, Apple Macintosh PC Exchange, Access PC DOS, DOS Mounter, and others. All of these programs allow a DOS disk to be inserted and read by a Macintosh computer. With so few images, it's usually not necessary to transfer the files from DOS floppy to Mac hard disk before processing.

For numerous images, a DOS formatted hard drive (up to 1 gigabyte in size) may be mounted onto a Macintosh by using a utility like PC Exchange. Debabilizer can process the images directly from the DOS hard drive for storage on a Mac hard drive.

2. Launch Debabilizer. The Image Info Window appears.

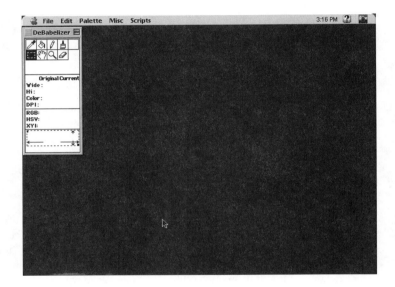

Figure 9.5 Image Info Window

This is displayed at all times, but shows information only when an image is open. The Debabilizer Menu Bar also appears.

3. Create a Script for processing the BMP files during the conversion. Scripts are used to automate procedures or series of processing steps.

From the Scripts Menu, choose New. The Edit Script dialog box appears.

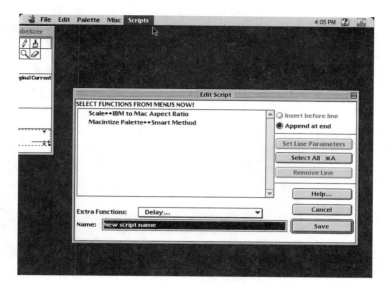

Figure 9.6 Edit Script dialog box

To create a script, commands are selected from the appropriate menus in the order they are to be performed.

From the Edit Menu, Choose Scale/IBM to Mac Aspect Ratio. The new command appears in the Edit Script dialog box. PC pixels are taller than they are wide, whereas Mac pixels are square. This command scales the image down to 83% of its original width. Otherwise, the PC image would look "squashed" when viewed on a Mac monitor.

From the Palette Menu, Choose Macintize Palette/Smart Method. The new command is added to the Edit Script dialog box. Palettes contain all of the individual colors used within an image and range in size from 256 to thousands to millions of colors. Palettes on non-Macintosh computers vary, especially in their placement of the pure black and pure white indexes. Macintizing the palette insures that these indexes are properly positioned within the palette so that all colors will be represented correctly.

Type in a name for the script and click on the Save button.

The Edit Script dialog box will disappear.

4.   Now create a batch list of images for the computer to process and convert. From the File Menu, choose Batch/Save.

The Batch Save dialog window appears.

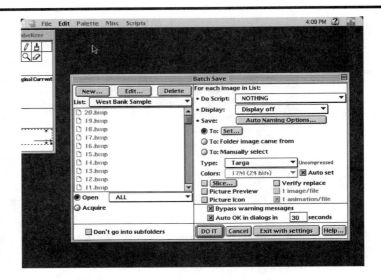

Figure 9.7 Batch save dialog box

On the left hand side of the window, information is displayed about the image files to be converted. On the right is information about how the files are to be processed and where the new images are to be stored. By default, Debabilizer opens with the last batch list used.

Click on the New button in the upper left hand corner. The Batch List Create/Edit dialog window appears.

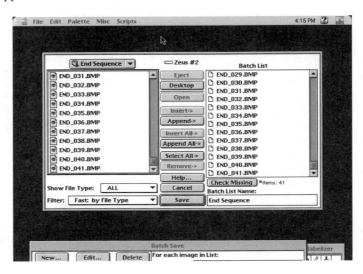

Figure 9.8 Batch List Create/Edit dialog window

The left window uses standard controls for searching volumes and folders for the files to be converted. These files are added to the batch list, which appears in the right window.

To add a single image file to a batch list, highlight the selected file by clicking on it with the mouse. Click on the Append Button in the middle of the screen. The file will now appear in the batch list.

To add an entire folder of images, open the selected folder so that the individual files are visible. Click on the Append All Button in the middle of the screen. All of the files will appear in the batch list.

Under Batch List Name in the lower right hand corner, type in a name for the batch list. Click on the Save button. The Batch Save Dialog Window will reappear. Notice that the batch list name and selected files are updated in the left hand window.

Select the Do Script pop up menu to the script just created.

Select the Display pop up Menu to the desired setting. This determines how long each image is displayed on-screen during the batch conversion. It is useful for monitoring the quality of processing. Display Off provides for the fastest performance.

Click on the Set Button. A standard Save dialog box appears. Select a destination folder for the new files.

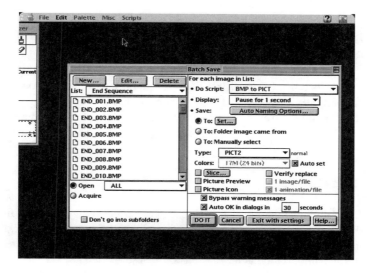

Figure 9.9 Batch Window–Action Controls

From the Type pop-up menu, select PICT2/Normal. This is the file format into which the BMP files will be converted.

Next to the Colors pop-up menu is an Auto Select checkbox. Make sure this is selected. This will convert the images at the same color depth as the original image.

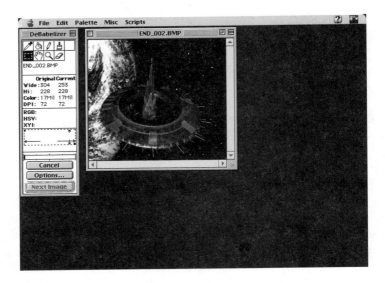

Figure 9.10 Batch Conversion in Process

Click the Do It button.

Processing and conversion will begin. When the batch is finished a beep will sound and no data will be displayed in the Image Info Window.

For all its power, Debabilizer does not support audio. It is also very time consuming to convert the video portion of a movie on a frame-by-frame basis, where no other processing is required. In cases where a PC AVI movie needs to be converted to Quicktime for use on a Mac, or vice versa, there are other utilities that more easily perform this task.

Video

Like graphics, video files need to be converted to a compatible file format for use on different computer platforms, for example, AVI for PC, and Quicktime on the Mac. To maintain quality, no recompression should be introduced during the conversion process. It's also important that the chosen codec is supported on both Mac and PC, otherwise the converted file may not be playable. For example, AVI files captured on the PC using the Intel Raw codec can be converted into Quicktime Intel Raw codec files with little or no loss in quality. Obviously, uncompressed files ("None" codec) will not suffer a generational loss either.

On the other hand, files that are created using proprietary hardware compression will not be playable on other systems. For the highest quality, these files should be output as uncompressed Quicktime movies, using an application such as Premiere. Quicktime is supported on both platforms and offers the greatest flexibility. This procedure is not recommended for general editing. Uncompressed files take up a great deal of hard disk space. Converting and transferring files is very time consuming. It is preferable to edit the bulk of a project on the same platform used to capture it.

Audio is also an issue. Generally, only uncompressed PCM audio may be converted safely. Audio interleave and format differences must also be addressed. See "Audio Interleave," Chapter 15 for further details.

For a complete description of video conversion tools and techniques, see "Cross-Platform Development" in Chapter 16.

Audio

Audio files themselves may also be converted. Standard PC audio files carry a WAV extension. Mac audio files are in the AIFF format. As with any conversion, it's best to use the same quality settings as the source file. Sample rates and bit rates should be maintained. For example, if the audio was captured at 22K and 16 bit, the converted file should be at the same setting. Converting to a higher sample or bit rate will not increase quality. It may, in fact, diminish it because of the processing involved.

Stereo files may be converted down into mono files. Mono files, however, are always mono. When converted into a stereo format, the end result is dual mono channels that use up twice as much disk storage space as the original.

Several applications and utilities on both Mac and PC can convert audio easily. SoundApp for the Mac is a basic utility that converts audio at the same sample rate and bit rate as the original.

To convert audio from one file format to another:

1.   Choose Convert from the File Menu. A Source File dialog box will appear.

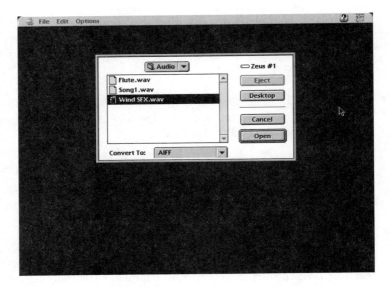

Figure 9.11 Source File dialog box

2.   Select a new audio format from the Convert To pop-up menu. SoundApp supports many of the most popular audio formats including WAV, AIFF, System 7, and Quicktime

3.   Using standard commands, select and open the source file.

4.   Depending upon your preference settings, you may choose a destination folder for the converted file to be saved or have SoundApp create one automatically. Click the Save button and conversion begins.

The converted file is now ready for importation and use in any compatible editing application.

Conclusion

In preparing to edit, the importance of thinking ahead can't be over emphasized. It is not an exaggeration to say that the quality of the final project is nowhere more affected than in the planning, organization and preparation of the assets for the edit process. The vision for the project must be reflected in the establishment of the project structure, and in the capturing and importing of all the primary assets into the system.

Chapter 10
Video Editing

Introduction

Once the project is established within the editing system, the actual editing and special effects creation begins. You have all your assets at your fingertips, in the correct format, ready to go. It's time to get down to the actual assembly of those assets into the look and feel of the final project.

Understanding a Timeline

The timeline is the heart of any edit session. All edits, transitions, effects, and mixes meet here. If anything is not in the timeline, it will not be in the final movie. All timelines are not created equally. Although they may be very similar in their layout and conventions, the way a timeline looks and how it is interacted with by an operator can make a huge difference in productivity. For some editors, it's the determining factor in deciding which system they will or will not use.

Timelines can get complicated very quickly. It's important to know where you are in a project, be able to move around, and make changes quickly. A good timeline is intuitive—it works like the editor thinks.

The best style of timeline is a matter of personal choice. Some prefer a very graphical interface with a loose "drag-and-drop" feel, while others are more comfortable with a precise "edit-by-numbers" approach. Most editing applications offer some control for creating an individual style that will feel right.

General Features

Let's examine the major features of a timeline by using Adobe Premiere 4.2 as our model. In Premiere, the timeline is referred to as the Construction Window.

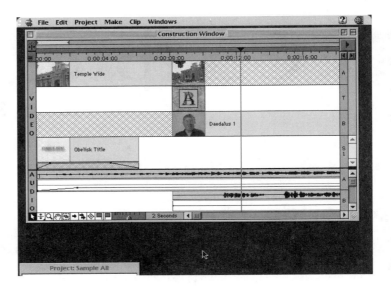

Figure 10.1 Construction Window

Elements are displayed sequentially in time from left to right. The size of the window may be enlarged by dragging the size box handle at the bottom right corner. To move through the edit sequence, use the scroll bar at the bottom of the window. To change the scale, (that is, how much of the edit sequence is viewable in the window), move the time unit selector. Moving it to the left will "zoom in" on the project showing fewer overall frames, while moving it to the right "zooms out" to reveal more frames.

Tracks are arranged vertically to indicate what elements are in use at any particular time. Each track contains different types of elements that make up a movie—video, audio, graphics, keys, and transitions. Video tracks are at the top of the Construction Window, audio tracks on the bottom. Key and graphic tracks are usually directly above or below the video tracks. In Premiere, all key (or superimposed) tracks are below the video.

All tracks may not be visible on the screen at the same time, even with the Construction window fully enlarged. In this case, use the scroll bars at the right side of the window to scroll through various types of tracks. The video and audio tracks each have their own control. It is also possible to adjust the number of tracks on display within each section by dragging the splitter between the two scroll bars.

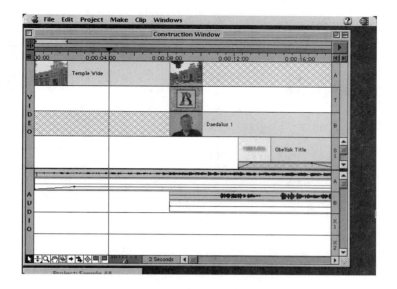

Figure 10.2a Adjusting the Track Splitter—before

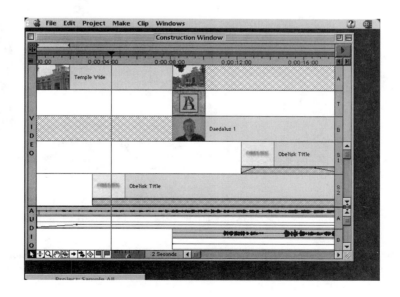

Figure 10.2b Adjusting the Track Splitter—after

The number of tracks available will depend upon what type of hardware/software configuration you have. Adobe Premiere can handle up to 99 layers of video and audio at any single time. Other high-end editing systems, like those from Avid Technology, Data Translation, and I-Mix, may limit you to two tracks of video, one graphics track, and 6 channels of audio. The power of these machines is in their real-time capabilities. To change the number of tracks, choose Add/Delete tracks from the Project Menu. Tracks will be added or deleted from the bottom of existing tracks for that type.

Construction Window Options

Just like the Project Window, the display of the Construction Window may also be customized.

1. With the Construction Window active, choose Construction Window Options from the Windows menu. The Construction Window Options dialog box will appear.

Figure 10.3 Construction Window dialog box

2. Select a track format by clicking on the appropriate button. The track format determines how video is displayed. There are three choices: Sample frames throughout the clip, first and last sample frames only, or filename only. For fastest performance choose filename only.

3. Select an icon size by clicking the appropriate button. This determines how large the video sample frames will be in the Construction Window. Selecting a smaller icon size will allow you to view more video tracks simultaneously.

4. Select which combination of tracks to display by clicking on the appropriate checkboxes.

5. Choose a frame numbering format from the Count pop-up menu. The choices includes SMPTE timecode, frame count, and feet of film.

6. When the numbering format has been selected, click on the OK button.

The Construction Window display may be altered at anytime during a project and does not affect the edit sequence. For example, disabling the superimpose track display doesn't affect any key effects that may have been created.

Putting Clips into a Sequence

The simplest way to create an edit sequence is to assemble clips in the order they are to play. Butted together, from left to right, the movie plays as a series of simple edits. Just drag the thumbnail icon of the clip from the Project window and onto the Construction window. Wherever the mouse button is released, that's where the clip will be placed. Clips must be of the proper type. An audio clip can only be placed on an audio track, a video clip can only be placed on a video track.

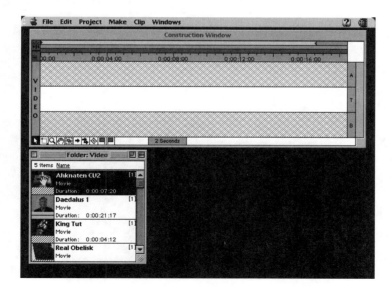

Figure 10.4a Dragging clips into Construction window

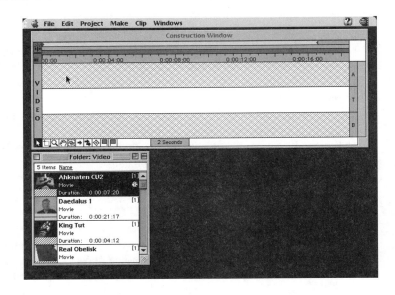

Figure 10.4b Dragging clips into Construction window—before

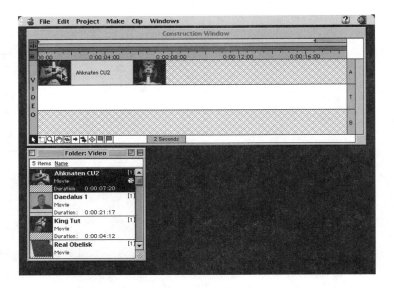

Figure 10.4c Dragging clips into Construction window—after

There are two ways to move several clips into the timeline. One is to hold down the Shift key while clicking on the desired clips. Then drag-and-drop all of them into the Construction window, just as you would for a single clip. The clips will be placed in the order they appear in the project window. Another way is to drag an entire folder from the Project window into the Construction window. This technique works particularly well with large sequence files, such as hundreds of PICT files that are to be made into an animation sequence.

Clips that contain both audio and video are referred to as linked or synched clips. When a linked clip is dragged into the Construction window, the audio and video together are placed in the appropriate track. Linked clips may be separated. That is, the audio and video may be moved and edited individually. It is also possible to re-link these clips. In fact, clips that were not originally linked may be linked together for editing purposes. This is useful when an audio track, because of a music cue or sound effect, must match perfectly with the video and may be treated as a single clip.

To delete a clip from the Construction window, simply click on the clip with the mouse and press the Delete key. Notice that with linked clips, only the portion selected will be deleted.

Clips may be moved within the Construction window in a variety of ways. To move a single clip, drag-and-drop it to a new location. The left edge of the clip represents where it starts, the right edge where it ends.

A very good feature to look for in any program is a "Snap-to-Edges" option. This means that when a clip is released with the mouse button, it will align itself to the next closest clip to the left. This insures that there are no empty frames between clips. It is also used to align clips with those in other tracks. When a clip is moved, vertical alignment guides will appear at the edge of a clip and extend through all tracks. The clip will have a natural "pull" or "tug" to line up evenly with the edge of clips from other tracks. In this way, clips can then be made to start or stop at the same time. This is important for timing effects and synchronizing audio to video.

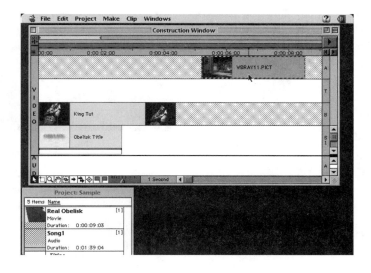

Figure 10.5a Snap-to-Edges—beginning

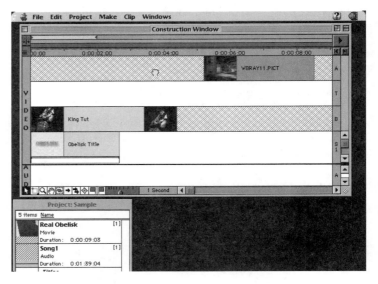

Figure 10.5b Snap-to-Edges—middle

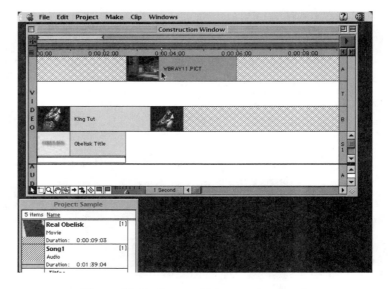

Figure 10.5c Snap-to-Edges—completed

In Premiere, Snap-to-Edges is the default setting. It may be accessed through the Construction Window Options under the Windows menu. In the dialog box is a checkbox for Snap-to-Edges. It can also be selected by clicking the snap tool in the upper left hand corner of the Construction Window.

There are controls for selecting and moving several items on a single track or multiple tracks. To move clips on a single track, click the track tool at the bottom of the window.

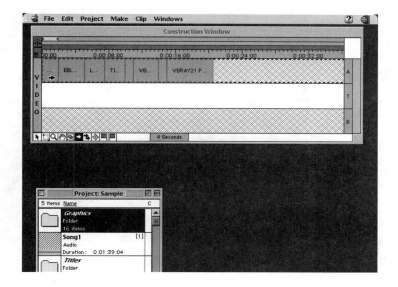

Figure 10.6a Track tool

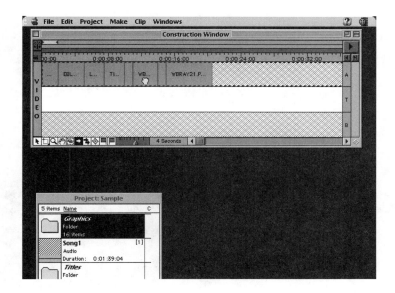

Figure 10.6b Track tool

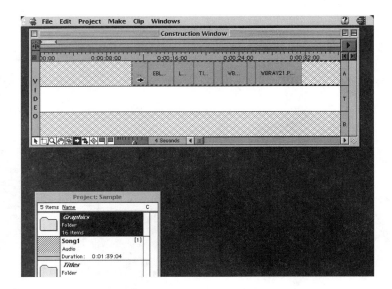

Figure 10.6c Track tool

Then click on the first clip you want included in the move. All following clips on that track will be highlighted. Then drag-and-drop to a new location in the timeline.

To move clips on all tracks, select the multitrack tool from the bottom of the Construction Window.

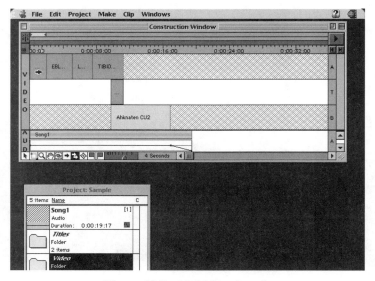

Figure 10.7a Multi-Track tool

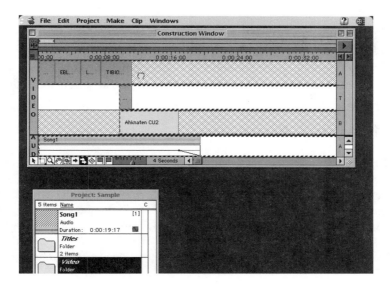

Figure 10.7b Multi-Track tool

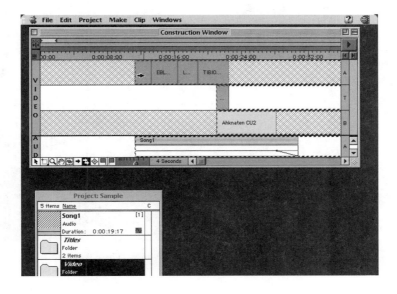

Figure 10.7c Multi-Track tool

Just like the track tool, selecting the first clip to move highlights all other clips to the right of it. It also highlights all clips on all other tracks. Then drag-and-drop to a new location.

Moving Through a Project

Now that you've got some clips in a sequence, there are a few other windows Premiere offers for use in editing. Variations of these appear in most other editing applications.

Preview Window

The most important of these windows is the Preview Window. This is where all or part of the movie may be viewed for checking effects and edits. Previews may be compiled or uncompiled. Compiled previews take processing time but give an accurate preview of transitions and effects. Uncompiled previews don't take any time to create, but aren't very detailed or accurate in timing. The choice of which to use will depend on the situation. If you just want to get a rough feel for the pacing of the program, then an uncompiled preview may be just fine. For checking complex video effects or timing with audio, then a compiled preview will be necessary.

The simplest way to preview is by dragging the cursor through the time ruler. Position the mouse cursor anywhere in the time ruler. The cursor will change into a down arrow.

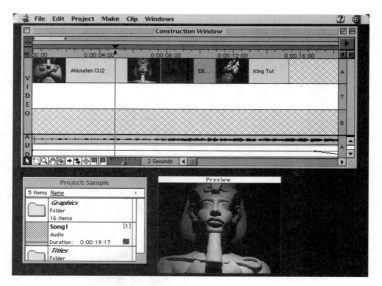

Figure 10.8a Preview Time Ruler

Drag the arrow along the time ruler. This is also referred to as "scrubbing." Clips under the arrow play in the Preview Window. It may not be possible to scroll through all frames smoothly, depending upon the complexity of the edit. Processing is done in real-time and may take several moments just to create one

Figure 10.8b Preview Time Ruler

frame. Since the mouse is controlling the speed of playback, it won't give you an accurate sense of timing. There is also no audio playback with this type of preview. It is, however, extremely useful for doing a quick check of specific frames of video effects such as transitions, keys, motion settings, and filters. In many cases, this is enough to get an idea of what the finished effect will look like. When all adjustments are made, a more detailed compiled preview can be made.

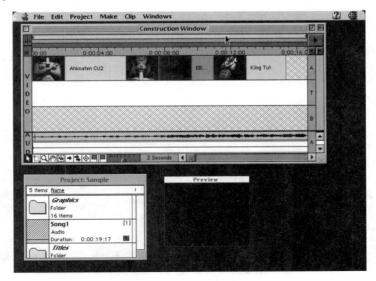

Figure 10.9 Work area bar

A compiled preview movie gives an accurate presentation of effects, transitions, and audio synchronization. Preview movies require processing time and are saved to a hard disk for repeated playback. To make a preview movie:

1. Double-click the work area bar above the time ruler in the Construction Window. A yellow bar with red triangles on each end will appear.

2. Drag the red triangles to create a start and stop point for the preview.

3. Press the Return button. Processing will begin and a progress bar will appear. When processing is complete, the preview movie will play.

4. To stop the preview, press the space bar. To play again, press the Return button.

Controller

The Controller works much like a playback unit for the Construction window. It controls a playback head through the video, which is displayed in the Preview window. No compiling is done when using the Controller. It can only playback effects and transitions that have been previously compiled in a Preview movie. Otherwise, a large "X" will appear over scenes that have not been compiled. It is useful for getting a sense of flow in a movie, especially when audio is present.

To use the Controller, choose Controller from the Window menu.

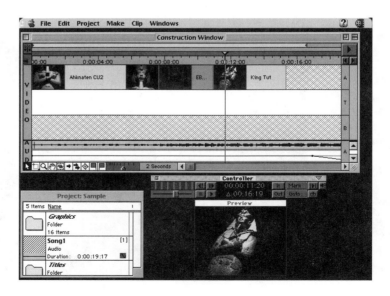

Figure 10.10 Controller

Make sure the Preview window is open. Drag the playback head through the timeline to scrub through the movie. A better way is to use the standard playback controls available through the Controller itself. These include play, jog, step-frame and loop modes.

Preview Settings

To a large degree, the usefulness and importance of previewing depends upon several factors. First you must determine how much to preview. Is it really necessary to preview every dissolve in a movie or would it be just as helpful to check a few for timing? Is it necessary to view the entire duration of a special color-tinted clip or will a few frames suffice? As you become more comfortable and confident with your editing techniques, the need for previews will lessen.

When you do preview, the biggest factor will be the settings used to compile the preview movies. Compiling can be very time-consuming and can have a major impact on the time-efficiency of an edit session. It is very frustrating to have a complex effect take several minutes to process each time a small change is made to it.

There are advantages to processing previews at the same resolution as the final output. Premiere can use these preview files in the final compilation, thus saving processing time. This strategy only works if you're confident that the previews will be very close to finished form. Otherwise, a great deal of time and hard drive space will be used up, which will far outweigh any final compression time savings.

Generally, it's best to preview at something less than final output resolution. This is especially true for full-screen video where playback may be impeded because of the large data throughput.

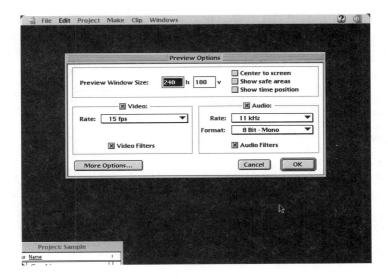

Figure 10.11 Preview Options Dialog box

Preview settings are initially set as part of the Project preset. To modify the major settings:

1.   From the Make menu, choose Preview Options. The Preview Options dialog box will appear.

2.   At the top of the dialog box are controls that affect the Preview window. Input an appropriate preview image size in pixels. Remember, the smaller the window, the less processing time required and smoother possible playback. The Preview window defaults to the same aspect ratio as the final movie. By inputting a horizontal or vertical setting, Premiere will automatically update the other field.

3.   At the left are controls for video. The Video checkbox may be de-selected if you wish to preview audio only. Select a video frame rate from the Rate pop-up menu. 15 frames per second is sufficient for most applications. De-select the Video Filters checkbox to turn off the effect of filters in previews.

4.   At the right are audio controls. The Audio checkbox may be de-selected to preview video only. Select an appropriate audio bit sample rate and format from the appropriate pop-up menus. Setting these to anything higher than the original source material will only take more processing time without increasing the quality of the audio. De-select the Audio filters checkbox to turn off the effects of audio filters in previews.

5.   There are also advanced option settings. These are accessed by selecting More Options from the lower left hand corner. See the Adobe Users Guide for detailed information about using these.

Info Window

The Info window is a valuable part of any edit session. It displays information about a selected clip or transition. This includes its name, type, speed, duration, and image size. To display the Info window, choose Info from the Windows menu.

It also displays the clip's starting and ending points. This is useful for accurately aligning clips in the Construction window.

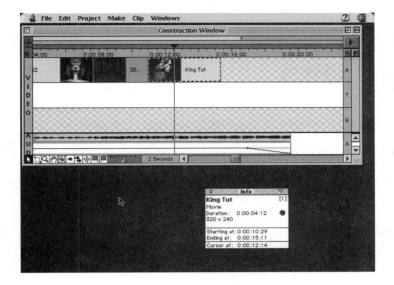

Figure 10.12 Info Window

Commands Palette

The Commands Palette is a convenient way to access commonly used functions. Instead of pulling down menu windows or using keyboard commands, functions in the Commands Palette can be selected with the click of a mouse. To display the Commands Palette, choose Commands from the Windows menu.

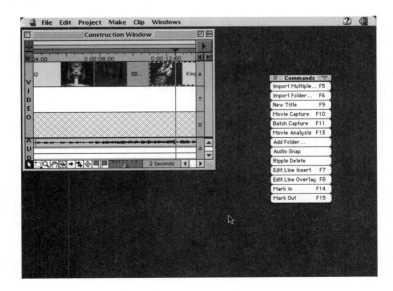

Figure 10.13 Commands Palette

It may be customized for personal use. The number of columns and order of commands may be altered. Commands may be added and deleted. These customized palettes can be saved for use in particular situations or projects.

Conclusion

Now that the flow and timing of the project has been established, the next step is the refinement of the clips and the transitions. If you have done your homework, this stage will flow smoothly. Remember that a clear vision, while always open for revision, is essential at every stage of a successful project.

Chapter 11
Trimming Clips

Introduction

Now that you have your work under your hand, it's time to finalize the design—by trimming and rearranging until you are satisfied that you have the best possible order of the clips. You will have clips that are too long, others that are not long enough. Some parts of a clip will not work, and you will want to edit it out. You will also want to mark your clips so you can align video with audio, and place special effects at certain points.

Clip Mode

The clip window is a quick way to view your clips in their entirety, from beginning to end, as originally recorded. It also provides you with a variety of information about each clip, including duration and frame count. The clip window is an accurate way to edit your clip; that is, to change the beginning or ending of the clip, to alter the duration of a still image, or even to set "marks" in your clip to help you find certain portions.

Opening

To open the clip window, double click on the clip you want to view. You can open a clip from the project window or when you have it already placed in the construction window. The clip window will display movie clips (video, with or without audio attached to them) and audio clips. If you have the clips already placed in the Construction window, and you want to view the whole movie (see the video and hear the audio), double click on the part of the clip that is on the video track. That way you will be able to see and hear it. If you just want to look at the audio portion in a wave form representation, double click the part of the clip on the audio track—but remember, although you are only looking at the audio portion, if the audio and video are linked (as in a movie clip), and you alter the in and out points to the audio, Premiere will automatically adjust the corresponding in and out points on the video portion as well.

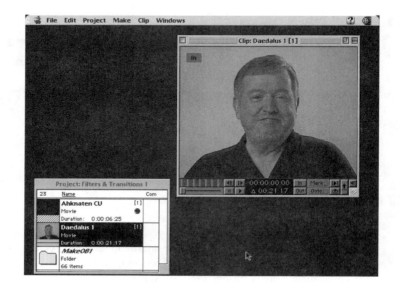

Figure 11.1 Clip Window

If you want to adjust the size of the clip window, put the cursor on the bottom right corner until you see the double-headed arrow and then click and drag it to the size you want. Be aware that if you make the video clip viewing square too large your playback speed may be decreased.

To close the clip window, click on the top left Minimize button. Since Premiere automatically opens a new window each time you open a clip, it is important to close clip windows when finished. If you don't do this, you'll have several windows open at once and your screen will not only be cluttered, but your program may run slower since it is using so much memory keeping those clip windows open.

Controls and Playing

The play controls on the clip window are very straightforward, utilizing universal symbols for basic features like Play and Stop. The slider bar on the bottom left acts like a jog/shuttle so you can quickly scan through your clip by dragging the slider bar left or right. The other control buttons on the clip window are for more advanced editing tools that will prove useful in any project and will be discussed in more detail.

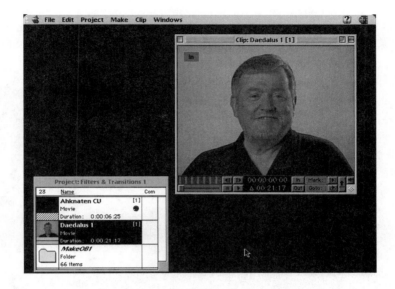

Figure 11.2 Clip window controls

The <| and |> buttons advance your clip one frame at a time, which will help you make more precise edits. When you play through a movie clip one frame at a time you will also hear the corresponding audio. This is particularly helpful when editing clips of people because you don't want to cut off your talent's first word, or on the other hand, you may want to edit out a tongue click and start your clip at the first important word.

The box in the middle with the numbers provides you with information about the duration of the clip. You can choose to view clips by time duration (SMPTE time code = minutes / seconds / frames), film feet or by frame count. The clip window will default to SMPTE timecode but you can change it to frame count by selecting Clip Window Options under the Windows menu. You can go back and forth between time and frame count without affecting the clip.

The top line of numbers tells you what frame you are currently looking at. The bottom line tells you the length of the entire clip.

Selecting In and Out Points

When you find the frame you want to use as the new beginning of the clip, click on the In button. You will see a square flash in the upper left corner showing you that this frame has been selected as the in point. Additionally, when you select the frame you want as the final one, the Out button will select your new out point of the clip, and you will see a square flash in the upper right corner. If you opened the clip from the project window, you will see the duration numbers update to the edited length. If you opened the clip from the Construction Window, you will see the clip change sizes to reflect the duration changes in the edited clip. Note: If you want to view the new In and Out points of the clip, click on the |>| button. If you click on the Play button, you will see the clip from its original beginning and end.

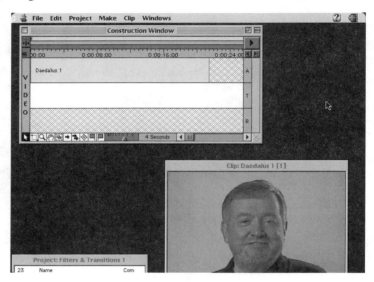

Figure 11.3a Setting In Points

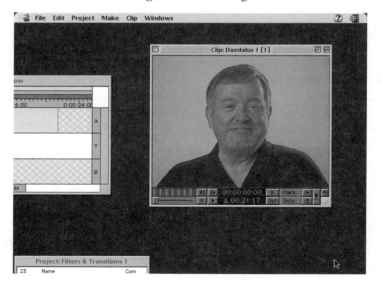

Figure 11.3b Setting In Points

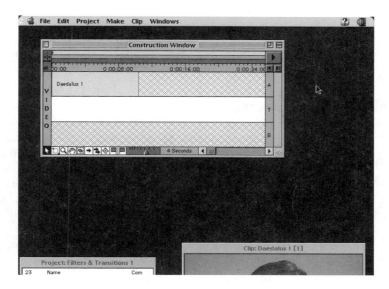

Figure 11.3b Setting In Points

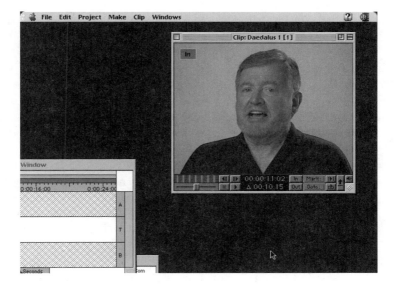

Figure 11.3c Setting In Points

To quickly see the In or Out point, click on the Go To button and choose either In or Out from the pull down menu. The corresponding frame will be in view in the clip window.

The bent arrow button will loop the clip from the In and Out points—that is, play the clip continuously from beginning to end.

Video can be "marked" for specific video cues or syching with audio. Since place markers are so commonly used with audio, this technique will be discussed in the next chapter.

Trimming Mode

If you want to trim clips with the most precision and attention to detail, use the Trimming window. Once you have placed your clips on a track in the Construction Window, the Trimming window lets you view the exact frames on either side of your edit points. It is a good way to fine tune your edits once you've done your preliminary editing in the Clip window. Trimming is adding or subtracting a couple of frames at a time to adjust an edit point. It is useful when viewing clips in relation to each other. You may have already edited each clip, but you have not seen how one edited clip looks next to the other. The trimming mode lets you see it this way to make sure your cuts are visually appealing.

Using the Trimming mode is especially useful when cutting from a medium shot of a person ("talking head") to a close-up of them. Adjusting a frame or two on either side of the edit point can make the difference between a jumpy cut or a smooth one. Hint: when editing talking heads from medium shots to close-ups, be aware of the position of their heads, the direction their eyes are looking and the position of their mouths (closed or speaking). You want the edit to look seamless as if the camera moved in closer instead of cutting in a different take of the shot.

Trimming Window Options

To open the Trimming Window, select Trimming from the Windows menu. If you want to change the display, select Trimming Window Options from the Windows menu and a dialog box will appear.

You will have three options for how many frames you want to view on either side of the edit point; one, three or five (Premiere defaults to five). Your preference on Window options will probably depend on what kind of edits you're making. For our 'talking head' example, three or five frames is probably a good choice so you can see any body or head movement that may affect a smooth edit.

You can select the number of seconds of the clip (the ones surrounding the edit point) you want to play when you preview a new edit point through the Trimming Window options menu.

You can also adjust the size of your Preview window by selecting Play Preview at Maximum size from the menu. When you have chosen all your options click OK.

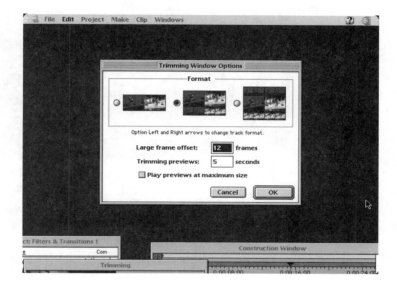

Figure 11.4 Trimming Window Options dialog box

Selecting Edit Points Using the Trimming Window

The picture you see on the left side is the frame on the left side of the edit point, and the picture on the right is the frame on the right side of the edit point. The numbers in boxes below the pictures let you easily add or subtract frames in increments of either 5 (+ or -) or

You can use the jog control to add or subtract larger numbers of frames. The numbers on the bottom of the Trimming Window (the ones preceded by a triangle) show you how many frames were added to or subtracted from your original edit point. If you know how many frames by which you want to alter the edit point, click on the numbers and type in the number you want.

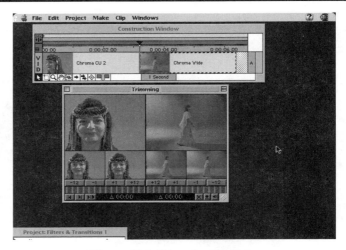

Figure 11.5 Trimming Window

Some of the icons on the control buttons in the Trimming window are similar to those in the Clip Window, but they are utilized slightly differently. The |< button brings you to the previous edit point on the timeline instead of to the previous frame. Correspondingly, the >| button brings you to the next edit point on the timeline. The play (>|>) button lets you preview the new edit.

Changing the Edit or Reverting to Original

When changing edit points using the Trimming window you do not alter the duration of any other clips on the track. All the clips (in all tracks) to the right of the edit point are moved along the timeline to correspond with the change in the clip you just trimmed. If you don't want all the other tracks to move with it, you can lock the track to prevent it, but the track with the clip you just trimmed will still move to accommodate the changes. A nice feature of the Trimming Window (and a frequently needed one) is the X button that allows you to return to your original edit points at any time while the Trimming Window is open.

Ripple Edit

A ripple edit changes the length of the clip you are looking at while maintaining the duration of all the other clips on the track. (Just like trimming clips through the Trimming Window.) Remember that a ripple edit also adjusts all clips on unlocked tracks to the right of the edit point to correspond with the changes in the clip on the rippled track. Because changing the duration of one clip changes the positioning of other clips, be aware that your total movie duration will be changed to reflect the frames you added or subtracted from the clip you ripple edited. Tthink of ripple edits like editing film. All the frames are connected into one long reel of film, so adjusting the edit point of one edit caused all the following frames to move together to reflect that adjustment.

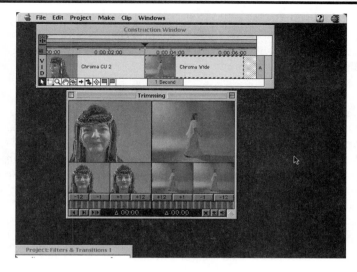

Figure 11.6a Ripple Edit in Trimming Window—before

How to do a ripple edit in the Trimming Window:

Once you have your clips lined up on tracks in the Construction window choose Trimming from the Windows menu. Click on the <| or the |> buttons to see the edit point you want to change. Click on the Add or Subtract buttons on the side of the edit point you want to adjust (either the right or left side). When you have trimmed the clip as you want it, click on the Play button to preview it. If you're not happy with how it looks, simply click on the Reset button and start all over.

Figure 11.6a Ripple Edit in Trimming Window—after

You can also do a ripple edit by choosing the Ripple Edit tool in the construction window. That will be discussed later in the section on Editing in the Construction Window.

Rolling Edit

A rolling edit differs from the ripple edit because it only adjusts the duration of the two clips on either side of the edit point. A rolling edit will adjust the adjacent clip to reflect the duration change in the one you trimmed, but it will not alter the duration of the two-clip sequence or the rest of clips on the track or any other track. For example, let's say you have edited together a two-minute movie of nature clips. You have a voice-over track that is also two minutes long, so you want to keep the edited piece at that duration. After you preview your movie you decide you want to stay on the sunset shot a little longer and you want to shorten the following clip of the ocean. By using a rolling edit, you can make the sunset clip longer (by extending the out point) and make the shot of the ocean shorter (by choosing a later in point) without changing anything else in the movie.

How to do a rolling edit through the Trimming Window:

1. Once you have placed your clips on a track in the Construction Window, select Trimming from the Windows menu.

2. When you see the Trimming window click on the |< or >| to view the edit point you want to adjust.

3. Move the mouse pointer to the line between the two frames shown in the window, and the pointer will change to the Rolling Edit tool (a two-sided arrow with a line in the middle). Drag it to the left or right to trim the clips. If you drag it to the left, the first clip is shortened and the adjacent clip is lengthened. If you drag it to the right, the opposite happens. Using the nature movie example, you would want to drag the Rolling Edit tool to the right to lengthen the sunset clip and shorten the ocean clip.

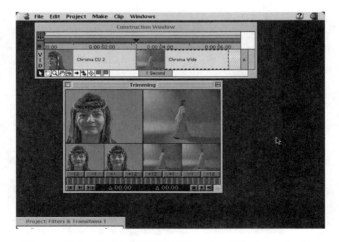

Figure 11.7a Rolling Edit in Trimming Window—before

To preview the new edit points click on the Play button.

You can also do a rolling edit right on the Construction Window by selecting the Rolling Edit tool which will be discussed in the following section.

Figure 11.7b Rolling Edit in Trimming Window—after

Construction Mode

Editing in the Construction window is a quick way to edit together clips which allows you to see just how the clips in your program relate to one another. In one location you can view all the tracks of audio and video you have working. The Construction window also allows you to see them in relation to the timeline, which is often a necessity.

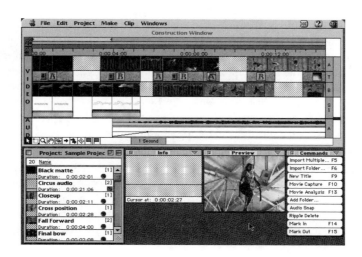

Figure 11.8 Construction Window

Editing within the Construction window is not as precise as editing clips in the Clip window or the Trimming window, but it can be very helpful, especially if the pieces have already been trimmed prior to being imported into your project.

Two tools that will make editing in the Construction window a lot easier are the Info box and the Preview window. If they are not displayed, select Preview and Info from the Window menu, and make sure they are in a location where they can be easily seen. The preview window will bring itself forward when it is in use, but the info box can be covered by other windows such as the project window or the preview window. Make sure you can see it because it provides valuable feedback.

Editing Individual Clips

There are several different ways to edit within the construction window, including dragging a clip, using the In and Out-point tools, and using the Rolling and Ripple Edit tools.

Dragging Clips to Lengthen or Shorten

The dragging method is especially useful when you are more concerned about the clip's duration than the specific frame that begins or ends the clip. If your clip is non-sychronized footage, like landscapes or still images, then precision editing of in and out points is unnecessary. When editing shots of people, be sure to carefully double check the edit points you created.

To edit by the Dragging method, verify that the clip is not touching or very close to an adjacent clip, because you will only be able to drag it until something gets in its way. To edit by dragging a clip, simply select the clip and put the cursor arrow on the edge of the clip that you want to change. The arrow will turn into a stretch pointer (a skinny double headed arrow with a line in the middle). When the cursor becomes the Stretch tool, drag it in order to lengthen or shorten the clip, and release the mouse button when you have reached the desired point. The info box will tell you how long the clip is, and you will see it update the information as you drag the clip. If you cannot drag it to the increment you want, zoom in the view of the Construction window so each movement is easier to control. Thus if you want to shorten a clip by exactly seven frames, and when you drag it you can't hit that number precisely, zoom in to a closer view (perhaps 1 or 2 frames), and it will be easier to control the dragging motion.

To make this type of trimming more accurate, select the edge viewing option which allows you to see the frames in the preview window as you are dragging. The Info box will also update as you drag. You can select edge viewing by clicking on the Edge Viewing tool icon in the upper-left corner of the Construction window, or you can select it from the Construction Window Options box in the Windows menu.

If you are lengthening clips, remember that a movie clip will only drag to the length of the original clip. A still frame or graphic can be extended to whatever length is desired, provided there is not a clip on the same track that will get in the way.

Also keep in mind that when you drag one portion of a movie clip (video with audio), the other portion will adjust with it. If this is a problem, a way to get around it will be discussed in the section on linking clips.

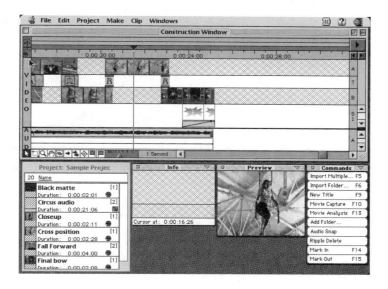

Figure 11.9 Edge viewing option icon

Using Construction Window In and Out Tools

In order to use this method for trimming clips accurately, you need to be in a close view of the Construction window, probably at least a four frame view for the greatest accuracy. If you are not in a close view, you will not be able to differentiate between adjacent clips.

Selecting Edge viewing (as discussed above) will also make it easier. Select the In point tool icon (the one with the flag facing left) and then click on the left edge of the frame of the clip, where you want the In point to be.

To select the Out point, click on the Out point tool icon (with the flag facing right) and then click on the right edge of the frame which you wish to be the Out point.

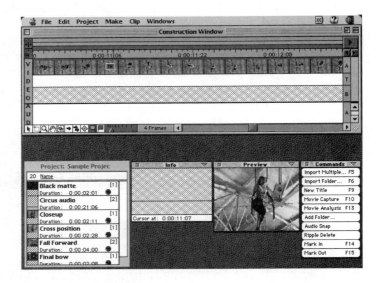

Figure 11.10 In/Out flags

Using the Rolling Edit Tool

The rolling edit adjusts the clip being edited and the clip adjacent to the edit point without effecting the rest of the clips. Thus, if you lengthen one clip, the one next to it will be shortened to accommodate the new edit point, and vice versa.

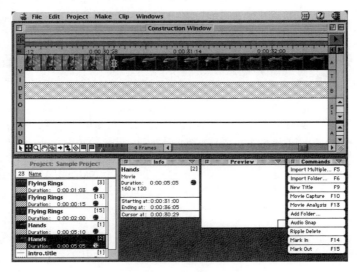

Figure 11.11 Rolling Edit tool

When performing a Rolling edit in the Construction window it is best to have the Edge viewing Option selected and to be in a Construction window view close enough so that the frames being edited are clearly visible. To do a rolling edit, select the Rolling Edit tool from the Construction window extended tools pop-up menu in the lower left section of the window.

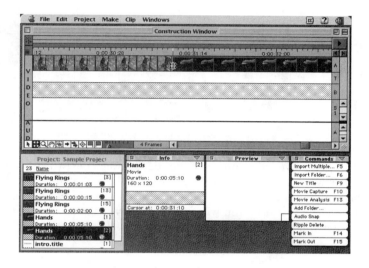

Figure 11.12a Rolling Edit usage

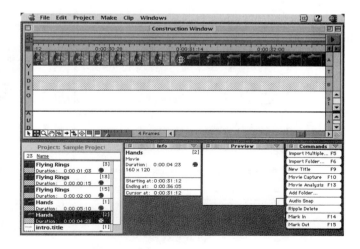

Figure 11.12b Rolling Edit usage

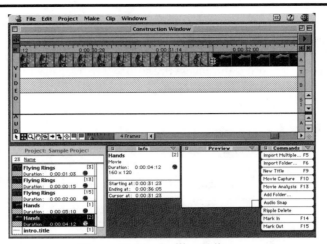

Figure 11.12c Rolling Edit usage

Once you move the mouse up to the edge between the two clips you want to edit, your cursor will change to the Rolling Edit tool. Drag the clip to the right if you want to lengthen the first clip and shorten the second one, or drag it to the left if you want to shorten the first one. You will see the frames changing as you drag the mouse in the preview window.

Doing a Ripple Edit in the Construction Window

A Ripple edit adjusts the clip you are editing and then moves every clip to the right of it on the same track to accommodate the changes just made. But remember that the total program duration will be altered when the clip is lengthened or shortened with the Ripple Edit tool, since the whole track is affected.

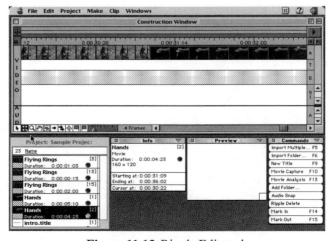

Figure 11.13 Ripple Edit tool

As with the rolling edit, it is helpful to have the edge viewing option selected when performing a ripple edit so that the frames in the preview window are visible (see previous section on Edge viewing).

Select the Ripple Edit tool from the Construction window extended tools pop-up menu. Move the mouse pointer over the edge between the two clips and drag to adjust the clip you want either to lengthen or shorten. Only the clip adjusted will be altered. All other clips to the right on the same track will move over to accommodate the change, but they will maintain their duration.

Editing Multiple Clips

There is a way to move a block of clips to another location within a program which has already been edited together (even including audio, transitions and any effects), and to accomplish this without changing anything else. Just use the Block Select tool found in the Construction Window extended tools pop-up menu. This makes it possible to move an entire sequence to a different location in your program without reediting the entire thing.

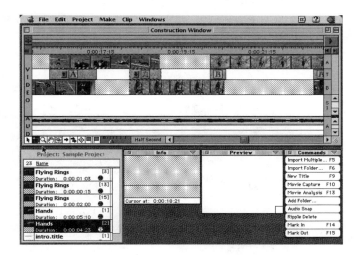

Figure 11.14 Block Tool

To move a block of clips to a different location, select the Block tool from the Construction window extended tools pop-up menu. Place the cursor, which changes to the icon, on the first clip you want to move and drag it until a box is created around all the clips to be included in the move. Release the mouse button. A dotted line surrounds all the clips you selected. This tool will take the whole area of the block selected so that empty spaces will also be moved if clips are not all of the same duration. If the dotted line does not surround all the clips to be moved together, try again and remember to start dragging at the clip that is earliest (farthest to the left) in the window. Once all the clips to be moved are selected, click on one of the highlighted clips and drag the block to its new location. Black squares appear on the tracks when the block reaches a place where all the clips in the block can fit. When the desired location is found, release the mouse button.

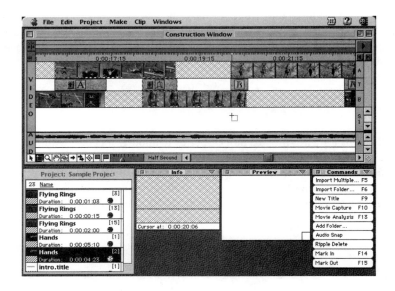

Figure 11.15a Block Tool Usage

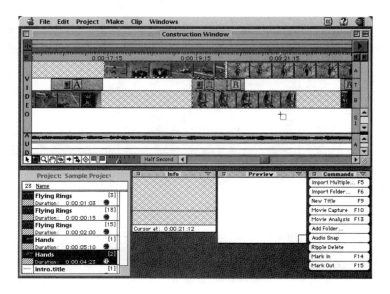

Figure 11.15b Block Tool Usage

This tool can also be used to apply commands from the clip or edit menu to each clip in the block selected. For example, a whole sequence, once selected, can be converted to black and white simply by choosing the black and white filter from the Clip menu (which of course does not affect audio clips). This tool can save a lot of time because it avoids the need to select each individual clip and to apply filters one at a time.

Splitting and Linking Clips

If you have a movie or audio clip and you want to make it into two or more clips, you can split it. Think of this as cutting a long reel of film into smaller sections. Shorter sections will be easier to handle when trying to find certain portions of a clip. In the magic world of digital editing, you are actually making copies of each clip but are seeing only a certain portion of each. You cannot rejoin clips, but you can get around that by dragging one of the clip pieces back to its full length.

Why would you want to split a clip? Perhaps you captured a long clip of a panel discussion, and within that clip three different people are interviewed. By splitting the clip into three separate pieces, different in and out points for each person can be established. This can also be helpful when you want to have these three different people speak at three different points in your program—perhaps the first one at the beginning, the second one at the very end and the third one somewhere in the middle. Split into separate pieces, appropriate sections of the clip can be relocated to any desired location within the program. Remember that if your clip has audio attached to it, splitting the video will also split the audio and vice versa.

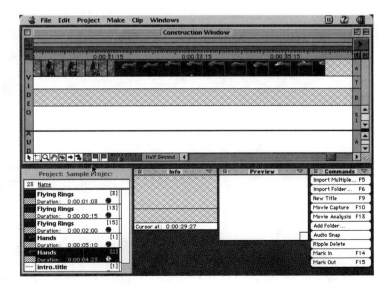

Figure 11.16 Razor Tool Icon

You perform a split by using the Razor tool from the Construction window. When the Razor tool is selected, the cursor appears as the razor icon. Place it over the clip you want to edit and click where you want the clip to split. In order to make an accurate split, zoom in your view of the Construction window timeline to increments of just a few frames so you can more accurately see where you are placing the tool. Once you have split a clip, you can trim it like any other clip by using either the Clip or Trimming window.

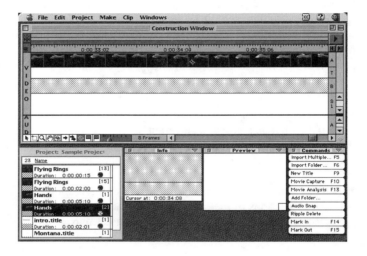

Figure 11.17a Razor Tool Usage

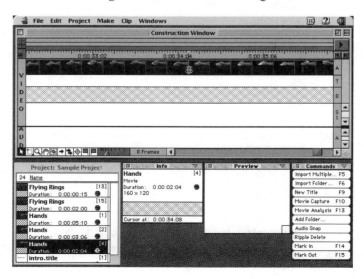

Figure 11.17b Razor Tool Usage

You can also use the Razor tool to edit audio clips, although it is tougher to determine the location of a good split.

Links

Within a movie clip, the video has a hard link to the audio, which means that when one piece of the clip is moved, the corresponding piece moves with it. This is also true of trimming movie clips. Generally this is extremely helpful, as with a clip of a person talking, because it ensures that the synchronization of lips and speech remains in tact. But there are times when you will want to break that link. There are also times when you may want to link clips together which were not originally linked, perhaps a music track with a piece of video or a graphic.

If you have a movie clip and you are not going to use one part of it (either the audio or the video) at all, you can simply delete that portion of it by clicking on it and pressing the Delete key. Once you delete it, you cannot bring it back, so be sure you will not be needing it.

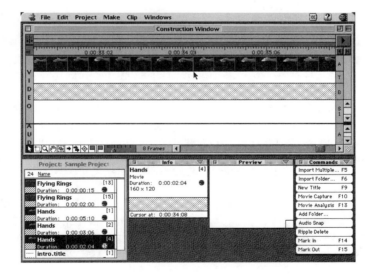

Figure 11.18 Broken link on clip

If you want to retain both portions of the clip, but also want to be able to move them separately, you can break the link by selecting the clip and choosing Break Link from the Edit menu. When this is done, Premiere places a marker in the newly separated clips so that you will know that they used to be linked. These markers can be realigned at a later time if it is necessary to synchronize the clips once again.

You can also break a link temporarily in order to move clips independently. Choose the Link Override tool from the Construction Window extended tools pop-up menu.

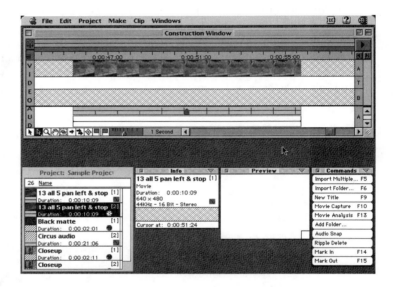

Figure 11.19 Link Overide Tool

Select the Link Overide tool, then select the video or audio portion of the clip and move it to where you want it. The portion selected will move independently of the other portion to which it was previously linked. Red triangles on both portions of the previously linked clip indicate the clip is now out of sync. You can click on either of these red arrows and learn by how many frames they are out of sync.

This tool can also be used to perform what is called a split edit or L-cut edit. By this means it is possible to start a clip with just one portion (perhaps the audio), and have the other (the video) enter, correctly synched, at a later point. Imagine an interview with the owner of a business who is talking about her company. You may wish to hear her talking about the company while, for the first ten seconds, we see the outside of the company head-quarters. By using the Link Override tool, it is possible to drag the video portion to the right in order to shorten it ten seconds and add a different video clip in that space. When the interview video rejoins the audio, it will be perfectly synched. By double clicking, each portion can be shown independently with an indication of the different in points.

Links between video and audio clips which were not originally linked can be created by using the Soft Link tool. First, click on an audio or video clip which you want to be part of the soft link, and then select the Soft Link tool from the extended tools pop-up menu in the Construction Window. Next, click on the clip it is to be linked with. A soft link icon (two chain links) flashes when the soft link has been established. Soft links can be established only between clips that are not already part of a hard link. When a clip which is already part of another soft link is chosen for a new soft link, the newly linked pair will replace the older one. A soft link can also be used to rejoin a clip that was previously hard linked.

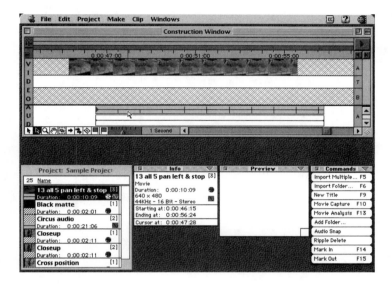

Figure 11.20 Soft-Link Tool

Conclusion

The primary editing has been completed at this stage and the final integration with audio and effects needs completion. Of course, the audio and effects are always considered, and usually the basic audio track sets the pace of the project, but they need to be brought together.

Chapter 12
Video Sound Editing

Introduction

It's impossible to edit successfully without at least a preliminary sound track. We have covered the basics of audio acquisition and clip editing, but now we must consider the integration and layering of the audio with the video elements of the project, and their refinement into a final product. The audio editing functions of most video editing software is very sophisticated and can, in many cases, be used as the primary audio editing platform. When more sophisticated audio effects are required, the use of specialized audio editing packages is warranted, with the final integration taking place in the video edit. In this chapter, we will consider the integration of audio into video.

Audio Clip Window

The audio wave form clip window is much like the movie clip window, in that the controls are similar and you select the In and Out point the same way. There is also another slider bar that helps you visually scroll through different sections of the clip, as you scroll through a word processing document. The jog/shuttle works the same way as in a movie clip but with this slider you can hear the audio as it shuttles through.

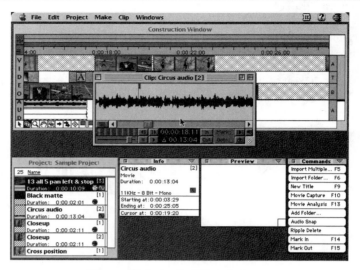

Figure 12.1 Audio Clip window

You will see your selected In and Out point with a flag marking a spot on the wave form display. The wave form control button allows you to view your clip from four different displays: expanded, normal, condensed, and extra condensed. For the most precise detail and information choose the expanded view. If you want to see a larger portion of the clip at one time, choose the condensed view. You can also expand the size of the clip window with the mouse by pulling out the bottom right corner.

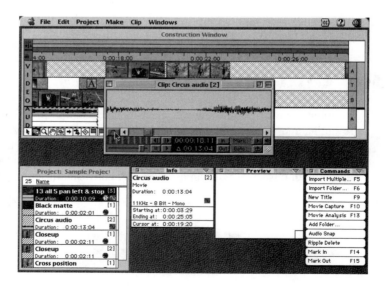

Figure 12.2a Waveform view

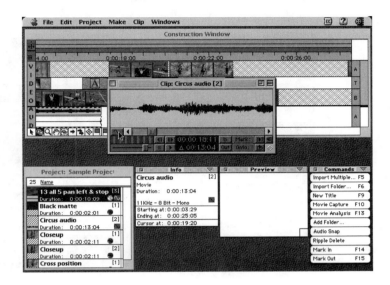

Figure 12.2b Waveform view

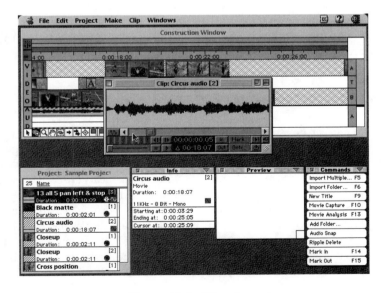

Figure 12.2c Waveform view

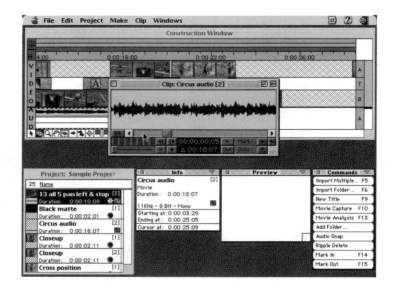

Figure 12.2d Waveform view

Editing to Marks

Place markers or "marks" are a way to help you identify a certain portion of the clip, much like turning down the corner of a page in a book to mark your place. Marks do not alter your clip or change the in and out points, they are merely a way for you to visually mark areas of your clip for easy identification.

Using Place Markers

Marks can be especially helpful when trying to edit several different pieces of video and audio together. For example, if you're editing a sequence of images to music you may want to have your cuts correspond to the beats in the music. By placing markers on the audio clip you can easily identify where those beats are located, and line up the video clips to those marks. These marks are also useful when marking areas in a video clip that need a sound effect. For instance, let's say you had video of a street scene in San Francisco with its natural street sounds. As the shot of the cable car is in the distance, you didn't pick up the sound of the cable car's bell on your microphone, and you want to add it in as a sound effect. You could put a place marker on the part of the video where the cable car is visible and then simply line up the audio clip of the bell sound to the marker.

These are just a few examples of the many different uses for place markers and each editor has his or her own way of using them. The more you use them, the more you will understand how helpful they are in developing your own editing style. You can place up to 1000 marks on one clip, ten of them (numbered 0– 9) can have a number on them for your reference.

Setting Place Markers

1.   To set a place marker, you must be viewing your clip in the clip window.

2.   Use the jog/shuttle or frame-by-frame buttons to find the desired frame.

3.   Click and hold on the Mark button and choose a number from the pop-up menu. You may assign it any number, in any order, as it's only a reference for you, but each mark must have a different number. If you want to use unnumbered place markers simply strike the + or = key on your keyboard.

There are only ten numbered marks available within a single clip, so use judiciously. Use the numbered marks for major cues and unnumbered marks for lesser cues. For example, the numbered marks may be reserved for the beginning of a new paragraph of narration, and the unnumbered marks for the beginning of each sentence within the paragraph.

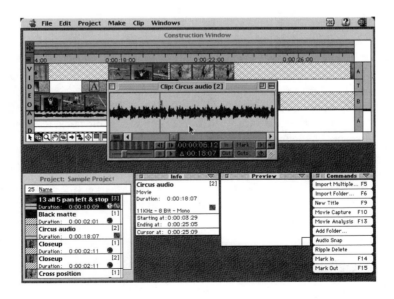

Figure 12.3 Setting Marks

You will see the marks (little blue arrows with the numbers on it) when the clip is in the Construction Window.

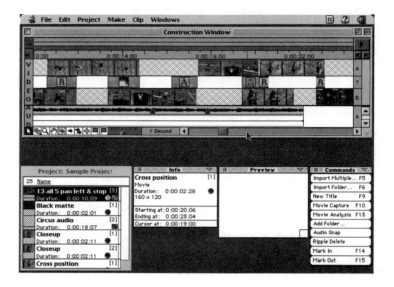

Figure 12.4 Markers in Construction Window

If you can't see them clearly, zoom in your view of the Construction Window by adjusting the time line. If you still don't see the marks in your clip, select Clip Window Options from the Windows menu and click on Show Markers. With the markers visible, you will be able to line up your video track with the marks on your audio track. Remember, placing markers does not change your in and out points, it only gives you a visual index to simplify your editing process.

To line up clips with markers easily, click on the marker (the pointer arrow will turn blue), and by dragging, you will be able to align the markers in the two tracks. You will see a vertical line appear that will make lining up the marks more precise.

Setting Marks During Playback

You can also mark your clips "on the fly" by listening or viewing your clip in real time (its regular speed, not frame by frame). This is helpful if you're trying to mark the beats in a long piece of music. For this purpose it is probably quicker and easier to use the unnumbered markers because you know each mark is a beat. Listen to the song in the Clip Window and strike the + or = key whenever you hear the beat. By the end of the song you will have all your edit points already marked on your music track.

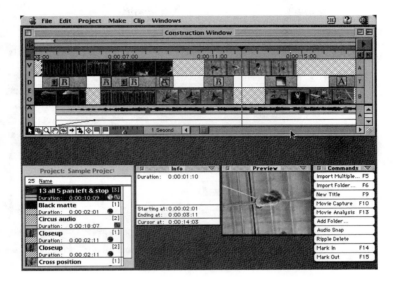

Figure 12.5 Unnumbered Marks in Construction window

Deleting Marks

The method for deleting place markers is the same in both the movie and audio wave form clip window. Open your clip in the Clip Window and use the Go To button to find the mark you want to erase. When you have found it (and a square with the mark number appears in the middle of the clip window), strike either the "c" or "x" key and it will erase that mark. You will notice that the blue arrow mark on your clip in the Construction Window will disappear. If it's an unnumbered mark you want to erase, locate the proper mark, click on it and strike the "c" or "x" key.

Synching Clips

To align marks in the Construction window make sure that you have selected Show Markers from the Construction Window dialog box from the Windows menu.

Choose the Selection tool (the cursor arrow) icon and click on the mark you want to line up with another mark (the selection tool turns gray). Now that the mark is selected, drag it towards the other mark. An alignment line will appear making the alignment of these two marks easier. If you have Snap to Edges chosen, the two will easily snap together with the marks lined up. Release the mouse button once you have them properly aligned.

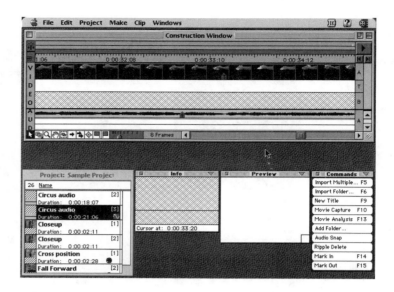

Figure 12.6a Synching Clips using markers

In Premiere, you have the capability of having ninety-nine audio tracks playing at once. You can add tracks to your Construction Window to accommodate the number of audio tracks you want. Of course it will be highly difficult to see all ninety-nine at once, but you can scroll down through them to see each clip.

You can adjust the level of each clip, create fades and even add audio filters to your clips. Mixing audio is often necessary when you have many different tracks playing within a program. You have to watch volume levels and make sure that, if you have audio tracks layered, you can hear what you need to hear, i.e., that the music is not drowning out the narration.

Rubber Bands

As with many digital editing programs, Premiere uses the rubber band method to make it easy to see any changes in fade and volume levels (so called, because the controls used in this process may be stretched and moved). If you want to see your audio clip, choose Show Waveform.

As you look at your audio clip (whether you have the waveform showing or not) you will see the Audio Fade control area at the bottom of the clip with a black line in the middle of it. The middle point represents 0 dB on the meters of a tape deck. This is the mid-volume point.

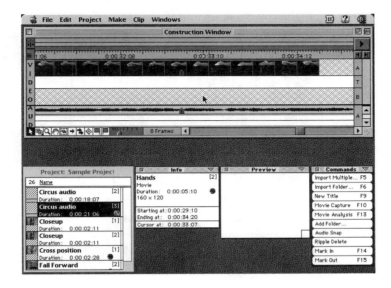

Figure 12.7 Audio Rubberband Default setting

To adjust the levels of an audio clip, move the cursor over the line in the middle and the arrow will change to a finger pointer. When you click on the line you create a dot that appears on the line. This is a handle that you can use to adjust the volume level by dragging it up or down. You can create as many handles as you need, and you can erase them by dragging them up and out of the clip. These are often referred to as rubber bands because you can move and stretch them as much as you want.

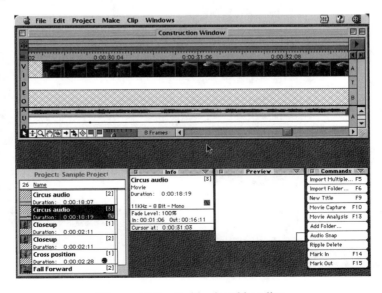

Figure 12.8a Rubberband handles

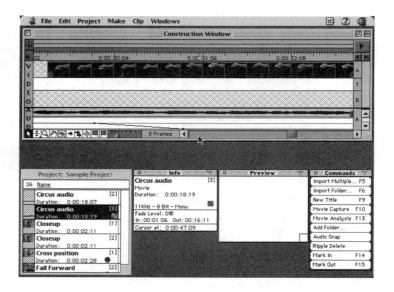

Figure 12.8b Rubberband handles

As you drag the handle, look at the information in the Info box (if the Info box is not showing, choose Info from the Windows menu) which shows the audio level percentage in 10% increments.

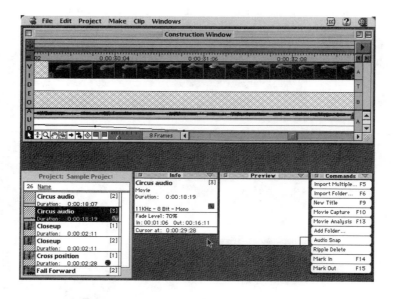

Figure 12.9 Info box and Fade control

Fade In

One of the most common adjustments you will be making to an audio clip is a "fade in." (Fade in means the gradual increase of volume from inaudible to the full sound level.)

1. First, determine how long a fade you want, for example a 15 frame fade up.

2. Click on the line near the beginning of the clip.

3. Look at the Info box and drag the mouse with the button still depressed until you see the In info numbers reach 00:00:15. At this point you will want the fade level to be at 100%

    (0 db / in the middle).

4. Go to the very beginning of the clip and click on the line to create a handle and drag it to 0%. You have just created a fade up from nothing to regular volume level. If 100% is not loud enough, you can drag that handle at the end of your fade up to a level you like.

To preview the audio fade and level, drag the yellow work area bar along the top of the Construction window to cover the length of what you want to preview and hit the return key. This is a quick way to listen to what you have created.

You can also use handles to raise or lower the level of the audio during certain portions of the clip by simply creating handles at the points where you want to make adjustments and moving them up or down as necessary. This can be useful when a loud part of your soundtrack drowns out the narration track. Instead of having to find a new soundtrack, you can bring this loud portion of the clip (easily identifiable by any markers you placed) gently down a little. This long fade down to the new level will not be noticeable and your audience will still be able to hear the narrator.

Fade Scissors Tool

An easy way to create two handles next to each other is to use the Fade Scissors tool found in the Construction Window pop-up menu. By using this tool, you can make a cut in the audio fade portion of the audio track and two handles (black dots) will be automatically created next to each other. This is useful when you want to increase or decrease the volume sharply at a certain point in the audio track.

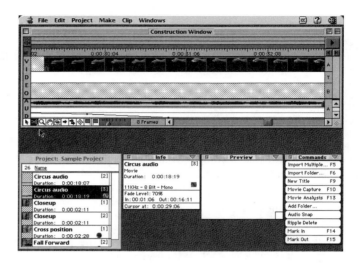

Figure 12.10 Fade Scissors tool

To use the tool, select the scissors icon and position your cursor over the portion of the audio track where you wish to create the handles. The scissors icon will appear when you place the mouse over the audio fade portion of the track. Click where you want to make the cut.

You will see the two handles appear. In order to adjust the levels, be sure to select the Pointer tool (the arrow) before attempting to grab the handles. This prevents inadvertently making more cuts and handles than are necessary. Once you see the finger icon you will be able to adjust the levels at the handles.

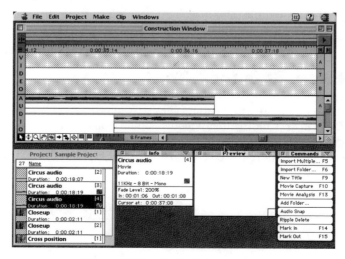

Figure 12.11a Fade Scissors usage

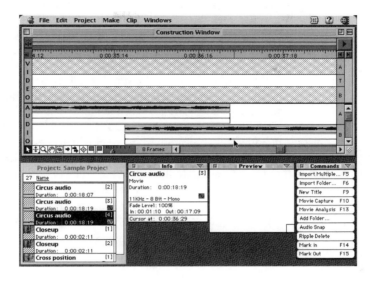

Figure 12.11b Fade Scissors usage

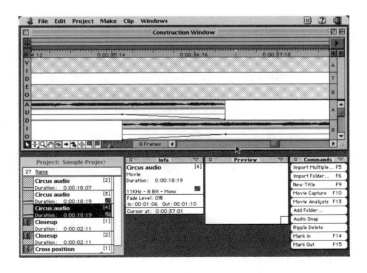

Figure 12.11c Fade Scissors usage

Cross Fade

A common need in editing audio tracks is a cross fade, where one track fades out simultaneously while another track fades in. A smooth cross fade usually needs to be at least 15 frames to one second long. To create a cross fade, you must have two clips on different tracks that overlap by at least the length of the cross fade. Create a one-second fade out on the first clip by creating a handle and using the info box to be sure the duration and level are correct. Grab the following audio clip, on another track, and line up the beginning of the clip to the handle on the first clip, which marks where the fade out begins. Create a handle in the second clip and make a one-second fade in, ending just where your first clip ends. Thus the first clip fades out while the second one is fading in, which usually creates a smooth (and unnoticeable) transition from one clip to the next. This is a great trick when using more than one piece of music, or when trying to extend a piece of music by simply repeating part of the first piece. In the latter case you would need to make a copy of the first clip, paste it onto another track, and overlap it for the cross fade.

A even quicker way to create a cross-fade is to use the Audio fade tool from the extended tools pop-up menu in the Construction Window.

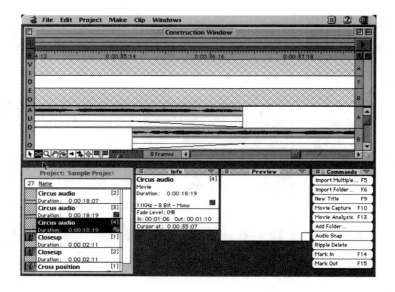

Figure 12.12 Cross-fade Tool

To use this tool, overlap the two audio clips for the desired duration of the cross fade and select the Audio fade tool. Click on the first audio clip and then on the second. The rubber bands automatically move to show the cross fade.

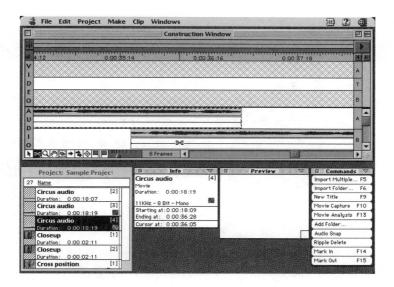

Figure 12.13a Cross-fade Tool Usage—before

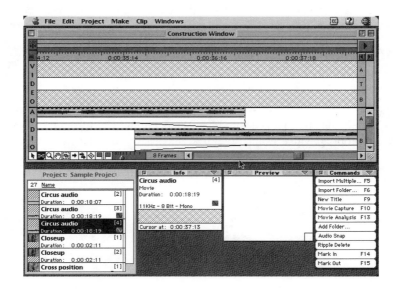

Figure 12.13b Cross-fade Tool Usage—after

To adjust levels in a clip uniformly without having to create a lot of handles, use the Fade Adjustment tool from the extended tools pop-up menu in the Construction window.

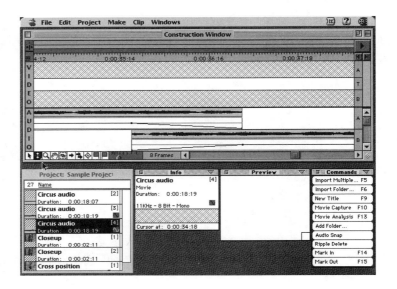

Figure 12.14 Fade adjustment Tool

Select the tool and place it in the Audio Fade control section of your clip. The cursor changes to a two-headed vertical arrow with a horizontal line in the middle. Drag the line up or down; the info box indicates the level. This tool, which creates no handles, is particularly helpful for adjusting the entire level of a clip.

If your clip is recorded so low that you want the whole thing to be louder, raise the gain level.

Select the clip that needs to be boosted, choose Gain from the Clip menu, and enter an appropriate value from 1 to 200% . Excessive boost may create some added noise (like static), so be wary when large increases are required.

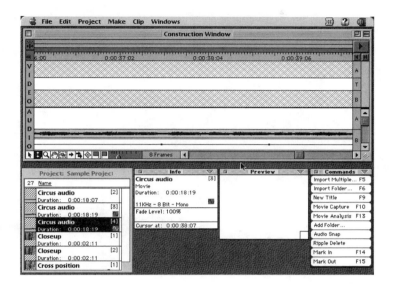

Figure 12.15a Fade adjustment Tool usage—beginning

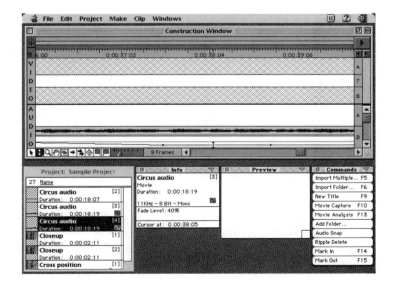

Figure 12.15b Fade adjustment Tool usage—middle

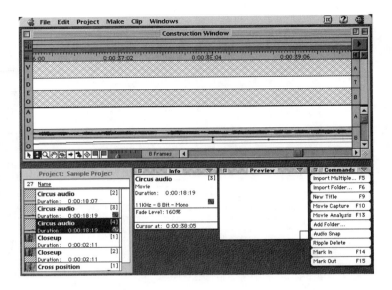

Figure 12.15c Fade adjustment Tool usage—completed

Effects

You can add effects to audio much like you would add special effects to video. While some special effects may radically change the sound of an audio clip, most audio effects and filters are used to "clean-up" the sound. As most people who shoot video with consumer camcorders know, you have little control over the audio being recorded by your camera microphone. Even when an additional microphone is used, the quality of the recorded audio usually sounds flat. Although Premiere has some basic filters you can apply to help the audio sound better, truly improving the sound will usually require that the clip be moved into another, more extensive sound program (to be discussed later in this chapter).

Using Filters in Premiere

In the basic Premiere package you have few audio filters, but you can purchase additional plug-in filters that will really add to your audio capabilities. Once installed, plug-in filters will show up in the usual filter menu so they are no more difficult to use than the original ones. To apply a filter, click on the audio clip and select Filters from the Clip menu. You will only see the Audio filters listed (the video filters are only listed when a video clip is selected). Scroll through and find the filter you want to try.

If you want to apply an echo to your clip, for example, click on Echo and then click Add. The Echo dialog box will appear, and you can adjust the setting of the echo. Once you have made the settings, click OK, and then click OK again on the Filter Dialog box. You will see a colored line on your audio clip indicating that a filter is being applied. Not all filters have a dialog box; those which do not are either on or off. Those which have variable settings allow for trying different settings in order to get the desired effect.

Echo is one of the filters included with the basic Premiere package. The others are Backwards (which make the audio clip play backwards), and Fill and Pan. The Fill filter lets you put the audio on just one channel and the Pan channel lets you move the sound left and right.

Cybersound FX

Additional plug-in filters, such as Cybersound FX, from InVision, have much more variety and have their own dialog boxes. Once you have added a filter to the current list by clicking on Add, you can double click on the filter to get to the settings. With the plug-in Settings Window you can preview an effect before you choose it which makes it easier to try out different types of effects.

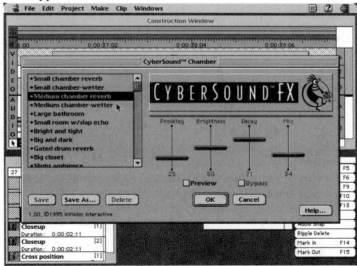

Figure 12.16 Cybersound FX dialog box

Effects and Filters

Although there are far too many effects and filters to detail here, there are basic types such as echo & reverb, pitch shift, compression and equalization.

Echo

Echo & Reverb add a sort of presence to the sound which may be needed to make it seem more realistic. An actor recorded in a studio, using a good microphone, should sound strong as if he or she were sitting next to you. Suppose, however, your final video will, utilizing special effects, show the actor standing in an empty castle. You would then need to apply a filter to make the voice sound as it would if the actor were actually standing in a castle. Adding some echo and reverb would make the sound of the voice more believable. You can layer filters, actually creating your own effect. It is often necessary to try out different setting before finding the "right" sound, but the end results are worth the extra effort.

Pitch Shift

Pitch Shift alters the audio to sound either lower of higher in pitch. You could take a female voice, lower the pitch and disguise it to sound like an alien. Effects can be as subtle or dramatic as you want.

Compression and Equalization

Compression and Equalization are ways of balancing the audio by cutting or boosting the treble, midrange and bass. Compression can be useful if there is a wide range of volume levels in your clip — someone who is talking quietly some of the time and then loudly at other times. Although these filters give you quick results, you will find even better results by using other more extensive sound programs.

There are several sophisticated sound programs on the market which provide the tools needed for achieving the best possible audio. These will be discussed in detail in a later section. Hint: Although Premiere will accept audio files in a variety of different formats (ex. Aiff, wav, snd), be sure that the program you are using can create a file which will import into Premiere.

Exporting to Sound Programs

It is often necessary to export sound blended or mixed in the video editing program to external sound edit programs. This is done simply by selecting the sound clip and using the File/Export function of Premiere to send a portion of all of the mixed audio track to an external file. It can be used for other purposes or can be processed and imported back into the video editing package.

Conclusion

The audio track is done and integrated fully with the visual elements. There may still be adjustment, adds and deletions when adding effects and once feedback is provided by clients or previewers. Be sure to retain all your notes and backup all your source files and edit lists "just in case."

Chapter 13

Basic Effects

Introduction

Basic effects, as listed here, are available in some form in almost every editing application. They include clip effects, filters, transitions, and titles. Some may be standard, while others require additional software upgrades. Just because we label these basic effects, don't consider them unworthy of your finest productions. These are the most common effects, used in every type of production, including feature films. Used alone or in combination, they can be just as emotionally powerful as any 3-D animated, flying, morphing, chroma-key composite.

Clip Effects

Clip effects change the way a clip appears to play. This can be a change in speed or direction, creating a single freeze-frame, or altering the frame rate.

Speed & Direction

Clips playing at normal speed and direction have a default setting of 100%. Changing this percentage to a negative number creates a clip that plays backwards. Changing the clip speed adds or subtracts frames from the original clip. A clip set for 200% playback will have half its frames removed for double speed playback. Alternately, a clip set for 50% playback will have twice as many frames (and double the duration) as the original. Therefore, clips used for slow-motion effects should be captured at the highest possible frame rate so that when slowed down, there will still be smooth motion between frames.

To set the speed of clip in Premiere:

1. Select the clip from the Project or Construction window.

2. From the Clip menu, choose Speed. A Clip Speed dialog box will appear.

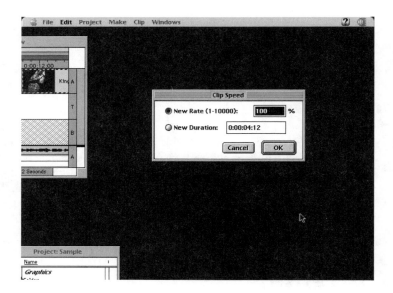

Figure 13.1 Clip Speed dialog box

3. Enter a desired rate in the New Rate box. If a duration is entered for the clip, Premiere will calculate and enter an appropriate rate automatically. Click the OK button.

If you're using 60 field-per-second clips, perform these additional steps. Doing so will eliminate possible jerkiness during playback.

4. From the Clip menu, choose Field Options. The Field Options dialog box will appear.

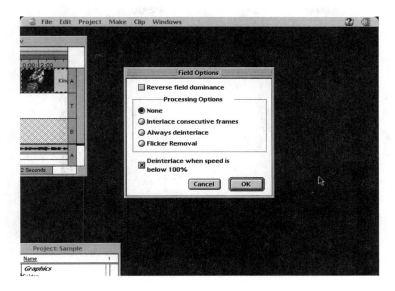

Figure 13.2 Field Options dialog box

5.   If you have reversed the direction of the clip, make sure that the Reverse Field Dominance checkbox is selected. If a clip has been slowed down, make sure the De-interlace When Speed is Below 100% checkbox is selected. Click OK.

Freeze-frame

Freeze-frames create a still image of a specified frame from within a clip. The duration of the freeze will be the same as the clip itself.

To create a freeze frame:

1.   Set the in or out point on the frame to be frozen. Or you may place Marker 0 at the desired frame.

2.   Select the clip in the Construction window. From the Clip menu, choose Frame Hold. The Frame Hold dialog box will appear.

3.   Click the checkbox next to Hold On and select the frame to freeze from the Hold On pop-up menu. Select Hold Filters if you don't want applied filters to change over time. (See Filter Effects, later in this chapter) Select De-interlace if working with 60 field-per-second video. This will eliminate any jittering during playback. Select OK.

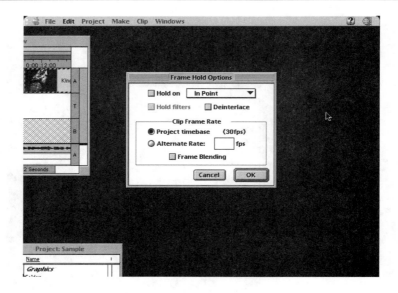

Figure 13.3 Frame Hold dialog box

Remember, this effect creates a freeze frame for the duration of the clip. For example, if you want a clip to play and then freeze on the last frame, you will need to create the effect using two clips and an edit, as follows:

1.   Place the clip to play at normal speed onto a video track in the Construction window.

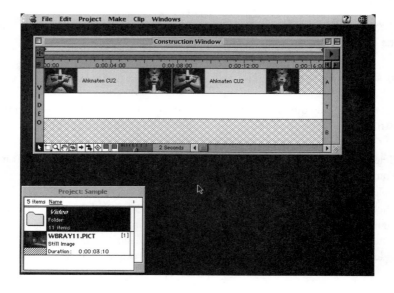

Figure 13.4 Play & Freeze effect

2. Copy & Paste a duplicate to the right of the original clip. This will be the freeze-frame clip. Select this clip from the Construction window.

3. From the Clip menu, choose Speed. Enter a duration for the freeze-frame. The dialog box will automatically disappear.

4. From the Clip menu, choose Frame Hold. Click the checkbox next to Hold On and select Last Frame from the Hold On pop-up menu. Select OK.

Now when the movie plays, it will play the first clip at normal speed. When it reaches the edit point it will play the second clip, which is really just a freeze-frame of the last frame from the first clip. Using other combinations of this technique, it's possible to have clips freeze-play or play-freeze-play, all in seamless fashion.

Frame Rate

There is one part of the Frame Hold Options we haven't covered yet. That is the Clip Frame Rate settings option.

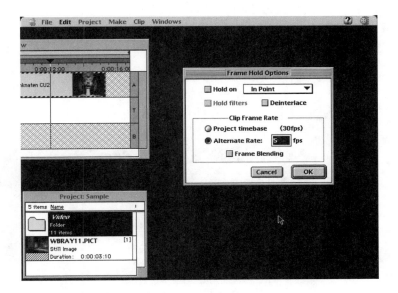

Figure 13.5 Clip Frame Rate settings

Dramatic changes in settings create a series of freeze frames from a clip. Subtle changes create a hi-tech stop-action look. This can also be used for simulating an old-time movie feel. When the Frame Blending option is selected, Premiere will automatically create a series of dissolves between frames, depending upon the frame rate. This is an easy way to smooth out the jerkiness of normal stop-action effects.

Filters

Filters are software generated treatments of individual clips. They let you distort, warp, blur, posterize, and texturize video and graphic images. More than one filter may be applied to a clip at a time. Some filters can be changed over time, through the duration of a clip. For example, a twirl filter can be applied so that the video starts normally and then spins itself into a whirlpool.

There are literally hundreds of different filters available for use. Dozens come standard with many editing applications, such as Premiere, Avid Videoshop, and In Sync Razor Pro. Many of these programs are designed to work with filters from other packages. Kais Power Tools can be used within Razor Pro. Any Photoshop compatible filter will work with Premiere or After Effects. Depending upon the application, some controls and features of a particular filter are not available. Custom filters may be created using tools available in editing applications.

Filters require extra processing and take longer to make into a finished movie than unfiltered clips. They can also add small distortions to video, even at minimal settings, so use them carefully.

Applying Filters

To apply a filter to a clip:

1.   Select a clip in the Construction window.

2.   From the Clip menu, choose Filters. The Filters dialog box will appear.

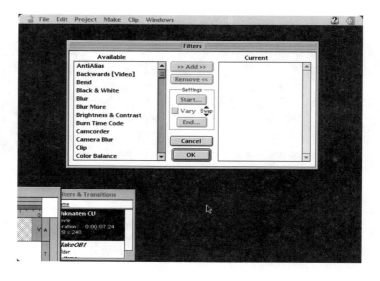

Figure 13.6 Filter dialog box

The left-hand window displays a list of available filters. The right-hand window displays the filters currently applied to the clip.

3.   Using the scroll controls, select a filter from the Available list. Click Add or double-click on the filter in the list.

4.   If the filter has settings, a Settings dialog box will appear.

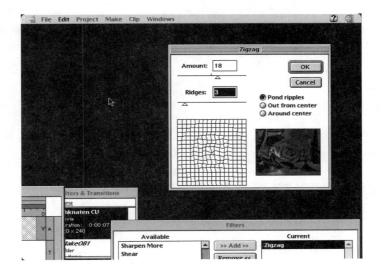

Figure 13.7 Filters Settings dialog box

5.   Adjust the settings as desired and click OK.

For filters that adjust over time, the Filters Settings dialog box may have slider controls.

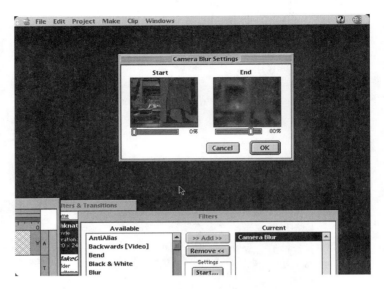

Figure 13.8 Time-change Filters Settings dialog box

Use the slider controls to adjust the start and end frames of the clip. If the effect is to remain constant over time, set the sliders to the same setting. The Start and End sliders may be locked together by holding down the Shift key while making adjustments. When finished, click on OK.

The same filter can be applied to the same clip, over and over again. This multiplies the the intensity of the effect.

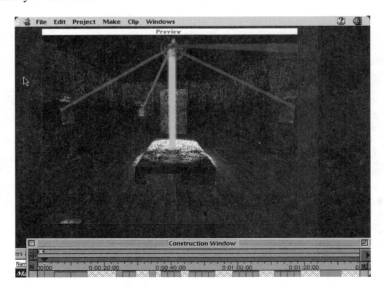

Figure 13.9a Original clip

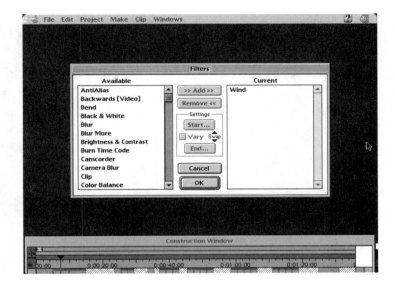

Figure 13.9b Single selection of filter—wind

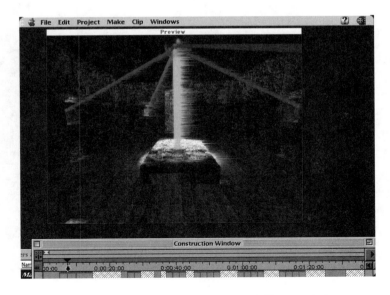

Figure 13.9c Single application of filter—wind

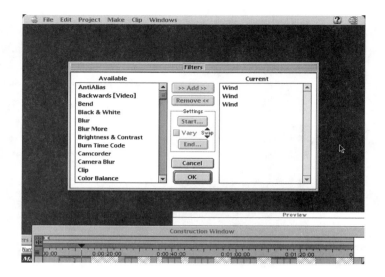

Figure 13.9d Multiple selection of same filter—wind

Figure 13.9e Multiple applications of same filter—wind

You can change a filter's settings at any time. Just select the filter in the Current list. Click the Start or End button in the Settings area.   Double-clicking on a filter in the list will always take you to the Start Settings dialog box.

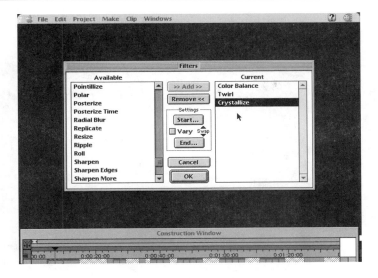

Figure 13.10 Multiple clips in Filters dialog box

Settings for the start and end frames may be reversed by using the Swap button in the Settings area.

If the Vary button is deselected, the filter will be applied at a constant level, based upon the start settings.

The order of clips can have a big impact on the final effect. For example, the Crop filter (which trims away unwanted pixels from the edge of a frame) and Horizontal Flip filter can be applied together. If placed on top of the Horizontal Flip filter, cropping takes place on the normal image. If placed below, cropping will be done on the flipped image.

Figure 13.11a Original clip

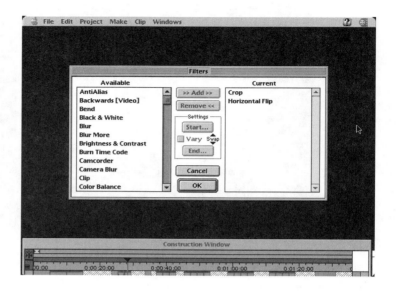

Figure 13.11b Filters dialog box—crop, horizontal flip

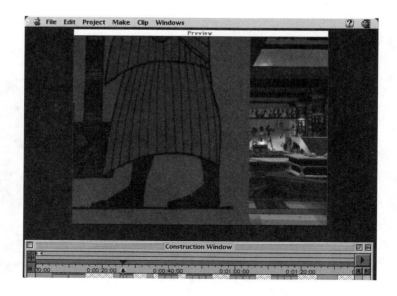

Figure 13.11c Application—crop, horizontal flip

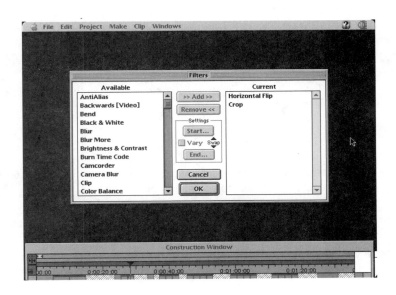

Figure 13.11d Filters dialog box—horizontal flip, crop

Figure 13.11e Application— horizontal flip, crop

To change the order of filters, select the filter from the Current list. Holding down the mouse button, drag the filter to a new location in the list. To delete a filter, select it from the Current list and click on Remove.

Filters in the Construction Window

Clips that have filters applied to them are displayed in the Construction window with a blue border at the top.

To view which filters have been applied to a clip:

1.   While pressing the Option key, move the pointer over the clip in the Construction window. The pointer changes to an icon of a miniature menu.

2.   Hold down the mouse button to display a pop-up menu of the applied filters.

3.   To view or change a filter setting, drag the mouse to the selected filter and release the button. To apply additional filters, select Filters from the bottom of the pop-up menu.

Working with Clips

Filters that don't change over time can be made to appear to do so through the use of transitions within the Construction window. For example, a normal clip can be dissolved into a filtered clip of the same video. (See more information on Transitions later in this chapter.)

For filters that do change over time, an edit will be necessary to start or stop the effect in the middle of a clip.

1.   Use the Razor tool in the Construction window at the point the effect should start.

2.   Apply a time-adjustable filter to the clip on the right. Make sure the start settings are at zero for no effect.

Now the clip will play normally, then transition into a filtered effect.

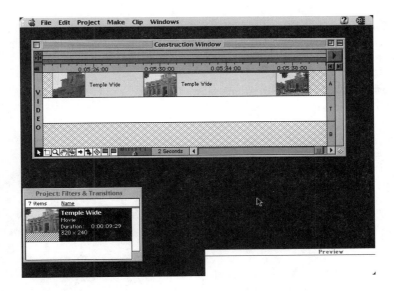

Figure 13.12 Starting a Filter Effect in the middle of a Clip

Adjustment Filters

It would be impossible to describe in detail every filter available on the market today. There are just too many of them. New ones are being created every day—some available through on-line services. Filters that have the same name may have subtle differences in output or setting controls, depending upon the editing application in which they are found. We can, however, break them down into basic categories and give a sample of the most common filters and suggested uses.

Filters may be placed into two major categories: Adjustment filters or Modifying filters. Adjustment filters are tools that fix or enhance a clip, maintaining the basic look of the original. Modifying filters change the elemental look of a clip and are more obviously an effect. Please note that these are categories of con-venience. Just because we've classi-fied a filter as an Adjustment filter, doesn't mean that, at extreme settings, it couldn't qualify as a Modifying filter.

Adjustment filters themselves can be divided into two groups: Frame filters and Image Control filters. Frame filters determine how much or what part of an image will be used. Image Control filters determine how those pixels are displayed.

Frame Filters are often used for cropping, scaling, flipping or otherwise changing the display area of an image.

- The Clip filter trims rows of pixels from the edge of a clip. The trimmed area is then filled with a selected color. This is useful for eliminating noise or pixel skew from captured video.

- The Crop filter is similar to the Clip filter in that it also trims unwanted pixels from the edge of an image. The difference is that the Crop filter automatically resizes the trimmed clip to it's original dimensions, filling the entire frame area. Uneven cropping can result in distortion, as pixels are stretched. Excessive cropping can result in pixelization because of pixel enlargement to fill the frame.

- Horizontal & Vertical Flip reverses the image left to right, or flips it upside down. The clip still plays in a forward direction.

Figure 13.13a Original Frame

Figure 13.13b Clip Filter

Figure 13.13c Crop Filter

Figure 13.13d Horizontal Flip Filter

- Image Pan is one of the great all-purpose filters. Image Pan allows you to crop any part of an image and then change the position and size of the crop through the duration of a clip. This can be used to create rolling titles, simulate pan and zoom movements on static images, or scale an image for output.

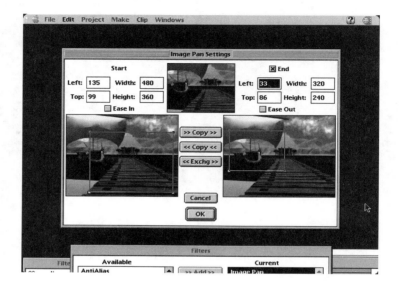

Figure 13.14 Image Pan Settings dialog box

Image pan works best on clips that are larger than the output frame size. As long as the cropped image is equal to or greater than the output size, no pixalization will occur. If the cropped image is smaller than the output size, then Premiere will use interpolation to scale the image up.

Image Control filters change the pixel properties of clips. Video can be captured at a normalized setting and then adjusted individually using these filters. This allows for the greatest amount of technical and creative control.

- The Black & White filter creates a black and white image by reducing all colors to shades of grey.
- Brightness & Contrast, Hue & Saturation, and Color Balance filters provide control over the individual elements of the color values of an image.
- The Broadcast Colors filter reduces luminance and saturation levels so that the image may be accurately displayed for television broadcast. Home video equipment can't handle the high amplitude signals commonly found in computer generated colors. This filter reduces

the signals to a safe level.

- The Gamma Correction filter controls the brightness of an image without substantially affecting the base black or white levels. This very useful when Mac images are to be eventually displayed on a PC. Because of the difference in monitors, Mac images can appear overly dark. A setting of .7 or .8 is usually sufficient for eliminating this problem.
- The Levels filter combines all of the features of Brightness & Contrast, Hue & Saturation, Color Balance, and Gamma Correction into one filter.

Modifying Filters

Modifying filters significantly alter the way a clip appears compared to the original. The effect may be subtle or dramatic. These can be used as stand-alone effects or used in combination with other elements. There are two major groups of modifying filters: Style filters and Distortion filters.

Style filters create abstract or impressionistic effects by altering and displacing pixels and manipulating an image's color scheme. Popular Style filters include:

- The Blur filter is available in a variety of strengths. A blur, applied over time, can simulate the de-focusing of a camera lens.
- The Ghosting filter overlays previous frames of a clip to create a ghost-like effect.
- The Lens Flare filter simulates the refraction of a bright light shining directly into a camera lens. This is great as a highlight on a moving object within the screen.
- The Solorize filter blends a negative and positive image, resulting in a "halo" effect.

Figure 13.15a Style Filters—Blur

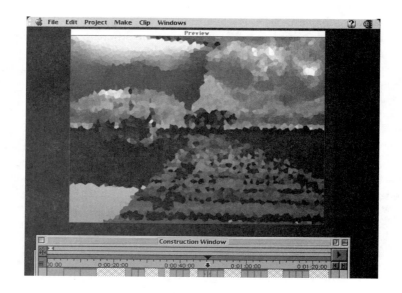

Figure 13.15b Style Filters—Extreme Blur

Figure 13.15c Style Filters—Lens Flare

Figure 13.15d Style Filters—Solarize

- Artistic Simulation filters simulate artistic styles, tools, and techniques. Charcoal, Crayon, Fresco, Mosaic, Paint Daubs, Pastel, Sponge, Stained Glass and Watercolor are just a few examples.

Figure 13.16a Style Filters—Charcoal

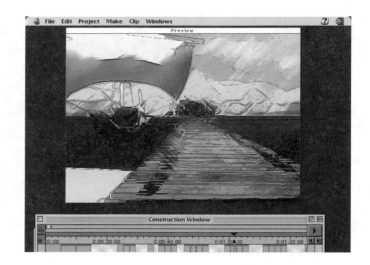

Figure 13.16b Style Filters—Crayon

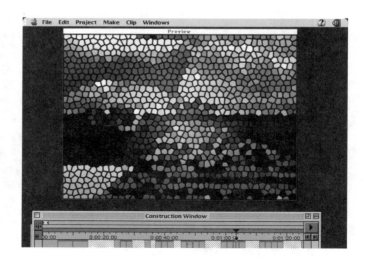

Figure 13.16c Style Filters—Mosaic

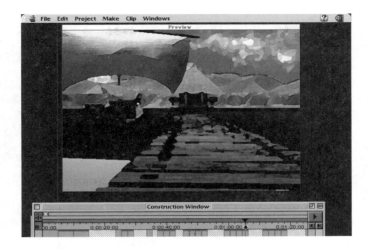

Figure 13.16d Style Filters—Watercolor

Distortion filters geometrically distort an image. They are often used as part of transitions between clips. Distortion filters include:

- The Pinch filter contracts or squeezes an image from the edges toward the center of the frame.
- The Ripple filter creates a rhythmic wave pattern, like ripples on the surface of water. Both vertical and horizontal settings, with many variations.
- The Roll filter rolls the image, in any direction, into a cylinder.
- The Twirl filter rotates an image around the center, creating a cyclone effect.

Figure 13.17a Distortion Filters—Pinch

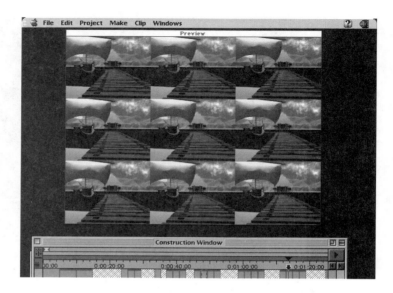

Figure 13.17b Distortion Filters-Multiple

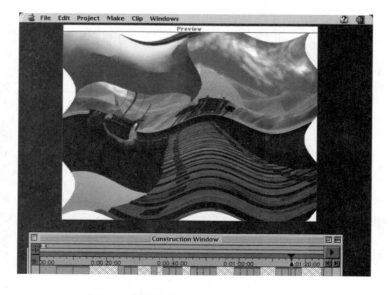

Figure 13.17c Distortion Filters—Ripple

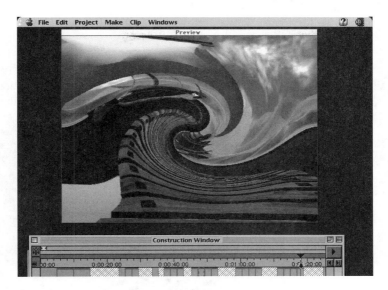

Figure 13.17d Distortion Filters—Twirl

Transitions

A transition is any part of a movie used to make a change between clips. By far the most common transition is the cut. When one clip ends, the next one immediately begins. This is what happens in the Construction window, with one clip butted up against the other. The clips play, in succession, from left to right. The next most popular transition is the dissolve. It provides a smooth blending between clips. As one image fades out, the next one fades in. Cuts and dissolves represent probably 99.5% of all transitions. The other half percent are more elaborate special effects. The reason for this is simple.

Good communication is dependent upon an audience that is interested and involved with the subject material. The key is content, story line, and plot. Everything else that goes into a movie (camera, lighting, sound, editing, effects) support the basic plot and keep attention focused on it. Think of it like a frame around a painting. The frame is necessary. It sets the picture apart, often complements and highlights colors and mood, and helps hold the picture up on the wall. The frame can enhance the painting, in color, texture and style. But the frame is not more important than the painting and should not draw attention to itself. Taken to an extreme, a frame strung with flashing neon lights, glitter, and bursting fireworks would destroy the message of the artwork. (Unless that's the message itself.) It is the same with video and film. Well made cuts and dissolves create the least amount of visual distraction. When an effect is used, it should fit seamlessly within the context of the story, helping it along. Gratuitous effects, or too many effects can create viewer strain and boredom. In fact, an otherwise decent production can look "cheesy" and unprofessional if effects are used injudiciously or are poorly integrated. Although there are dozens of unique transitions to choose from, restrain yourself. Keep your special effects "special."

Applying Transitions

To create a transition between clips in Premiere:

1.   Overlap two clips in the Construction window. Place one clip on Track A, the other on Track B; the longer the overlap, the longer the duration of the transition. It doesn't matter which track is first in the timeline; it's possible to transition from either track to the other.

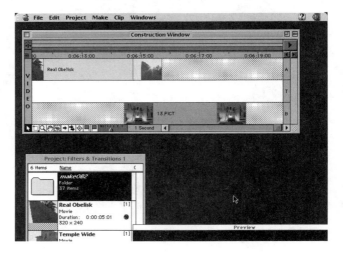

Figure 13.18 Setting up clips for Transitions

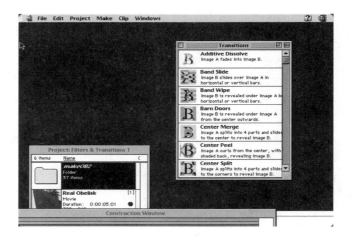

Figure 13.19 Transitions window

2.   From the Windows menu, choose Transitions. The Transitions window will appear. Use the scroll bar to view available transitions.

3.   Select a transition with the mouse and drag it to the T track in the Construction Window,

between the two clips. Premiere will automatically size the transition for the duration of the overlap.

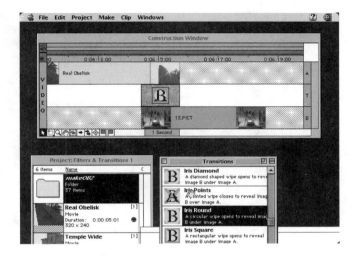

Figure 13.20 Transition in Construction window

You can change the length of the transition using the same tools and techniques as you would with a clip. Be sure to check that the transition completely fills the overlap area. Transitions that are longer or shorter than the overlap area can result in undesired playback.

4. To replace one transition with another, use the Copy and Paste to Fit commands from the Edit menu. To delete a transition, select it in the Construction window and press Delete.

Transition Settings

Transitions have many possible settings. These are helpful for customizing a particular effect. Major settings can be accessed on the transition icon itself in the Construction window. It may be necessary to zoom in on the project range to make the icon big enough for the controls to become visible. More detailed settings are found as follows.

To change transition settings:

1. Select the transition in the Construction window and double-click on it. The Transition Settings dialog box will appear.

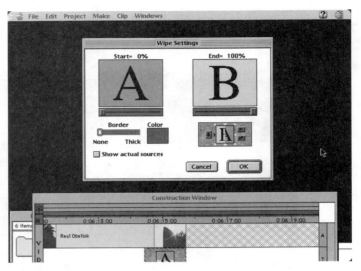

Figure 13.21 Transitions Settings dialog box

A small sample of the transition continually runs in the lower right-hand corner of the dialog box.

2. Click the Track selector arrow, next to the transition sample, to change the direction between clips. For instance, if the arrow is pointing down, the transition will go from Track A to Track B. Premiere automatically assigns a transition direction, based upon how the tracks are aligned in the Construction window.

3. Click an Edge selector to change the orientation of a transition. These are the small triangles bordering the transition sample. The transition will appear from the corner or side selected.

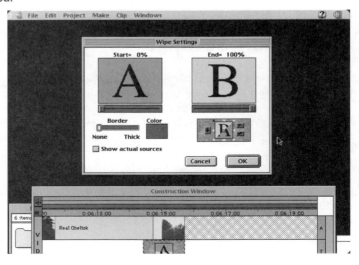

Figure 13.22 Transition Icon Area

4.   Click the Forward/Reverse selector to determine whether the transition itself will run forward or backward. For example, the Clock Wipe transition can play clockwise or counter-clockwise.

5.   Click the Anti-Aliasing selector to adjust the smoothness of a transition's edges. This is located directly below the Forward/Reverse selector. Clicking it toggles between three settings—Off, Low, and High.

Figure 13.23a Anti-Aliasing Transition Output—before

Figure 13.23b Anti-Aliasing Transition Output—after

The Transition Settings dialog box defaults using a graphic "A" and "B" for the respective track start and end points. This provides the fastest performance while working within the dialog box.

6. To see the clips as they will appear during the transition, select Show actual sources.

7. Use the Start and End sliders to change the start and ending positions of the transition itself. These can be used to create interesting "window" effects. Holding down the Shift key while using the a slider locks both start and end sliders together.

8. Drag the Border Slider, if applicable, to set the width of a transition border.

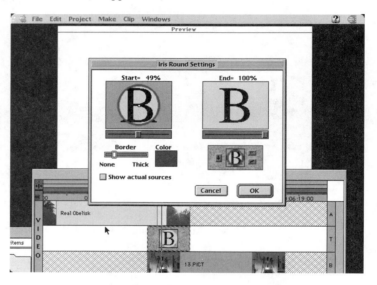

Figure 13.24 Transition Border Settings—color swatch

9. Click on the Color swatch to change the border color.

10. Certain transitions can be started at positions other than the direct middle of a frame. If this is possible, drag the small, white repositioning box to the desired starting point.

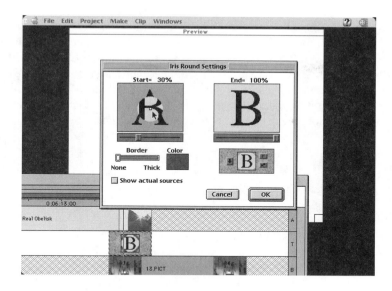

Figure 13.25a Transitions Repositioning box—Center frame selected

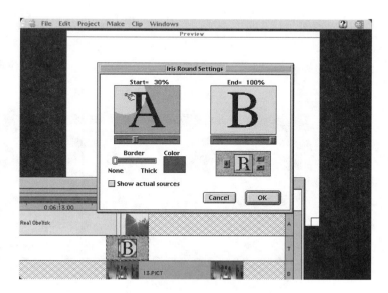

Figure 13.25b Transitions Repositioning box—Upper left corner selected

11. Some transitions have additional custom settings. For example, the number of bands used in the Band Slide transition can be changed. If available, click on Custom Settings to adjust these. When finished, click on OK.

Types of Transitions

Just like filters, there are many more transitions than can be fully described in this book. Besides the ones that are standard within an editing application, additional transitions are available as add-on features. Transjammer 1 & 2 from Elastic Reality is a set of plug-in transitions that works with both Avid Videoshop and Adobe Premiere on the Mac. There's also a version that works with In Sync's Razor and RazorPro for Windows. Most of them are very complex and could provide the right touch in a special situation. In addition, it's also possible to create your own custom transitions.

Transitions can be divided into two groups—2D and 3D.

Following is a small sample of what's available.

2-D Transitions

2D transitions are those that wipe between clips in a flat plane. These include more traditional film and video wipe, iris, and banding effects.

- Band Wipe: Image B is revealed under Image A by horizontal or vertical bars.

- Checkerboard: Two sets of alternating boxes or squares move to reveal Image B.

- Clock Wipe: A wipe from the center of Image A in a circular motion revealing Image B.

- Dissolve: Image A fades out, while Image B fades in.

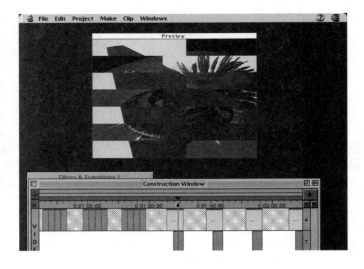

Figure 13.26a 2D Transitions—Band Wipe

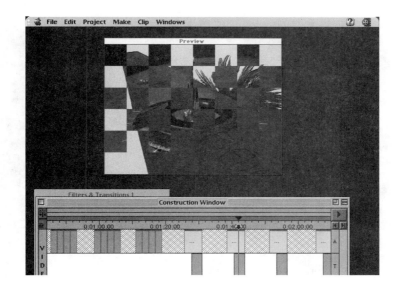

Figure 13.26b 2D Transitions—Checkerboard

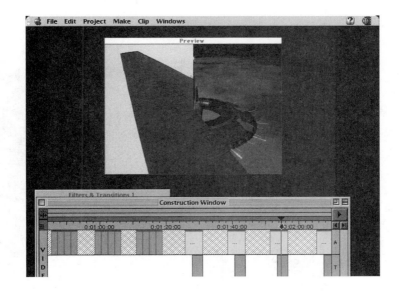

Figure 13.26c 2D Transitions—Clock Wipe

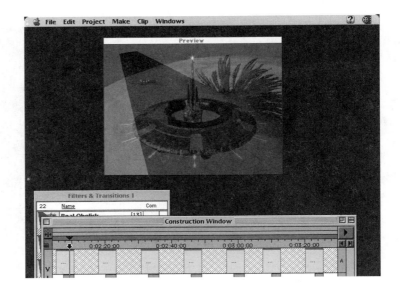

- Iris Cross, Diamond, Round, Square, & Star: Geometrically shaped wipe reveals Image B under Image A.

- Wipe: A moving wipe reveals Image B.

- Rocket: A rocket lauches from the bottom of Image A, revealing Image B in its jet trail.

- Cows: Falling cows, containing Image B, fall from the sky obscuring Image A.

Figure 13.27a 2D Transitions—Diamond Wipe

Figure 13.27b 2D Transitions—Wipe

Figure 13.27c 2D Transitions—Cows

3D Transitions

3-D transitions create the illusion of depth and perspective.

- Doors: Image B swings over Image A on vertical or horizontal doors.

- Funnel: Image A is pulled through a funnel, revealing Image B.

- Page Peel: Image A peels away with a shaded back to reveal Image B.

- Push: Image B pushes Image A off to one side

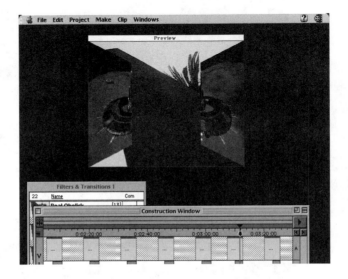

Figure 13.28a 3D Transitions—Doors

Figure 13.28b 3D Transitions—Funnel

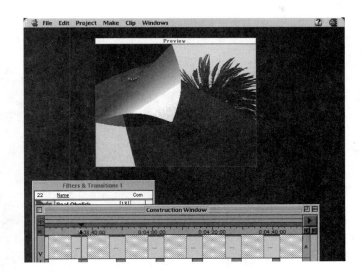

Figure 13.28c 3D Transitions—Page Peel

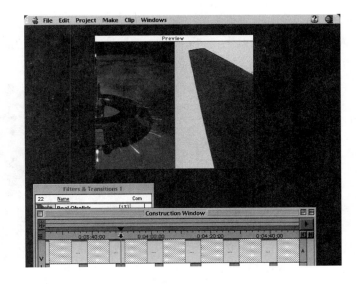

Figure 13.28d 3D Transitions—Push

Here are some samples of 3-D transitions available through Avid Transjammer 1 & 2:

- Big Fish: Image A warps into a small fish, which is then eaten by a big fish containing Image B. The big fish then expands to fill the screen.

- Billiard Balls: Image A warps into a rack of billiard balls that are then shot off the screen, revealing Image B.

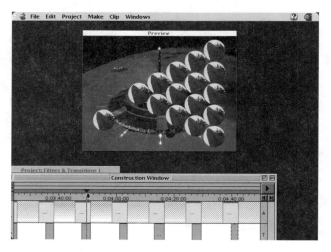

Figure 13.29a 3D Transitions—Billiard Balls

- Column Tumble: Image A breaks into columns that tumble toward the viewer, revealing Image B underneath.

- Gears: Image A pulls back and warps into a gear shape. It is joined by a gear shaped Image B. Image B then expands to fill the screen.

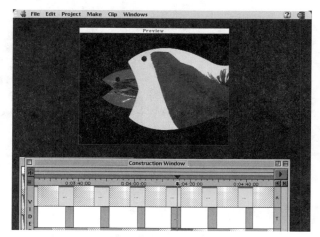

Figure 13.29b 3D Transitions—Big Fish

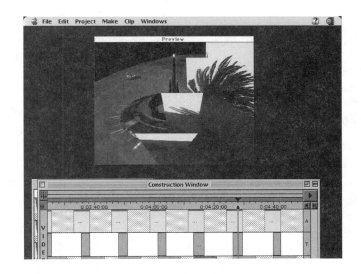

Figure 13.29c 3D Transitions—Column Tumble

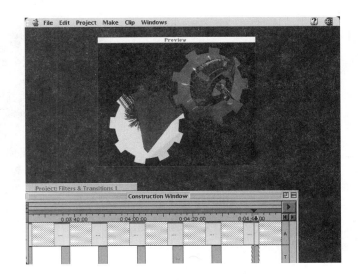

Figure 13.29d 3D Transitions—Gears

Using Titles

Titles are used in everything from the opening credits of a major motion picture to disclaimers for used-car ads. They can contain text, lines, and geometric shapes. Titles may be used full-screen, as self-contained clips, or superimposed over other clips.

Many editing applications have title creation features built into them. More complicated titles and graphics, like logos, can be imported from 2D (e.g. Photoshop) and 3D applications (e.g. Strata 3D). Using Premiere 4.2 for the Mac as our model, let's take a look at the basic process of creating a title.

Title Window

1. From the File menu, choose New/Title. The Title window will appear. Note that two new menus appear in the menu bar, Title and Font. The Title menu has options for text and objects drawn in the Title window. The Font menu is used to select a font for text.

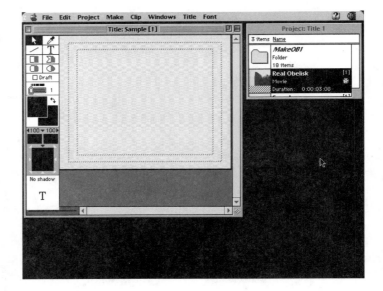

Figure 13.30 Title Window and Menu Bar

2. Use the text and object tools to create the title.

3. From the File menu, choose Save.

4. While holding down the Control key, drag the title from the Title window directly into the Construction window. Or you may import the saved title into a project, just like any other clip.

Tools & Techniques

There are many different tools and techniques used in creating titles. We'll cover each of these briefly.

It's often desirable to use a frame of a clip as reference for positioning a title.

1. Select a clip and set Marker 0 to the frame you want displayed in the Title window. If no Marker 0 is chosen, the in point will be used by default.

2. Drag the clip from the Clip or Project window into the Title window.

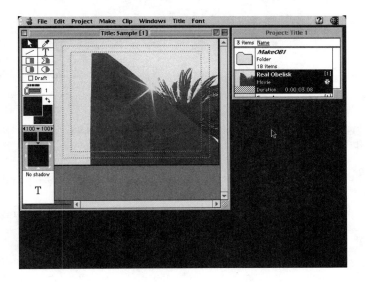

Figure 13.31 Background Clip in Title Window

3. To remove the frame from the Title window, choose Remove Background Clip from the Title menu.

Once you're in the Title window, your first task should be to set the options for the drawing area.

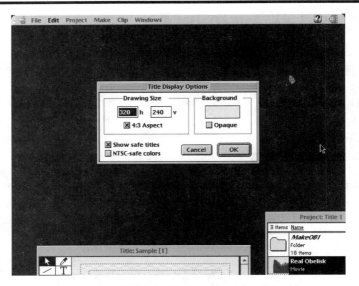

Figure 13.32 Title Window Options dialog box

1. From the Windows menu, choose Title Window Options. The Title Display Options dialog box appears.

2. Select a Drawing Size. Generally, this should be set to the same as the output frame size.

3. Select a background color for the clip by clicking on the color swatch. Choosing a contrasting color is useful for previewing text and object effects.

4. By default, the background is transparent. This is the necessary setting when the title will be keyed over another clip in it's final use. To make the background opaque, click on the Opaque checkbox.

5. Click on the Show Safe Titles checkbox to display Title Safe and Motion Safe areas. Television picture tubes are generally overscanned and don't show every part of a screen. In addition, every TV set is adjusted slightly differently. If your final output is videotape, make sure this box is selected. Keeping text and objects within the Title Safe area insures that all elements will be visible on all television sets.

6. Click on NTSC Safe Colors checkbox to restrict colors used in the Title window to NTSC-safe standards. Computer generated colors often have more saturation and signal amplitude than home video equipment can reproduce. This results in color "bleeding" and distortion. When finished, click OK.

Creating Text

The Title window comes with a compliment of standard drawing tools for creating framed and filled objects. See the Adobe User Guide for more details.

To create text:

1. Select the type tool (T) from the Title window toolbox.

2. Click to position the text in the Title window. Type the desired text. When finished, click anywhere outside the text entry box.

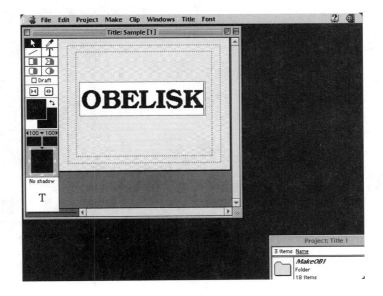

Figure 13.33 Typing Text

3. To adjust text attributes, begin by selecting the text.

   Use the Font menu to change the font.

4. Use the Title menu commands to change type style, justification, and shadow.

5. To change type size, choose Size from the Title menu and select a point size.

4. To center type or objects, choose Center Vertically and/or Center Horizontally from the Title menu. To center an object in the lower third of the screen, choose Position in Lower Third from the Title menu.

Now that the basic text and objects have been created, additional highlights may be added, like shadows and gradated color.

To create a shadow for text or an object:

1.   Select the text or object.

2.   Drag the Shadow Offset control to position the shadow. The offset coordinates, shown in pixels, will be displayed above the control. For no shadow, drag the control to the center or outside of the control box.

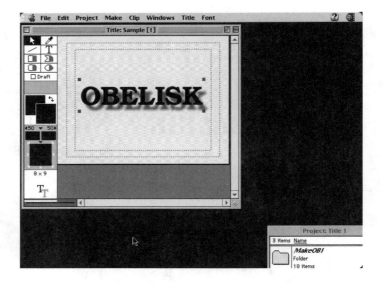

Figure 13.34 Shadow Offset control

3.   Click the shadow color swatch in the toolbox to select a shadow color.

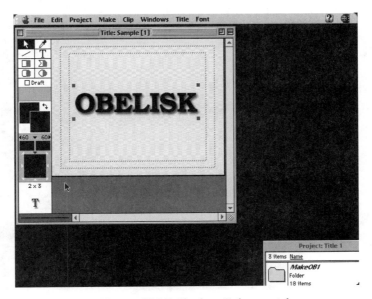

Figure 13.35 Shadow Color swatch

4.   Use the pop-up opacity sliders to adjust the transparency of the shadow.

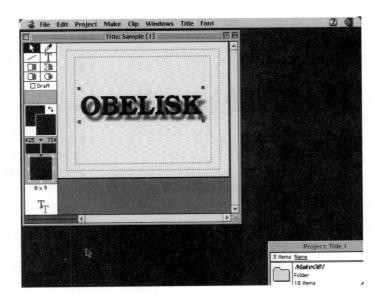

Figure 13.36 Opacity Sliders

5.   Choose Shadow from the Title menu to select one of three shadow styles - Single, Solid, or Soft.

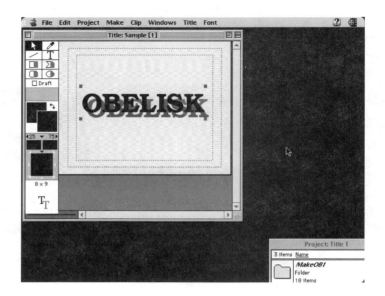

Picture: 13.37a Shadow Style—Single

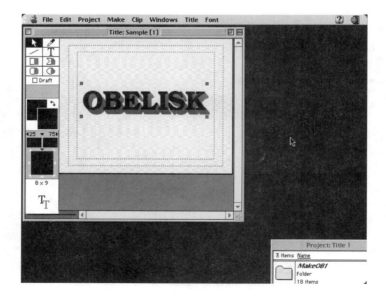

Picture: 13.37b Shadow Style—Solid

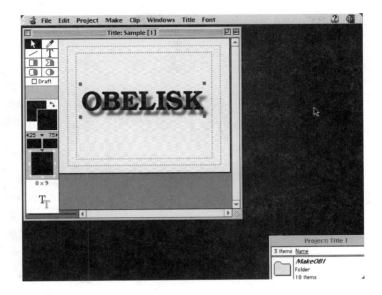

Picture: 13.37c Shadow Style—Soft

To create a gradient fill across text, object or shadow:

1. Select the object.

2. Click the object color swatch or shadow color swatch, as appropriate.

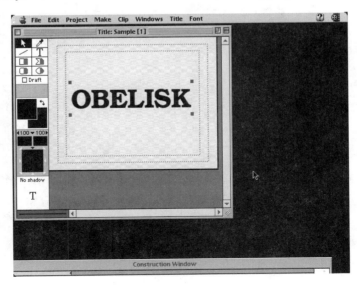

Figure 13.38 Color & Shadow Color swatch

3. Select a starting color by clicking the left color swatch in the gradient controls. Select an ending color by clicking the right color swatch. A preview of the gradient will appear in the box below the color swatches.

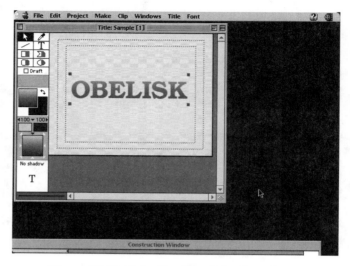

Figure 13.39 Color Gradient Color Swatches

4. Change the opacity of the starting or ending point by clicking the small black arrow above the respective color swatch and dragging the opacity slider to the desired setting.

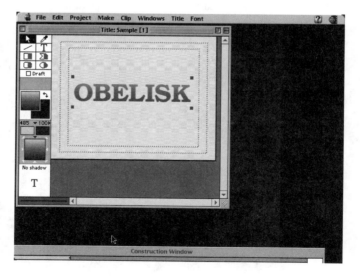

Figure 13.40 Opacity Sliders

5. Set a common opacity for the starting and ending points by clicking the small black triangle between the swatches and adjusting the slider control.

6. Change the direction of the gradient by clicking one of the small arrows around the preview box. The gradient will start from the location of the selected arrow.

Conclusion

You could spend a lifetime learning to use all of the latest effects and there would be still more to learn. Remember the content, the story or message of the video is the point, not the technical pyrotechnics. Don't obscure the main point with pointless effects. Usually less is more!

Chapter 14
Advanced Video Effects

Introduction

In Chapter 13 we considered basic video effects, or those most commonly found in all editing applications. It is important to have a thorough understanding of those basic skills and techniques before going further. In this chapter, we'll be covering more complex effects, like motion control, compositing, and morphing. Many of these effects, or advanced control of them, can only be done in third-party applications. That is, the video is treated, a new clip is created, and then imported into an editing application for final placement in the movie. As much as possible, we'll continue demonstrating each concept through Premiere. Unique features from other selected applications will be discussed at the end of each section.

Motion

Premiere comes with a versatile collection of motion control settings. These can be used to start, stop, rotate, zoom, and move a clip through a predetermined motion path. Note that the entire clip moves. To create the illusion of flying objects, movement needs to be combined with key effects. This will be discussed later in the chapter.

Applying Motion

To apply motion to a clip:

1.   Select the clip in the Construction Window

2.   From the Clip menu, choose Motion. The Motion Settings dialog box will appear.

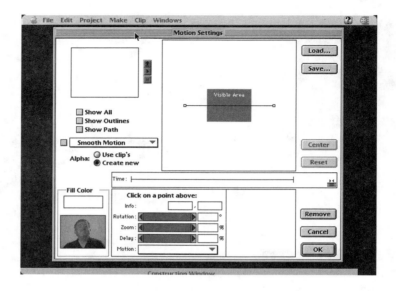

Figure 14.1 Motion Settings dialog box

The upper left-hand corner contains a sample and controls for previewing the motion settings. There is a large graphic motion path work area for setting points of movement. At the bottom, motion options are set for each point.

3.   Set the points of movement. These points of movement are commonly referred to as "keyframes." (Note that the usage is different from "keyframes" as used in video compression terminology.)

4.   Set any motion options. Click on OK when finished.

Movement is now applied to the clip and can be changed or deleted at any time. To change motion settings, repeat the Motion Settings process as necessary. To delete motion settings for a clip, click on Remove from the Motion Settings dialog box.

Keyframes

The basic functions of defining a motion path include creating, selecting, and adjusting keyframes. A keyframe can be the frame at the start or end of the path, or any point in between where motion properties need to change. It's helpful to create a motion path with as few keyframes as necessary to accomplish the effect. Adjustments can be made much more quickly and the effects of such adjustments are more obvious for viewing. Even if an effect is to have many keyframes, it's good to start with the major movement points, establish the basic feel, and then fill in with more keyframes as needed.

Premiere defaults with a start point that is off-screen to the left and an end point that is off-screen to the right.

To create new keyframes:

1. Position the pointer on the motion path in the work area. The pointer will turn into a pointing finger. Click to add a keyframe to the path.

2. Position the pointer above the timeline. The pointer will turn into a downward pointing triangle. Click to add a keyframe at the desired point.

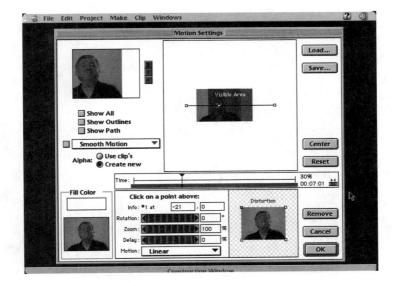

Figure 14.2 Keyframes

Whenever a new keyframe is added to a motion path, it will be represented by a small white box in the work area and a vertical mark in the timeline. Changing either one will dynamically change the other.

To select a keyframe:

1. Click a keyframe in the motion path work area or from the timeline.

2. Press Tab to advance from keyframe to keyframe in motion path. Holding down the Shift

key while pressing Tab will reverse the direction of advance.

To adjust the position of a keyframe along a motion path, select the keyframe and then use one of the following techniques:

1. Drag the small white box in the motion path work area to a new position. Release the mouse button to set in place.

    or

2. Press an arrow key to move the keyframe one pixel in the direction of the arrow. Holding down the Shift key while pressing an arrow key moves the keyframe in 5-pixel increments. This is useful for fine adjustments.

    or

3. Enter coordinates for the keyframe's new position in the Info field below the timeline.

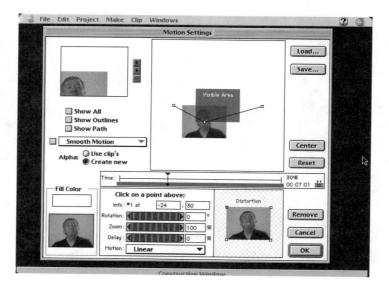

Figure 14.3a Adjusting Keyframe Position

To center a keyframe in the visible screen area, select the keyframe and choose one of the following:

1. Enter the coordinates (0,0) in the Info field below the timeline.

    or

2. Click the Center button at the right-hand side of the Motion Settings dialog box.

    To delete a keyframe, select the keyframe and press Delete.

Preview

A preview of movement is shown in a sample window in the upper left-hand corner of the Motion Settings dialog box. This shows what's happening to the chosen clip. To see how this movement interacts with other video clips playing concurrently in the Construction Window, click on the Show All checkbox. Because of the extra processing involved, performance can be impeded with Show All selected. Generally, it is best to use this option only as needed.

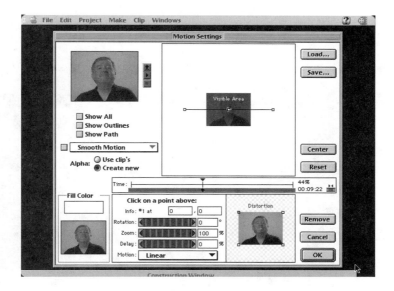

Figure 14.4 Motion Settings Preview controls

Selecting Show Outlines displays the edge of the frame in the work area. This is useful for positioning the clip, as when it might need to be off-screen.

Selecting Show Path changes the connections between keyframes in the work area from solid lines to a representation of the number of frames between keyframes. This is a graphic way to examine speed changes through the effect.

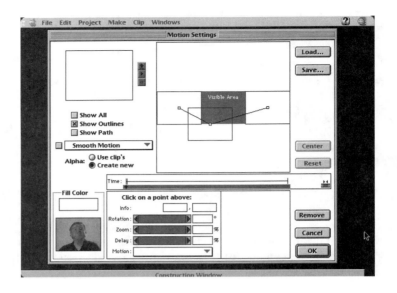

Figure 14.5a Show Outlines & Show Path

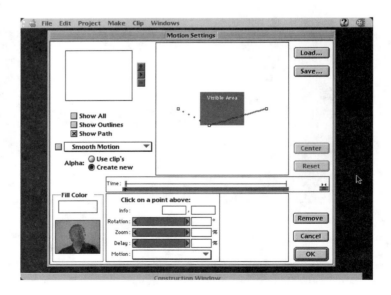

Figure 14.5b Show Outlines & Show Path

The preview may be paused and started by using the appropriate buttons next to the preview window. Alternately, pressing the Space Bar on the keyboard will perform the same function.

To scroll through a preview by hand, drag the mouse, while holding down the mouse button, through the gray bar below the timeline.

To preview selected frames of a motion path, click Pause next to the preview window. Then click on the gray bar below the timeline.

The timeline is a representation of the duration of the clip. Keyframes appear as vertical marks along the timeline. At the right of the timeline the location of the keyframe is indicated, as the percentage of the entire clip its location represents (in the example in Figure 14.6, thirty percent into the timeline), and the actual time that a keyframe occurs within a clip. To adjust the speed between keyframes, drag the keyframe markers closer together or further apart.

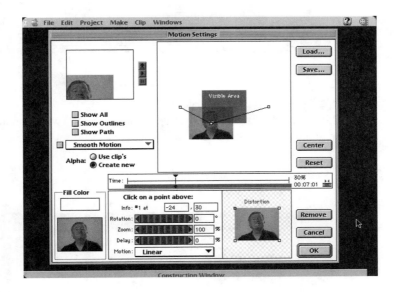

Figure 14.6 Timeline

There are a variety of motion options that may be applied to keyframes. Individual settings are found at the bottom part of the Motion Settings dialog box. Select a keyframe to apply one of the following:

- Rotation: This determines the angle of a clip at a particular keyframe. The clip will rotate from the previous keyframe to the selected point. It can also be used to make spinning movements or full revolutions. Use the treadmill slider control or type in an angle for the rotation.

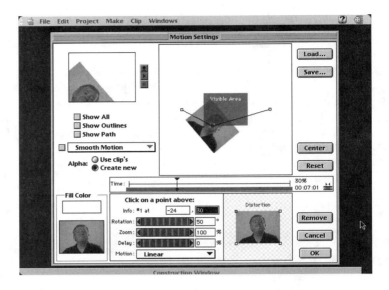

Figure 14.7 Rotation

- Zoom: This adjusts the size of the clip at a keyframe. The clip will zoom from the previous keyframe to the selected point. Use the Zoom controls to set a size percentage.

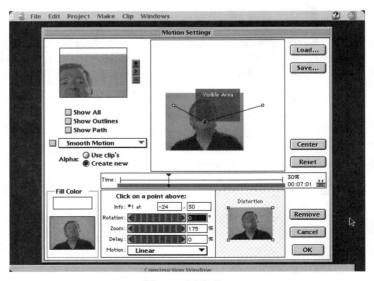

Figure 14.8 Zoom

- Delay: This creates a pause along the motion path at the selected keyframe. Use the Delay controls to set a delay percentage, based upon the total length of the clip. A blue bar will also appear on the timeline.

- Motion: This gives the option of slowing down or speeding up movement between the previous and selected keyframes. It works especially well in conjunction with Zoom to create the illusion of depth. If a clip is zooming from small to large, select Accelerate. If zooming from large to small, select Decelerate.

- Distortion: This allows the four corners of a clip to be individually adjusted at a keyframe. This can be used to simulate 3D perspective effects. Drag the corners of the clip from within the distortion box.

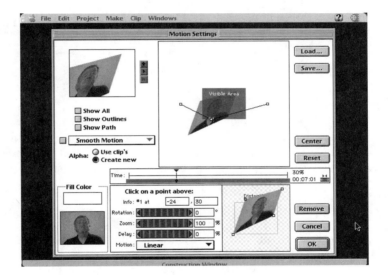

Figure 14.9 Distortion

To remove all individual keyframe settings, click the Reset button from the right side of the Motion Settings dialog box.

There are Motion settings that can be applied to all keyframes within a clip:

- Fill Color: This is used to select a background color for the clip. This is a vital part of setting up certain key effects. The color may be chosen directly from a sample of the clip. When placed over the clip, the pointer will change into an eyedropper. Click on the desired color. Alternately, a color may be chosen from the color swatch above the clip sample.

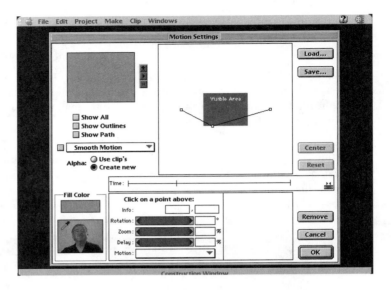

Figure 14.10 Fill Color

- Smooth Motion: Select the checkbox next to Smooth Motion to access a pop-up menu of motion attributes. By default, motion between keyframes is in a linear path. That is, the clip travels from keyframe to keyframe in straight lines. Selecting one of the motion attributes can smooth out sharp corners, giving a more natural feel.

- Alpha: This determines whether to use the clip's alpha channel for keying or to create a new one. This option will only affect clips that are using an alpha key type in the Transparency Settings dialog box. (See "Keys," later in this chapter, for more information) Select Use Clip's for titles and graphics that have been created with their own alpha channel in third-party applications, like Photoshop. Select Create New to create an alpha channel in the shape of the clip as it moves.

After Effects Motion Controls

Adobe After Effects provides additional control and features for motion effects. Many of these are tools for precision timing and motion path adjustments. Some of these include:

- Wireframe Preview: This provides real-time motion preview, using the actual clip sources, is very difficult to achieve. The calculations necessary to process each frame are just too overwhelming for most computers. However, by using a clip's alpha channel, a wireframe of the motion can be created in real-time. An optional selection is to leave an outline trail of each frame. This is useful for seeing the entire path of an object.

Figure 14.11 Wireframe Preview

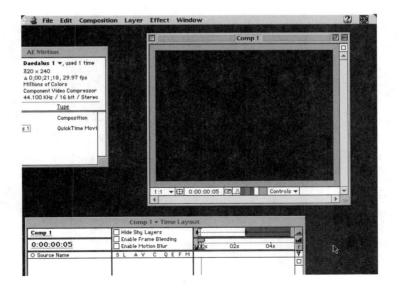

Figure 14.12 Wireframe Preview

- Bezier Interpolation: Motion paths in Premiere are fairly straightforward. Some rounding of the path from keyframe to keyframe is possible, but for the most part, the clip moves in a linear fashion. Motion occurs instantly and evenly. Bezier curves offer more control over the motion path. They're also harder to work with and require some experience to use effectively. The shape and speed of a path between keyframes can be customized for more natural or unique movement.

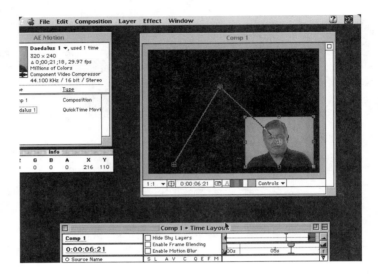

Figure 14.13a Bezier Motion Path

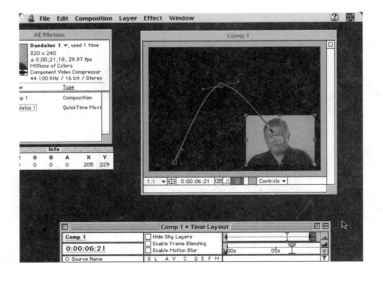

Figure 14.13b Bezier Motion Path

Figure 14.13c Bezier Motion Path

- Auto-Orient Rotation: Assume that you have a clip of a jet plane, and, as it moves, the nose follows the direction of the motion path. When the jet goes up, the nose goes up. In Premiere, the clip rotation would need to be set manually for each keyframe. After Effects has an auto-orient rotation feature that does this automatically for the duration of a motion effect.

Figure 14.14a Auto-Orient Rotation

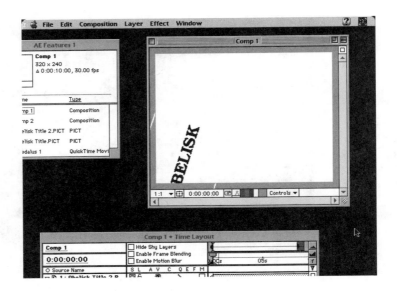

Figure 14.14b Auto-Orient Rotation

•   Motion Blur: This mimics the blur seen in video and film, yet is applied to 2-D animation. Computer-generated animation may produce a strobe effect. This makes the effect appear smoother and more realistic.

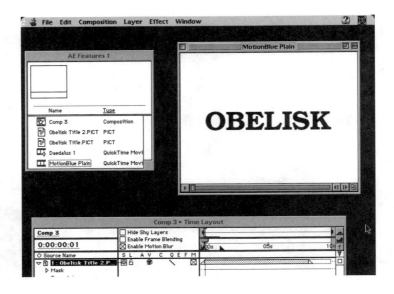

Figure 14.15a Motion Blur

Figure 14.15b Motion Blur

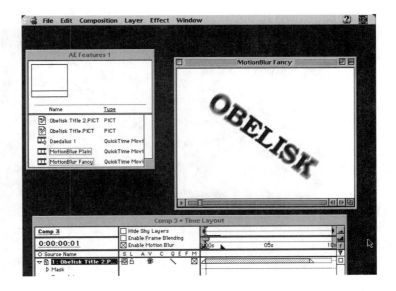

Figure 14.15c Motion Blur

Compositing

Compositing is the process of selectively playing parts of one clip over another. Compositing is also referred to as keying or matting. Areas of a superimposed clip are made transparent to reveal a background clip underneath. This layering technique is used to add titles, create video-within-video boxes, and combine live-action talent into a synthesized or virtual set.

Figure 14.16a Compositing example

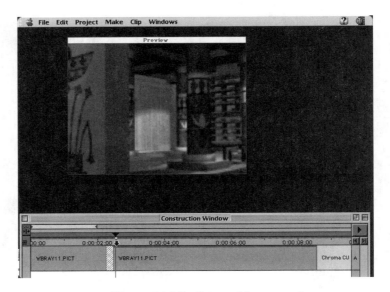

Figure 14.16b Compositing example

Figure 14.16c Compositing example

If any effect symbolizes the power of desktop video, it's compositing. Traditional video and film compositing required several passes to build up the complex effects. Each layer would be added, one at a time, and then used as the background clip for additional layers. This was time consuming, it was not always possible to see what the finished composition would be like, and there was generational loss during the transfers. On top of all that, if a change had to be made to specific layer, the entire process had to be repeated starting at that point. Not so with desktop video. Premiere can handle up to 99 layers of superimposed images simultaneously. Previews accurately display the finished effect. Changes in clips or order of clips can be made easily.

The base background for any key is the mixed effect of any clips on tracks A and B from the Construction window. Superimposed clips go on the numbered S tracks. Layering will be done in the order they appear in the tracks. That is, higher numbered S clips will be played over lower numbered S clips.

Creating a Key

To superimpose a clip:

1.   Drag a clip from the Project window to an S track in the Construction window.

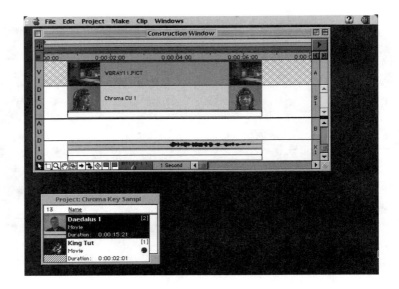

Figure 14.17 S track in Construction window

2.   Select the clip on the S track.

3.   From the Clip menu, choose Transparency. The Transparency Settings dialog box will appear.

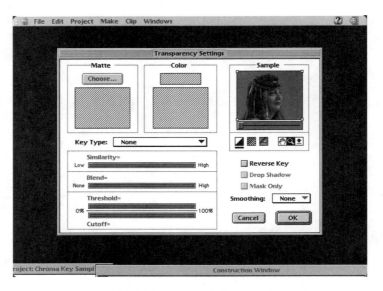

Figure 14.18 Transparency Settings dialog box

In the upper right-hand corner is a Sample box and controls for previewing the composite. The left-hand side contains controls for selecting and adjusting the key. In the lower right-hand corner are controls for how the key is to be applied.

4.   Make a selection from the Key Type pop-up menu.

5.   Make key adjustments as necessary. When finished, click on OK.

Key Types

There are many different key types from which to choose. Some images will work with only one key type while other images may work with several. Selecting the right one can make a big difference in your ability to control and set the key properly. Here is a sample of the major key types:

•   Luminance: This key uses a clip's gray scale values to determine the key. Darker parts of an image will key out first. It can often provide softer edges for objects shot against a black background.

Figure 14.19a Luminance Key

Figure 14.19b Luminance Key

- Chroma: In a chroma key, a color or range of colors from a clip are selected to be transparent. There are special Blue Screen and Green Screen key types available as well. These are the most commonly used colors in video and film production for chroma key compositing.

Figure 14.20a Chroma Key

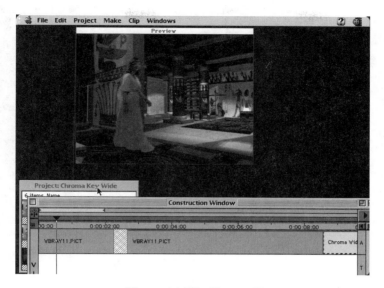

Figure 14.20b Chroma Key

- Alpha Channel: An alpha channel is an invisible gray scale channel assigned to an image. It is often used for creating masks or otherwise isolating a part of an image. The black areas become transparent, while the white parts remain opaque with the key image. Alpha channels are created in software applications like Adobe Photoshop. Premiere creates alpha channels for titles and clips with motion effect. Alpha channels produce super-fine keys and should be tried first, if possible.

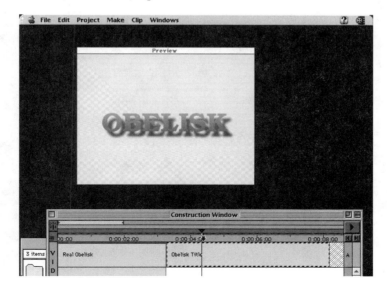

Figure 14.21a Alpha Key

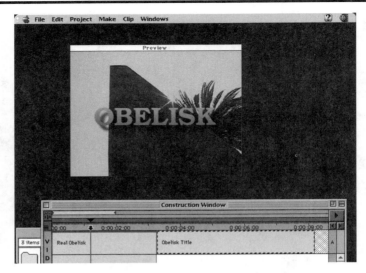

Figure 14.21b Alpha Key

- Track Matte: This key uses the clip on the next S track of the Construction window as a matte. Track mattes often use moving images as a key source and are called traveling mattes. Blue-screen Ultimatte productions would use a track matte, one for the actual blue-screen image, the other for the matte image. The clips are locked in frame-accurate synchronization and played together. This can result in a better looking composite than a straight chroma key because there is no color distortion of pixels between subject matter and background. The blue wall is incidental—the key is being created by the matching black and white mattes.

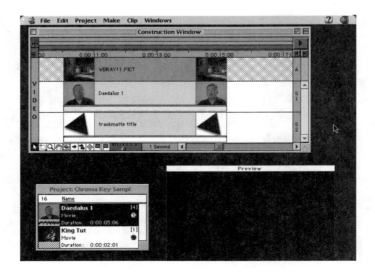

Figure 14.22 Track Matte Key

Adjusting Key Settings

Once a key type has been selected, other adjustments can be made. Certain controls and options will be grayed out if not available for that key type. Certain keys allow a still image to be used as a matte source. To select an image, click on the Choose button in the Matte sample box. Use the standard Open dialog box to open the desired file.

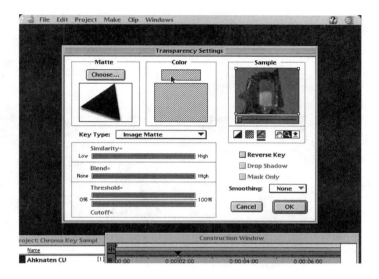

Figure 14.23 Matte Sample box

For chroma-based keys, the first thing that needs to be selected is the base color to be keyed. Position the cursor over the desired color of the clip shown in the Color sample box. The cursor will change into an eyedropper. Click on the color. Alternately, the color swatch above the clip may be used for selecting a specific color.

Figure 14.24 Color Sample box

The Similarity slider is used with chroma-based keys to select a range of colors to be transparent. The higher the Similarity setting, the broader the range of colors.

The Blend slider controls the degree of opacity between keyable and non-keyable colors. This can be used to smooth out rough edges or trouble spots.

The Threshold slider adjusts the amount of shadow present in an effect.

The Cutoff slider adjusts the shadow detail. It is used only with luminance and chroma-based keys.

Figure 14.25 Key Slider Controls

In the lower right-hand corner of the Transparency Settings dialog box are options for how the key will be applied to the clip.

The Reverse Key option reverses the transparent and opaque areas of a key.

The Drop Shadow option applies a 50% gray shadow to the lower right of the transparent portion of a clip.

The Mask Only option creates a black-and-white gray scale mask from the transparent portion of a clip.

The Smoothing pop-up menu is used to select a degree of edge softness between the key and background image in a composited clip.

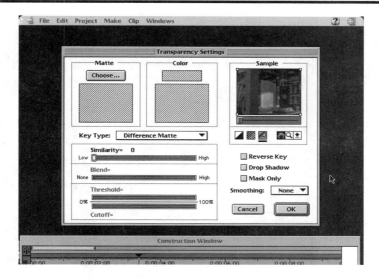

Figure 14.26 Key Output Options

Sample Box

To preview settings and options, use the Sample box in the upper right-hand corner of the Transparency Settings dialog box. There are three options for how a background will appear in the Sample box. The background can be toggled between black and white by clicking the black-and-white icon below the Sample box. A checkerboard background is created by clicking the checkerboard icon. To see the actual background image from the Construction window, click on the page peel icon.

Figure 14.27a Sample box

Figure 14.27b Sample box

Figure 14.27c Sample box

To zoom in on a sample image, select the Zoom tool and click the image. To zoom out, hold down the Option key while clicking the image.

A close-up view of an image may be repositioned using the Hand tool. Click on the Hand tool. Click on the clip, and while holding down the mouse button, drag the clip to the desired position.

If the clip is a movie, a slider bar under the Sample box can be used to scroll through the preview.

Garbage mattes are useful for blocking out portions of a clip that should not be keyed. They get their name from their common use

Intensity Adjustment

Once the Transparency Settings have been selected, the intensity of the key may be adjusted. Use the Fade control panel at the bottom of the S track in the Construction Window. These rubber band controls work just like those for setting audio fades. To adjust fading of a key:

1. Position the pointer over the top line in the Fade control panel of a clip. The pointer will change to a finger pointer.

2. Click to create a handle. It will appear as a black dot. Drag the handle to adjust the transparency. The higher the handle, the more opaque the image will be. If the handle is at the bottom of the control panel, the key will be invisible.

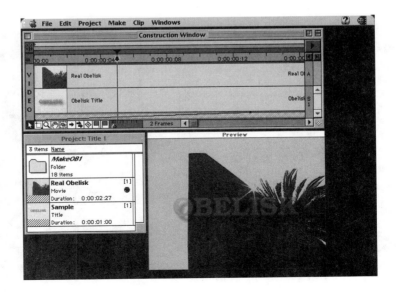

Figure 14.28 Intensity Adjustment

The handle may also be dragged horizontally to change the duration and speed of a fade. To delete a handle, drag it out of the Fade control panel.

3.   To create two handles close to each other, use the Fade Scissors tool. This is found in the extended tools pop-up menu in the lower left-hand corner of the Construction window. Click on the Fade control at the desired point. This is useful when quick transitions need to be made.

4.   Change the fade level between two handles by using the Fade Adjustment tool. This is also found in the extended tools pop-up menu. Drag the line segment up or down as desired.

After Effects Composite Controls

Adobe After Effects has many more fine-tune controls and options for the creation of composited effects. This is especially important when working with high-resolution images, like full-screen video. Examples of its output can be found in movies, television shows, and music videos. Following is a sample of additional features found in Adobe After Effects.

•   Custom Masks: These can be created directly within After Effects. Custom masks can be drawn freeform and adjusted for precision. Masks are often the only way to separate an object from a background. They also create very sharp, clean edges during compositing.

Figure 14.29a Custom Mask

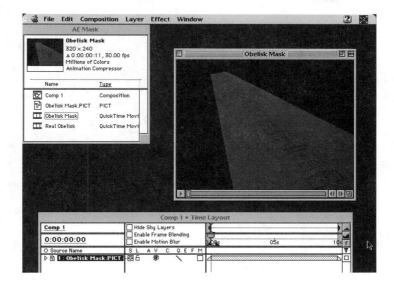

Figure 14.29b Custom Mask

- Edge Control: In Premiere a composited image may have its keyed edges smoothed one of three ways—Off, Low, or High. In After Effects, luminance and chroma-based keys have highly controllable slider bars for both edge border size and edge feather size.

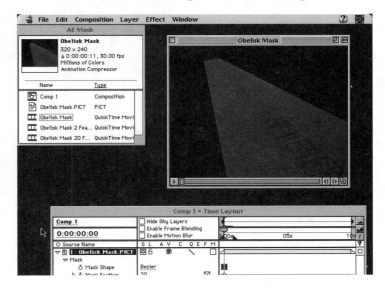

Figure 14.30a Edge Control

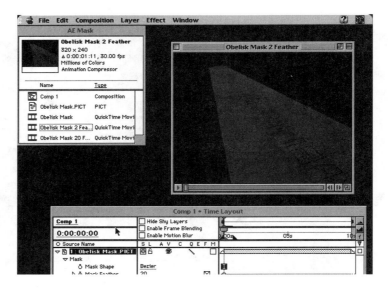

Figure 14.30b Edge Control

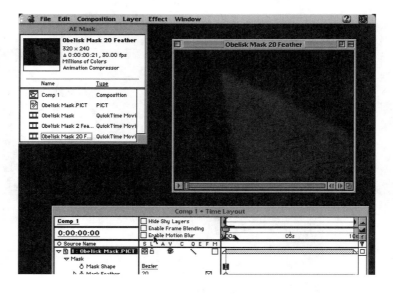

Figure 14.30c Edge Control

Production Bundle

After Effects 3.0 is available with a Production Bundle, especially tailored for film and video professionals. In addition to all the features and effects found in the standard package, the Production Bundle contains advanced motion controls and keying tools.

- Motion Pack: The advanced motion controls included in the Production Bundle are also called keyframe assistants because they operate by generating, removing, and manipulating keyframes. You can track motion, stabilize a wobbly image, or capture a motion path that you draw. Simpler utilities allow you to smooth out a curve, automatically ease in and out of movement, and reverse the flow of time.

- Keying Pack: This is an additional set of key types and matte tools that increase control over the always critical edges between key source and background. The Color Key and Luma Key effects included in the standard program generate a binary key in which the areas of the key image are either fully transparent or fully solid. The key is either on or off, there is no in-between. The resulting abrupt edges can be softened by feathering, but if you are working with subject matter that does not have sharp, clearly defined edges, the overall result can be less than ideal. This is very often the case with live-action video. The keying effects included in the Production Bundle generate a full range of alpha values, which make areas of the matte partially transparent. After Effects uses these semi-transparent pixels to achieve precise and clean edges around solid objects in the matte, yielding a more natural composite.

- Linear Key: Linear keys work by comparing each pixel in an image to a specified standard. This is usually the color of your keyable background. If the match is close enough, the pixel is made transparent. Very poor matches remain opaque. Unlike a binary key, however, intermediate values become partially transparent in proportion to how closely they match the key color. This gradual linear progression from opaque through semi-transparent to fully transparent give this category of keying effects its name. Linear keys are versatile and the Production Bundle includes a variety from which to choose. The choice of which one to use will mostly depend upon the quality of the source material.

- Color Difference Key: For images that contain transparent regions, such as smoke, windows, or water, a Color Difference Key is included. It generates a matte that is fundamentally different from that used by the Linear Keys. It is a variation of the optical method used in the traditional blue screening used in film production. The selected layer is first transformed into two gray scale components—one represents the amount of the key color present in each pixel and the other represents the amount of a color very different from the key color in each pixel. The final composite is created by combining these two partial mattes.

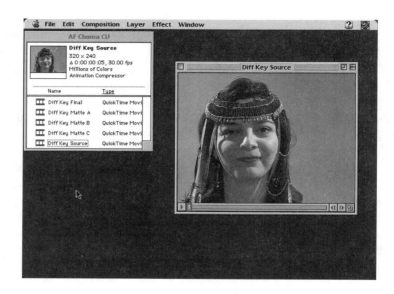

Figure 14.32a Color Difference Key

Figure 14.32b Color Difference Key

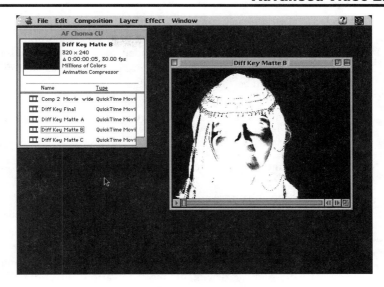

Figure 14.32c Color Difference Key

The Color Difference Key works best with well-lit footage shot in front of a blue or green screen. Although most blue-screen footage could also be keyed with a linear key, the Color Difference Key is designed specifically for such material and will produce a higher quality key. It also retains shadows, enhancing the natural look of a composite.

- The Matte Tools included with the Production Bundle are used to refine the edges between the key source and the background. The matte used to create the key may be shrunk or expanded in small increments to sharpen and soften the key's borders. Additional tools are used to clean up color spill or other trouble spots.

Included with the After Effects Production Bundle are fifty additional distortion filters that may be applied to clips. There's also a set of device control plug-ins for use with the digital disk recorders found in hi-end production editing suites.

Morphing

We've all seen it. We've all heard about it. It's the "effect of the 90s!" Yes, we're referring to morphing. Morphing is the illusion of transforming one image into another. Outlines of the images seamlessly bend, stretch, and mold themselves together over time.

The top morphing application on the market today is Elastic Reality, by Elastic Reality, Inc. (a division of Avid Technology, Inc.). It is available only on the Macintosh. This is the program used by all the top movie and television studios. It is a stand-alone product, the output of which can be played directly or incorporated into another editing environment.

To understand morphing, we must first explain the concept of warping. Warping an image involves creating Bezier curve shapes that describe the starting and ending shape, then linking them together to form a correspondence. These shapes describe areas or objects in an image. The correspondence between shapes describes the amount and direction in which the image will be "pulled" or distorted.

Think of your images as rubber sheets, having elasticity. The shapes allow you to push, pull, and restrict movement of the image.

The process of morphing two images together involves two steps—warping each image and then compositing the two warped images together. Normally, when you composite two images together, you are mixing a percentage of one image with the other image, as in a dissolve. Morphing adds the step of warping each image so that the composite will make it seem that one image is transforming into another.

Elastic Reality can be used to create other effects as well, for example, "break-aways," where parts of an image detach and move in various directions. Or it can be used for "tweening", that is, creating the in-between frames of animated line art, such as cartoons. There are also tools for page peels, twirls, and any other effect where areas of an image are being stretched, shrunk, or broken apart.

Conclusion

You should have one final reminder to not overwhealm the content of your production with effects. Even when the production is an "effects" based story, such as Star Wars, the story is still King. This is one of the restraints that seperates the artisan from the artist.

Chapter 15
CODECS for Computer & CD-ROM

Introduction

When video is processed within the computer it is usually compressed. Most editing systems utilize MJPEG compression. When video is to be incorporated into entertainment or business titles and games it must be compressed into forms that can be accessed by the programs and systems that will play them back. This chapter covers many of the standard compression schemes for this purpose.

Desktop Video Environments

Video for Windows

Video for Windows (VfW) is currently called ActiveMovie and is the standard which Microsoft Corporation has created for video. It carries an AVI extension and runs only on a PC. AVI stands for audio/video interleave. The audio and video are stored in one continuous stream which alternates rapidly between the two types of information and are, in effect, interleaved.

The video plays at its own clock rate and the sound is clocked to its own sample rate. This can lead to a slippage in synchronization between the two, especially in long movies. VfW also requires that a movie with video-only include a silent or *null* audio track in order to play correctly, thus wasting valuable data space which could be used for increased video compression.

Quicktime on the Macintosh

Quicktime (QTM) is the industry standard for CD-ROM video. Designed by Apple Computer, Inc., it became the first widely available desktop video technology to treat video as a standard data type. Prior to Quicktime, video data could not be cut, copied, or pasted in the same manner as text in a word processing program. With a time-based synchronization, it provides tracks and controls for multiple media types, including video, audio, music, and text. The file extension is MooV.

Quicktime for Windows

Quicktime for Windows (QTW) is the PC version of Quicktime and currently the only cross-platform playback environment. In Quicktime a single video file, properly compressed, can be played on either Mac or PC. The file extension is .MOV.

Compression Codecs

A 640 by 480 pixel full screen image totals 307,200 pixels, each requiring 3 bytes of data to contain all color and brightness information. One frame of video therefore requires 921,600 bytes of data storage. At a frame rate of 30 frames per second, one second of video would require more than 27 megabytes, and one minute of video, over 1.6 gigabytes! Even if sufficient storage capacity were available, playing back and manipulating that much data would require enormous computing power.

How then is it possible that even modestly equipped computers are able to capture and display video? How can full-screen, full-resolution video be squeezed into 150 kilobytes per sec for CD-ROM playback and still retain much of the quality of the original? By means of a "compressor-decompressor" or *codec*! Codecs may also be used for material other than video, such as graphics and animations.

The number of available codecs for computer and CD-ROM production continues to increase. The choice of which to use depends upon the type of material being compressed and the capabilities of the computer system for which it is designed. Since each codec takes advantage of different properties of an image in order to achieve compression, the type of material being compressed significantly effects both how much compression can be applied and how well the codec will reproduce the original.

Algorithm Speed

Codecs contain both compression and decompression algorithms. Rapid compression increases the speed with which movies can be created, and fast decompression increases the speed with which the user can display and manipulate the material.

It is desirable that both operations be performed as rapidly as possible, but faster decompression is generally the more important, particularly for CD-ROMs and for network based delivery applications. Compression and decompression times are often not equal for the same data streams. Codecs which provide higher compression ratios tend to require substantially more time to perform compression than to achieve decompression.

Codec algorithm performance depends mainly upon:

- the complexity of the compression algorithm,

- the efficiency of both hardware and software in implementing the algorithm,

- the speed of the utilized processor and ancillary hardware.

Image quality

The ultimate quality of an image depends upon the fidelity with which a codec recreates the original data. Compression algorithms are said to be either *lossy* or *lossless*. Lossless algorithms preserve all of the original data and are therefore usually preferred for still images and for storing archival records. They provide copies which are equivalent to the original, suffering no loss from one generation to the next. Minimal compression produces high quality results, but with files still extremely large, especially for video work.

Lossy codecs generally try to compress data as much as possible without noticeable deterioration of image quality. Because some of the image data is lost and cannot be recovered during decompression, they are best suited for moving images wherein the viewer is less likely to notice the loss.

A common method of conserving on data storage in a lossy codec is to record only the data which changes from one frame to the next. The background of a "talking head," for example, may not change at all, but only the pixels involved with movements of the face are altered in consecutive frames. Typically, the first frame records data for the entire image. In subsequent frames only data for those pixels which are different from the previous frame is saved, dramatically reducing file size. Obviously, static images can be compressed much more than those involving constant movement.

There are a number of codecs in use currently, each with its individual characteristics. Some, such as the Photo codec, even utilize algorithms allowing the user to choose a level of compression and quality. Thus, they may be either lossless or lossy.

Survey of Codecs

None

Ideal Source Material:	Any
Supported Bit Depths:	All
Compression Time:	Approximately 1:1
Supports Data Rate Limiting?	No
Supports Lossless Compression?	Yes

None, a codec which performs no compression at all, is appropriate for original video captures, the pre-conversion of animation, and for archival storage. Initial use of the None codec does not prohibit the application of a different compression codec at a later time. It can also be used to convert an image from one pixel depth to another, reducing image storage requirements in that fashion. Converting 32-bit movie data to 16-bit results in a 2:1 compression ratio, for example. Movies generated in the None codec are available for post-production editing with tools such as *Premiere*.

Note: When converting full-color data to indexed colors (25 colors or less) using the None codec, the Quality setting affects how the codec does the conversion. When the Quality setting is set to Most, a dithered image is produced, while a setting of Least results in a posterized image. (The Animation codec has the same quirk/feature.)

The None codec can also convert a 32-bit image to 24-bit format with no loss in quality by removing the alpha channel byte. 24-bit color depth is known as "Millions," and also as "True Color" in the PC world. "Millions Plus" is another way of referring to the 32-bit color depth, specifying 24-bits of color data with the addition of an 8-bit gray scale alpha channel. The alpha channel can be used for setting the transparency of keys between different applications, a feature which one rarely needs to use.

Never is it desirable to actually deliver a movie in the None codec, nor is it even the best choice for storing a series of still images. Use the Animation codec at the Most quality setting instead.

Animation

Ideal Source Material:	Computer Generated Animation
Supported Bit Depths:	All
Compression Time:	Approximately 3:1
Supports Data Rate Limiting?	No
Supports Lossless Compression?	Yes, at the Most quality setting

The Animation codec uses a compression algorithm well suited for animation and computer-generated video content. It may also be used to compress sequences of screen images, for example those captured by utilities such as *CameraMan* and *Spectator*.

The Animation codec stores images in a run-length encoded format which functions in either a lossy or lossless mode (when set at the Most quality setting). The Animation codec's performance and compression ratios are highly dependent upon the type of images being compressed. Very sensitive to picture changes, it generally works best on synthetically generated images. Images captured from videotape commonly contain visual noise which corrupts the inherent similarity of pixels and reduces the chances that the Animation codec can achieve good results.

The Animation codec, unlike the Graphics codec (to be discussed next), works at all bit depths and provides substantially faster decompression than the Graphics codec, but at the expense of reduced compression ratios. Sometimes it is simply necessary to experiment with both in order to determine which will work best in a CD-ROM application. Even though the Animation codec is faster at decompression, the Graphics codec may be preferable because of the time saved in accessing smaller files.

Graphics

Ideal Source Material:	Computer animation and video
Supported Bit Depths:	8-bit color/gray scale
Compression Time:	Approximately 16:1
Supports Data Rate Limiting?	No
Supports Lossless Compression?	Yes (at Most quality setting)

The Graphics codec is a good alternative to the Animation codec whenever performance is less of a consideration than the compression ratio (whenever it is more important to achieve reduced file size than to minimize compression processing time). The size of a compressed image generated by the Graphics codec will usually be a little less than one half the size of the same image compressed by the Animation codec. The Animation codec, on the other hand, can decompress an image twice as fast as the Graphics codec. Therefore, consider using the Graphics codec mainly with slower storage devices such as CD-ROM discs and across networks. In these cases, the Graphics codec has sufficient time to decompress the image or image sequence.

Movies created in the Graphics codec can vary in size from 80 x 60 pixels up to full screen at a depth of 8 bits (256 colors). It is also useful for video captured at 16 or 24 bits and then dithered down to 8 bits.

Photo-JPEG

Ideal Source Material:	Photographic still images
Supported Bit Depths:	24-bit color, 8-bit gray scale
Compression Time:	Approximately 1:1
Supports Data Rate Limiting?	N/A
Supports Lossless Compression?	Yes

The Photo codec, commonly identified as JPEG, utilizes a compression algorithm developed by an industry body known as the Joint Photographic Experts Group. It is best suited for use with photographs and images in which areas blend smoothly from one into another; sharp edges and fine detail are not its strong point. Thus it is not ideal for computer generated graphics and line drawings.

Photo codec compression ratios can vary widely, depending upon characteristics of the source images. The general range is between 5:1 and 50:1 for 24-bit images, with the best image quality in the range from 10:1 to 20:1. Well suited for most desktop publishing applications, the Photo codec excels at compressing high-resolution, photographic images and works well with 8-bit gray scale images.

Since it provides very high compression while maintaining quite good image quality, the Photo codec is appropriate for archiving video clips. But when archival image quality is of the highest importance, the None codec or the Animation codec at the Most quality level is a superior choice.

Video

Ideal Source Material:	Video
Supported Bit Depths:	16-bit color
Compression Time:	Approximately 7:1
Supports Data Rate Limiting?	No
Supports Lossless Compression?	No

The Video codec is best suited for digitized video content rather than synthetically generated images. It preserves reasonable image quality and delivers fast decompression of video content on both the PC and Mac platforms. Compression time for video is but a fraction of that for Cinepak (described below), which makes it excellent for trying out edits. This codec supports both spatial (size) and temporal (quality) compression. Using only spatial compression, it is possible to obtain compression ratios between 5:1 and 8:1 with reasonably good quality at a 16-bit pixel depth. By combining spatial and temporal compression, the compression ratio range extends from 5:1 to 25:1.

Even though a Video codec is available for both Macintosh and PC (it's called Video 1 on the PC), they are, unfortunately, not compatible. The Video 1 codec is available for QuickTime, which does allow for the direct reading VfW files.

Component Video

Ideal Source Material:	Video
Supported Bit Depths:	24-bit color
Compression Time:	Approximately 1:1
Supports Data Rate Limiting?	No
Supports Lossless Compression?	No

The Component Video codec, which is sometimes known as YUV, was originally produced for QuickTime 1.6 and is available only for Macintosh. It provides a better quality video than the regular Video codec and is well suited for editing and archiving. The compression ratio of only 2:1, while helpful compared to None codec's lack of any compression whatsoever, provides minimal relief from the need for huge quantities of digital storage space.

When the digitizing hardware in use is capable of generating Component Video data directly, recording in the Component Video codec using QuickTime shortens the process since the need to compress the video separately is eliminated and therefore the capture frame rate is accelerated.

Some digitizing hardware, such as the built-in digitizer in the 660AV and 840AV, generate Component Video data directly, so asking QuickTime to record in Component Video bypasses a couple of steps during digitization (since it doesn't have to compress the video). This can improve capture frame rate on some digitizing hardware.

Cinepak

Ideal Source Material:	Video
Supported Bit Depths:	24-bit color and gray scale
Compression Time:	Approximately 190:1
Supports Data Rate Limiting?	Yes
Supports Lossless Compression?	No

Note: It is necessary to keep horizontal and vertical frame size to multiples of 4 in order not to impede playback performance.

Well suited to compressing 16-bit and 24-bit video sequences, Cinepak is undoubtedly the most popular of codecs. It is highly asymmetrical, meaning that it takes significantly longer to compress a frame than to decompress it. Compressing a 24-bit 640 x 480 image, for example, can take more than 150 times longer than decompressing it.

Cinepak's popularity stems from its ability to obtain higher compression ratios, better image quality and faster playback than the Video codec. It is also able to hold data rates within user-definable limits for playback from CD-ROM discs.

To achieve the best results, start with the cleanest uncompressed captured video it is possible to obtain. Results will be quite inferior when the initial video data has already be subject to compression loss, as with movies previously compressed via the Video codec.

Tip: The Cinepak codec works well with all types of video source material, but is superior to any other codec in achieving low data rates and in the representation of motion. Cinepak images, though not perfect, are able to retain detail in cases where other codecs generate unrecognizable blur. On the other hand, other codecs are able to perform just as well, or better, in low-motion shots.

Indeo 3.2

Ideal Source Material:	Video
Supported Bit Depths:	24-bit color
Compression Time:	Approximately 45:1
Supports Data Rate Limiting?	Yes
Supports Lossless Compression?	No

Like Cinepak, it is necessary to keep movie size to multiples of 4 horizontally and vertically in order not to impede playback performance.

The Indeo 3.2 Codec is quite similar to the Cinepak codec in many ways. Compared to Cinepak, it requires about a third less time for compressing video, but a longer processing time for playback.

For "talking head" type video in which the background image remains static, Indeo 3.2 seems to be superior in quality and in image compression. But because it requires more processor cycles for playback to achieve this quality, it does not "scale down" on lower-end CPUs as well as Cinepak. Cinepak is probably the better choice for most digitized video work.

The recommended key frame interval for Indeo 3.2 is four regardless of the frame rate. It shares with Cinepak the characteristic that data rate and quality settings are mutually exclusive. It is possible to choose a certain quality setting or to set a data rate limit, but not both.

Note: When playing a movie back on QTW, Intel recommends attaching the Indeo video palette because it improves 8-bit video quality and playback performance. The Indeo palette is included with the codec release.

Indeo Raw

Ideal Source Material:	Video
Supported Bit Depths:	24-bit
Compression Time:	N/A
Supports Data Rate Limiting?	No
Supports Lossless Compression?	No

The Indeo Raw codec is designed to decode video files captured with the Intel Smart Video Recorder, which operates with Windows. Movie files can be compressed into this format as well. The Indeo Raw codec is best suited for high quality capture and for archiving video images.

The Indeo Raw format has the great advantage of not being hardware dependent. Once the video has been captured, any PC or Macintosh loaded with the appropriate software can play back Indeo Raw files without any conversion process. As a consequence several computers can be used for editing and compressing Indeo Raw codec video without the need to install duplicate sets of hardware on each.

Indeo Video Interactive

Ideal Source Material:	Video
Supported Bit Depths:	24-bit
Compression Time:	Approximately 90:1
Supports Data Rate Limiting?	Yes
Supports Lossless Compression?	No

Recently introduced by Intel, the Indeo Video Interactive codec is more than an upgrade to earlier Indeo codecs. Indeo Video Interactive utilizes an entirely new algorithm based on *wavelet* technology (which is also used in the high-end IMIX non-linear editing systems).

It is called interactive because new features allow compressed video or graphic objects of arbitrary shape to be overlaid onto either a video or graphics scene and interactively controlled during playback with a joystick, mouse or keyboard. Previously it was necessary to "marry" a keyable image to a background and a specifically defined area. Indeo Video Interactive allows the creation of a key source which is able to move anywhere on the screen, a feature especially desirable for multimedia and game applications.

Indeo Video Interactive is also a scaleable codec, which means that it is possible to scale between several different quality levels or bands, depending upon the capability of the host CPU. This makes it possible for faster computers to playback full screen, smooth motion video with even better quality. Earlier versions of Indeo video codecs allowed for frame rate and image size variation in order to achieve best results when running video across a range of CPU performance levels.

Proprietary Codecs

Proprietary codecs are those that check for and require the presence of specialized hardware on the host computer in order to operate. These are generally found on high-end capture boards that support full-screen, 30 frame, 60 field-per-second video processing. By using hardware assisted compression and playback, more data can be streamed through the computer resulting in greater image size and quality. Examples of proprietary codecs and hardware include Radius Studio and the Targa 2000.

The trade-off is that you are limited to editing and compressing this video on systems that are set up with like equipment. This can be quite expensive if your goal is to establish a render farm of multiple CPUs working with the same footage at the same time. (Some of these boards retail from 5–10 thousand dollars. Each.) It is also possible that video captured by a proprietary system may only work with a select set of software editing applications, or only with a lot of file conversion steps and hard drive space. For example, the Targa 2000 on the PC captures in a special file format that has the extension ".DVM." To use this footage in Premiere, it is necessary to save the captured footage as an AVI file format. Once the movie is edited and compressed in Premiere, it needs to be converted back into a .DVM file format for playback out of the Targa 2000. This double compression, however slight, does lower the video quality compared to the original image. Many systems are now trying to be sensitive to the needs for use of third-party software. Media 100 on the Mac captures in a proprietary codec, however, the file is a true QuickTime format. Although it's still necessary to have the installed hardware, it's possible to import the footage into any QuickTime compatible application, edit it, and bring it back out to the Media 100 without conversion.

Compression Options

The typical applications which allow you to create or export movies will display a standard image compression dialog which contains a standard set of controls. These controls are important and can have a substantial effect on the results achieved with the selected codecs. Let's explore these in more detail.

Spatial Quality Setting

Spatial compression is the process of compressing a frame by itself (the concept also applies to still images). A good example of this type of compression is JPEG, where it's easy to see the trade-off between an image quality and its size. Spatial compression eliminates redundant information within each frame in a sequence. In making movies, keyframes are spatially compressed.

You should leave this control's setting at normal default, unless the resulting image quality is insufficient. Note that higher settings quickly increase the data rate of the movie while increasing the quality of the individual frames. Some codecs, such as the Animation codec, will provide a lossless compression when the spatial compression quality is set to Most.

Codecs that allow you to limit the movie's data rate, like Cinepak and Indeo 3.2, dynamically adjust the movie's Spatial and Temporal quality in order to maintain a specified data rate. In cases where you are limiting the movie's data rate, you'll normally just set the Quality to Most.

Temporal Quality Setting

Temporal compression only applies to sequences of images, like video. This type of compression takes advantage of the fact that a given frame often has a lot in common with the frame before it, therefore, a codec only needs to store the changes since the previous frame. "Difference frames" (all frames that aren't key frames) are temporally compressed.

The standard image compression dialog will only display the Spatial Quality (sometimes just shown as "Quality") slider. On the Mac, you can access the Temporal Quality slider by holding down the Option key while dragging the slider. Not all codecs support temporal compression. You won't be able to access the Temporal Quality slider if this is the case.

If you select Key Frames for an image sequence, then the Spatial Quality slider will control both spatial and temporal quality. Note that the Temporal Quality setting may be adjusted automatically by the codec that has been selected so that it corresponds to a value that the codec supports. As with the Spatial Quality setting, some codecs will support a lossless temporal compression when the setting is placed at Most.

You should leave this control's setting at Medium unless there is a lot of motion frame to frame in your image sequence—in which case you should then try placing the setting Medium and Low to decrease the bandwidth needed to playback the compressed sequence. Of course, doing so will increase the number of artifacts and "blockiness."

Key Frames

"Key" frames are complete, stand-alone frames of video. The frames between key frames are called "Difference" frames, and just store the video information that has changed since the previous frame. You may be able to get away with less (or need more) key frames depending on the movement characteristics of your video.

The Key Frames setting controls the frequency with which key frames are inserted into the compressed image sequence. Key frames provide points from which a temporally compressed sequence may be decompressed. When using only Spatial compression, you can consider every frame a key frame, so you don't need to specify any key frame setting. If you are using Temporal compression, you must specify a key frame setting, otherwise you will not have the ability to randomly access any part of the image sequence or play it in reverse. The more key frames there are, the quicker a particular portion of a movie can be accessed. Additionally, you will have trouble playing the sequence from a CD-ROM or over a network. Remember, that key frames are the key for enabling QuickTime to keep video and audio synchronized during playback, particularly if it has to skip video frames.

A generic key frame setting for video is to have one key frame every second. So if your movie is to be compressed at 15 frames per second, the key frame setting should be 15. Note that Cinepak and Indeo work best at a key frame setting of 4, regardless of the number of frames per second. For image or animation content, try settings from 30 to 150. If the quality is being controlled by Temporal compression and there is no need for random access, you may even try just having one keyframe in an animation sequence. Simply find out the number of frames in the sequence and enter that number for the key frame setting. Note that not some codecs have limits on their key frame settings. For example, the highest that Indeo 3.2 can be set to is 60.

Natural Key Frames vs. Forced Key Frames

Natural key frames are simply defined as the first frame of a cut in the video or image sequence. Forced key frames are frames which are designated as key frames artificially (by a codec like Cinepak or an application such as MovieShop) in order to enable smoother playback and random access to a movie's contents. Note that QuickTime itself may create a forced key frame when it detects a 90 or more percent difference between the current frame and the previous frame. This automatic keyframing will not typically affect performance unless this situation occurs frequently in a given image sequence.

Frame Rate Setting

This controls the number of frames per second in the image sequence to be compressed. You need to decide the frame rate you desire on a case by case basis. This may take substantial experimentation because a successful selection is dependent on many factors.

First, your frame rate should be a sub-multiple of the source frame rate. If you digitize at 30 frames per second, you should use 30, 15, or 10. If your original source material is at 24 frames per second, consider 24, 12, or 8. If you don't do this, your movies may look like they're not playing back smoothly. This is because of an uneven selection of frames used in the final movie. For example, with an original source video at 30 frames per second, a 15 frames per second movie simply uses every other frame (frames 1,3,5,7,9, etc.) in creating the final image sequence. At 12 frames per second the frames used are unevenly distributed (1,3,6,8,11, etc.). This uneven distribution creates a choppy or stutter-step look that is quite noticeable.

Second, the best frame rate will depend on the type of material to be compressed. By most general observations, 15 frames per second is the minimum frame rate necessary to maintain the illusion of proper lip-synch for on-camera talent. Anything lower starts to give the impression of a poorly choreographed puppet show. Conversely, action sequences and animation can safely be compressed at 10 or 12 frames per second without a serious loss of continuity. The motion on the screen helps detract the viewers attention and the absence of frames is less noticeable.

Data Rate Setting

"Data rate" refers to the amount of data required at a specific moment in time to play a movie. Data rate is commonly measured in terms of kilobytes per second.

The primary limit to a movie's data rate is the storage device from which the movie is being played. The performance of the playback device also limits the maximum data rate. Standard double-speed CD-ROM drives support a maximum data rate of 300 kBs. (By contrast, hard drives fast enough to do Super-VHS quality video have to transfer data at over 4 megabytes per second.) Don't think, however, that your movies will always play back at the maximum speed. There are a number of other things that occur while your movie is being played besides simply transferring the data from the CD-ROM. Time is needed to seek the location of the data on the CD-ROM, decompress the video data using the corresponding decompressor, play the sound data, copy the image data to the display and for general overhead, to manage the movie's frames and tracks.

As a result, you get only about 150–200 kBs of sustained data rate from a CD-ROM on a base level multimedia computer. Fortunately, triple and quad speed CD-ROM drives have been developed. These drives provide higher maximum data transfer rates—up to roughly 450 and 600 kBs, respectively. However, even as faster CD-ROM drives become more commonplace in the market, multimedia producers need to deal with the reality of the installed base. That means planning carefully to squeeze maximum performance out of a double-speed drive's data rate.

If you are designing movies for playback from hard disk drives, then you can plan for a sustained data rate of a at least 300 kBs. Faster CPUs coupled with a fast hard drive can take you up to 600–800 kBs of sustained data rate.

Later in this chapter are suggested settings for typical applications.

Peak Data Rate

Depending upon the codec, the data rate within a compressed movie can be highly variable. The peak data rate measures the point of the movie with the greatest data throughput. If these peaks are more than the target computer can handle, then the system will automatically skip or drop frames in order to keep synch with time. Obviously, this is to be avoided. A movie created at 15 frames per second that suddenly grinds down to a random selection of 5 frames per second will be distracting to the user.

Motion as a Factor in Data Rate

The number one factor in determining the data rate is the amount of motion happening on the screen at any given time. This is especially true for the peak data rate. Apparent motion of any type implies that there is less similarity between consecutive frames of an image sequence. The greater the difference, the more data the difference frames need to store to reflect this change. Moreover, the difference may be so great that additional key frames are created by the codec. It's possible, at some points in the movie, to have nothing but a string of key frames, with no difference frames whatever. Only when the motion decreases enough, will the codec go back to its regular pattern of key and difference frames. Since key frames store pixel information for the entire frame, this can significantly increase the data rate.

Motion may be in the form of subject movement, camera movement, and transitions.

- Subject movement is movement within the frame. Examples would include video clips of a roller coaster or a speeding car. Subject movement coming directly towards the camera would have less apparent effect on the data rate than something traveling across the frame.

- Camera movement is movement of the frame itself. This includes pans, tilts, zooms, crane & dolly moves, and hand held camera shots. Be aware, the more abrupt or uneven the movement, the greater the probability for disproportionately high data rates. This is not to say that you can't or shouldn't use these, but you should use them in moderation.

- Transitions create movement between frames. This includes dissolves, wipes, and digital "flying box" type effects. The most computer-friendly transitions are those that have hard edges, straight lines, and a simple, direct path. A horizontal wipe or clock wipe would fit into this category.

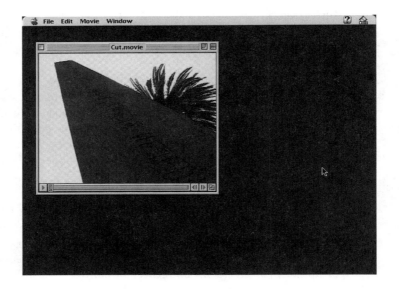

Figure 15.1a Horizontal and Clock wipe

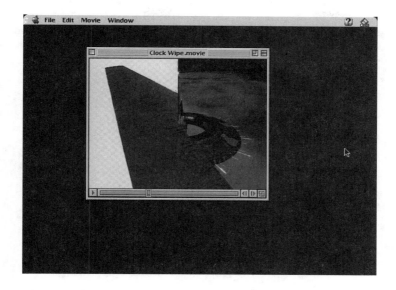

Figure 15.1b Horizontal and Clock wipe

Figure 15.1c Horizontal and Clock wipe

Assuming that the shots are static (no subject or camera movement) the only place there is a change in the picture is right where the wipe is occurring. Since the rest of the frame is the same, the codec has a better chance of keeping up and maintaining a regular pattern of key and difference frames. In contrast would be a Venetian blind wipe or digital "push".

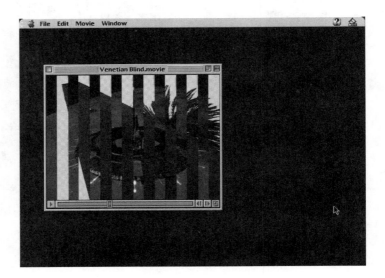

Figure15.2a Venetian blind wipe and digital "push"

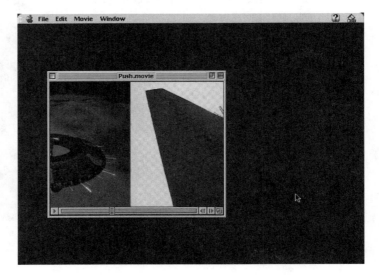

Figure15.2b Venetian blind wipe and digital "push"

Although the edges are sharp and straight, now there is movement occurring throughout the entire frame. In the case of the Venetian blind wipe, the sheer number of edges involved is the main culprit. The digital "push" is different from the horizontal wipe in that the entire "B" frame is sliding "over" the base "A" frame. Not only is there movement at the edge where the two frames overlap, but also wherever the "B" frame happens to be; as the "B" frame moves, the pixel-to-pixel information changes as well. Less frequently used effects include full-frame transitions such as dissolves and sci-fi "fizzle" effects.

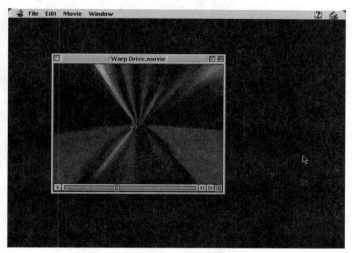

Figure 15.03a Dissolve and "fizzle" effect

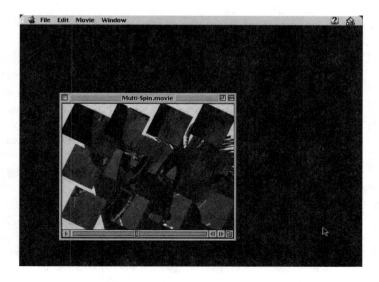

Figure 15.03b Dissolve and "fizzle" effect

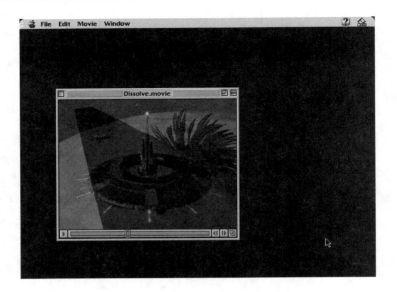

Figure 15.03c Dissolve and "fizzle" effect

Because there is change occurring everywhere, at the same time, these types of effects can put the most "stress" on a compression codec. The dissolve is the most popular transition of all time, and, with special care, can be made easier for the codec to handle. If both the "A" and "B" frames are static, there will be less apparent motion than trying to dissolve between two panning shots or where there is a lot of movement happening within the frame. If you're a real glutton-for-punishment, try the sci-fi "fizzle." Not only is there constant full-screen change, but the random nature of the pixelization will certainly drive up the data rate.

Detail as a Factor in Data Rate

Another factor in determining data rate is the amount of detail present in any given image. Certain codecs, like Indeo 3.2, are sensitive to edges between objects in a frame. This is part of how these codecs give the illusion of increased resolution and sharpness of picture. Taken to an extreme, a great amount of detail, i.e. many edges, can make for a very pixelized image. This pixelization is magnified with any kind of movement. Obviously, a pan across a checkerboard background would have a lot more compression applied to it than a pan against a neutral white background.

Codecs apply their compression indiscriminately. That is, they objectively analyze the entire frame, without regard to the main subject matter or its importance. If there is an area of the background with lots of detail, the codec will compress that just as equally as detail in the main subject matter. Knowing this, it's possible to "steer" the codec into compressing what's most important to telling the story. This can be accomplished by minimizing extraneous detail and increasing the size of the primary subject matter relative to the background.

Figure 15.4a Effect of detail on a compressed image

Figure 15.4b Effect of detail on a compressed image

Figures 15.4 a and 15.4 b show two versions of Indeo 3.2 compressed images. Image "A" is a tight head shot against a neutral background. Image "B" is a wide head shot against a busy background.

Audio

Audio Interleave

Movie files, AVI or MooV format, usually contain both video and audio data. With current technology, the video data is almost always compressed, while the audio data is seldom compressed. The video and audio have a direct temporal relationship. As the movie is played, audio accompanies the visual content. The audio must be played at the same time the video is decoded and displayed, or the movie looks like a foreign movie dubbed into your native language. The multimedia environment, QTM, QTW, or VfW, has the task of both reading and synchronizing the playback of the audio and video information. To make this task easier, the movie file contains chunks of audio followed by chunks of video. The movie has a series of these chunks interleaved so that audio is played followed by video, audio followed by video and so on, until the movie is completed. If there is too much video data between the audio data, then the lip-synch will be lost.

Under VfW, audio data should be interleaved with video data at a ratio of one-to-one (one frame of video for each sample of audio). For Quicktime files, optimal playback performance is achieved with a ratio of one-half second for every half second of video data (regardless of the frames per second).

Audio Sample Rates

The sampling rate, sometimes referred to as the sampling frequency, has to do with the conversion of an analog audio signal to its corresponding digital representation. This process of digitizing audio requires that every so often a snap shot of the audio signal is measured and stored. If the snap shot occurs every tenth of a second (1/10), then the sample rate is 10 or a frequency of 10 hertz (Hz). A sample rate of 11,025 Hz means that every 90.7 microseconds a sample is taken. The more samples taken of the analog signal, the more accurate the digital representation will be, although there is a point where the number of samples taken no longer increases the accuracy of the sample.

The audio format must be intelligently chosen because it will affect the overall playback performance of the video files. Sampling rates differ between the Macintosh and Windows platforms. There are even differences among Macintosh systems. If the audio sample rate is different from what the system expects, additional processing must be performed at playback time. This extra processing takes away processing from the decode and display of the video data and may affect the playback frame rate.

If the movie file is intended for playback on QTM and QTW, Apple recommends that PC sample rates be used. This is suggested because Apple's trend is to produce Mac systems which utilize the same sample rates as PCs. Macintosh computers with 8-bit sound chips use the Mac specific sampling rates. The newer Macintosh computers have 16-bit sound chips and use the same sampling rate as PCs. The data rate demands of 44khz audio are too great for practical use at this time. If you subtract the audio data rate from the total data rate, you have the data rate for the video track of your movies. The lower the data rate left for the video track, the lower the image quality. As faster CD-ROMs and better compression schemes become more commonplace, use of 44khz sampled audio will make this issue moot.

Sample Size

The proper selection of sample size is dependent on the audio material and target computer system capabilities. If most of the audio material is loud, then you can use 8-bit samples with good effect. For example, if you are creating a movie with Rock music, then 8-bit samples are appropriate. On the other hand, if your material has low volume, or more range in volume such as voice or classical music, then 16-bit samples are appropriate. Using 16-bit samples gives your audio better signal-to-noise ratios.

Stereo

The use of stereo audio in movie files is a design choice that should be made carefully. With the limitations of CD-ROM data rates, the use of stereo limits the data rate available to the video. For example, for a double speed CD-ROM playable movie file, the total data rate for the movie file is often around 150KB per second. The data rata, and hence, image quality available for the video decreases as the audio information increases.

If music is the most important element to your application, then perhaps using stereo is the right decision. Stereo realization is sometimes difficult because of the end user's proximity to computer and speakers. This proximity is such that perceiving stereo is difficult. For stereo imaging to be perceptive, the speakers should be at least three feet away from the listener. This distance allows one to perceive stereo optimally from the audio content.

Suggested Settings

The following are suggested settings for software codec compressed movies to be played back from CD-ROM drives. Note that these settings may need to be adjusted, depending upon the characteristics of the source material. Experiment with a variety of settings until you get acceptable results.

High-Motion Sequence

Double-Speed CD-ROM

  Codec: Cinepak

  Color-Depth: Millions

  Frame size: 320 x 240

  Frame rate: 10–30 fps (depending on action)

Audio: 22.05 kHz, 8-bit, mono

Data Rate: Less than 300 kBs, 150–200 kBs is typical

Low-Motion Sequence

Double-Speed CD-ROM

Codec: Indeo 3.2

Color-depth: Millions

Frame size: 320 x 240

Frame rate: 10–30 fps (depending on action)

Audio: 22.05 kHz, 8-bit, mono

Data Rate: Less than 300 kBs, 150–200 kBs is typical

Quad Speed CD-ROM

Codec: Cinepak or Indeo 3.2

Color-depth: Millions

Frame size: 320 x 240

Frame rate: 30 fps

Audio: 44.1 kHz, 16-bit, mono or 22.05kHz, 16-bit, stereo

Data Rate: Less than 600 kBs, 450-500 kBs is typical

Adobe Premiere CD-ROM Movie Maker

Adobe Premiere 4.2 is a major upgrade for multimedia producers. The CD-ROM Movie Maker plug-in optimizes movies for playback off CD-ROM by uniformly limiting the data rate and automatically flattening movies for cross-platform delivery. In the past, many Premiere users used third-party utilities, such as MovieShop, to optimize movies for CD-ROM playback. The CD-ROM Movie Maker eliminates this extra step. Now it is possible to optimize movies entirely within Premiere.

The CD-ROM Movie Maker offers the following major features:

1. Limits and smoothes the movie's data rate. By minimizing spikes in the overall data rate, it makes it easier for the host computer's CPU keep up with the data flow coming from the CD-ROM. This in turn, cuts down on the chances that frames will be dropped during playback.

2. Crop the movie. This is helpful in getting rid of unwanted pixels from the edge of the movie and either resizing it or scaling the image to fit the original frame size.

3. Gamma correction, noise reduction, and de-interlacing filters. Gamma correction, as explained in more detail in **Chapter 16**, compensates for differences in contrast between Mac and PC monitors.

   The noise reduction option may help the movie to appear to have higher resolution at very low data rates, especially when using Cinepak.

   The de-interlacing option is used when the original source material is 640 x 480 or larger and the final movie's frame size is smaller than 640 x 480. This removes the secondary field in each frame and doubles the lines of the dominant field. If you don't use this option, Quicktime will deinterlace the fields using a lower quality method.

4. Generates a specific color palette to optimize playback on 8-bit systems or attaches an optimized palette that's already been created. See **Chapter 16** for more details.

5. Allows batch processing of building CD-ROM optimized movies.

MovieAnalyzer

Although Premiere 4.2 comes with an upgraded Data Rate Analyzer, nothing beats the MovieAnalyzer utility available on the Mac. Not only does it provide basic information such as movie duration, frames per second, key frames, and audio interleaving, MovieAnalyzer also finds the peak data rate in the movie. An overall low average data rate may hide the fact that there is a particular scene or transition that may create play back problems. By knowing the peak data rate, it's possible to adjust settings so that the entire movie will playback well, without dropping frames. It also will troubleshoot the movie, warning you about potential problems and giving tips and suggestions to correct these problems, all in plain English.

To use *MovieAnalyzer,*

1.   Open the application. The MovieAnalyzer command dialog box will appear.

2.   Select Open Movie. A standard file browse window will appear. Select the movie to be analyzed. The movie will appear on the screen along with standard Quicktime controls for playback.

3.   Select Play on the Main Menu bar. After a few seconds a data rate analysis window will appear.

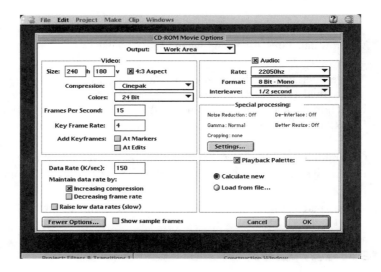

Figure 15.5 MovieAnalyzer Command dialog box

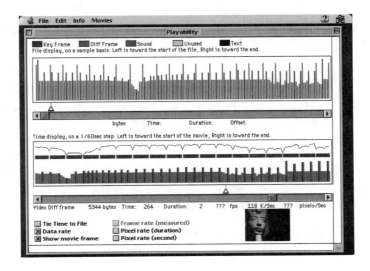

Figure 15.6 Data Rate analysis window

From here, it is possible to examine the movie frame-by-frame, check data and pixel rates, key frames, and audio interleaving. A preview frame of the movie can be opened for seeing trouble spots so you'll know exactly where in the video they occur.

5. Close the data rate analysis window. This will reveal the main window which now has any potential playback problems outlined in a list. These can be cross-referenced for further information along with suggestions for fixing them.

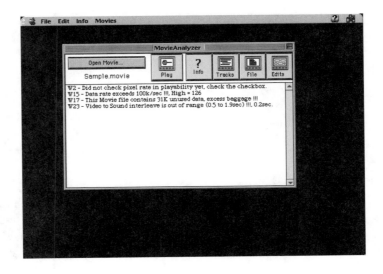

Figure 15.7 Potential playback problem list

There are other menu buttons for getting more detailed information about the movie, such as track information and file size. To exit MovieAnalyzer, select Quit from the File menu.

Conclusion

This chapter is only an introduction to key compression schemes for computer and CD-ROM playback and the technical and aesthetic issues associated with them. The producer should refer to the technical bulletins provide by the publishers of the various CODECS and tools as well as some of the excellent reference volumes listed below.

Bibliography

Ozer, Jan. *Video Compression for Multimedia*, Cambridge, MA: Academic Press, Inc., 1995.

"Cross-Platform Development Using Indeo Video," Intel Corporation, 1994.

Charles Wiltgen. "The QuickTime FAQ," Version 0.45, Apple Computer Corp, 1995.

"Indeo Video R3.2 & Audio Conversion Issues in Cross-Platform Development," Intel Corporation., 1995.

"What's New in Adobe Premiere 4.2," Adobe Systems, 1995.

Chapter 16

The Final Product

Introduction

The point of all the video shooting, audio recording and subsequent editing and processing is a finished video tape or digital video program for use on a computer or CD-ROM or on the Internet. This chapter helps you assemble the final product for video tape, computer and CD-ROM distribution. The next chapter will consider the technical requirements and tools for compression and distribution over the Internet.

Video Tape

Once you've gotten this far, this is probably the easiest part of the entire desktop video process—writing your digital video from your computer to video tape for distribution. This section covers the last minutes elements and technical issues as well as the standard formats required for a professional product.

Settings & Levels

Just like any traditional video duplication, it's vital that all output and input settings are properly adjusted. Make sure that colors are within the NTSC safe range. Check volume levels. Use the best signal connections available with your system.

Black, Bars and Leader

Many software programs have extra functions built into them for video output. High-end systems like Media 100 and Avid come with pre-built black, bars & tone, slate, and countdown. Others contain the raw elements, ready to be edited into your program. These allow proper set-up on analog video systems, especially if your tape is going to be used as a duplication master. On the other hand, a VHS copy may not need any of these.

Black, Bars and Tone

Black is first laid for 10–30 seconds. This gives the tape time to spool up to full speed and tension. Color bars and a 1K Hz audio tone are laid simultaneously for the next one minute. This gives an operator plenty of time to make any playback adjustments. Color bars ensure that luminance, hue, and saturation video levels are within spec. The audio tone is adjusted to a 0 dB level.

Slate and Countdown

An optional slate and countdown may follow. The slate gives important information, like the name of the project, length, and date it was produced. The countdown does just what it sounds like. Large numbers on the screen hold for one second each as they countdown from 10 to 2. At the 2 sec. mark, the number 2 is on the screen for only a few frames. Black then follows until the start of the program. A countdown is especially useful in situations where the tape must be cued and ready for playback at a moment's notice, as in news production or commercials.

Control, Time Code

High-end systems allow for control of the video record deck directly from the computer. This is a nice convenience, especially if the deck is not within arm's reach. This also means that you can begin playback from the computer and recording on the deck at exactly the same time, and therefore precise editing of the tape is possible. For even greater control, some editing systems support time code. As mentioned earlier, time code is an electronic timing system created for traditional video production. With deck control and time code, true frame-accurate editing is possible from the computer.

EDLs

Perhaps for your project you're working on the computer for a test run, and you plan to do the final edit at a traditional video facility. This is called making an "off-line" edit and it can make a lot of sense. First, it's a lot cheaper to use this method for deciding on edits than an expensive "on-line" editing suite where the clock is running and the costs are literally in the hundreds of dollars per hour. Second, it's often faster in a non-linear environment to see and place shots in order, re-arrange elements, and experiment to find exactly the right look. It's not enough to get just a rough idea of how things should go together. If you've spent the time trimming down to exact frames, you shouldn't have to go through all that again. The link between the off-line and on-line edit suite is the EDL, or Edit Decision List. It's a line-by-line computer generated account of your entire project. Every shot, every effect is put into a linear order for traditional tape-based video production. The EDL is a data file, saved on floppy disk, able to be read by the edit controller. The computer can generate the EDL in a variety of formats, the most common being CMX, Sony, and Grass Valley. You will need to match the EDL format with the specific edit controller brand and model number you expect to use.

MPEG Encoding

MPEG (Motion Picture Experts Group) is an emerging compression format designed with video in mind. Two different codecs are available. Both require special hardware and software for proper record and playback.

MPEG-1 is 30 frames, 30 fields per second at a resolution of 352 x 240. This is scalable to play at full-screen size. It is primarily used for consumer grade video and multimedia applications.

MPEG-2 is a true full-screen, full motion video codec. It runs at 30 frames, 60 fields per second at a resolution of 640 x 480. Users include broadcast and high-end video distribution applications. The new multi-layer Digital CD stand-alone unit available for playback of Hollywood titles uses MPEG-2 compression.

There are companies that provide MPEG compression as a service. Do-it-yourself systems, such as those created by Optibase, can cost upwards of $40,000. A low cost alternative is the RealMagic Producer from Sigma Designs. It retails for about $5000 and provides an excellent picture for the price. It is an MPEG-1 capture and compression board and software package, available only in a PC/Windows configuration. It not only lets you capture video in real-time, but also allows you to edit the footage before making a final compressed movie.

Cross-platform Development

Cross-platform development is the process of creating digital video for playback from computers and/or CD-ROM that are capable of being played by multiple computer systems such as MAC, Windows and UNIX. There are a variety of factors to consider for cross-platform development of compressed movies.

Desktop Video Environments

This section gives an overview of the major compression and file technologies such as Quicktime from Apple and Video for Windows or ActiveMovie from Microsoft. There are other systems being created and the systems listed below are constantly changing. Be sure to refer to the publisher's current technical standards and manuals when using any of the systems.

Video for Windows

Video for Windows (VfW) is Microsoft Corporation's standard for video on PCs. Files created carry an AVI extension. AVI stands for audio/video interleave. The video and audio are stored together in one continuous stream, interleaved in small pieces, first one then the other. The video plays at its own clock rate and audio is clocked to its own sample rate. This can lead to a slippage in synchronization between the two, especially in large movies. VFW also requires that a video-only movie include a "silent" or null audio track in order to play correctly. This wastes valuable data that could be used for better video compression.

Quicktime on the Macintosh

Quicktime (QTM) is the industry standard for CD-ROM video. It was designed by Apple Computer and became the first widely available desktop video technology to treat video as a standard data type. Prior to Quicktime, video data could not be cut, copied, and pasted like text in a page composition program. The file extension is MooV. Synchronization is time-based and provides tracks and control for multiple media types—video, sound, music, and text.

Quicktime for Windows

Quicktime for Windows (QTW) is the PC version of Quicktime. The file extension is MOV. Currently, QuickTime is the only cross-platform playback environment. Using Quicktime, a single video file, properly compressed, can be played on either a Mac or PC.

Compatibility

Creating cross-platform video entails more than simply converting the files from one format to another. File formats store information in different ways. Audio sampling rates and audio interleaving are slightly different in the PC and Macintosh and can degrade playback performance when not properly addressed. There are several different ways to assert color palettes under QTW, QTM, and VFW.

File Naming Conventions

On PCs, filenames consist of up to eight characters, followed by a dot (.) and a filename extension up to three characters. This is sometimes referred to the DOS "8.3" convention. Folder names are also limited to eight characters. Legal characters in a filename are restricted to the letters A–Z, the numbers 0–9, and a few special characters. Even with Windows 95, filenames are stored in the DOS 8.3 format. File names that share the first eight characters are truncated and given new names. Internally, filenames are stored as all uppercase characters.

FILENAME.PIC

On the Mac, filenames can be up to 31 characters in length and contain any character, including spaces and non ASCII characters. While filenames can include any mixture of upper and lowercase characters, case is not significant. For example *FileName, filename,* and *fileName* are identical filenames.

The Mac will accept any filename created on the PC. On the other hand, PC conventions should be used when naming Mac files that are destined to be moved to the PC. It is important to use an appropriate naming system from the beginning of the project to minimize confusion and avoid later naming conflicts.

File Type Identification

On the PC, many filename extensions are reserved by convention to identify the type of information contained within the file. Thus, the .AVI extension is reserved for VfW movies, and the .MOV extension is for QTW movies. A movie player application may reject a file whose extension does not indicate the type of data it expects.

On the Mac the file system maintains a "two 4-character" signature with the entry for each file: the file type and the file creator. The file type indicates the type of information stored in the file. As with the PC filename extension, it may be used by applications to accept/ reject files for processing. The file type of a QuickTime movie is "MooV." The file creator identifies which application created the file, the icon that will be displayed, and which application is executed by the Mac operating system when the file is "double-clicked." The file creator for a QuickTime movie is MoviePlayer, "TVOD." After a file is moved from the PC to the Mac, its file type and file creator must be set appropriately. Many utilities exist to perform this operation. One utility, MakeItMooV, specifically sets the file signature for QuickTime MooV files.

Self-contained and Single-forked Files

There are two fundamental differences in the way QuickTime files are stored on the Mac vs. the PC. On the Mac, data can be split between files and between forks. On the PC, all data must be contained in a single file. The PC can only create the equivalent of Mac self-contained and single-fork files. Therefore, no further manipulations for Mac playback are required. But Quicktime files created on the Mac must be made self-contained and single-forked before they can be played back or compressed on the PC.

On the Mac, a Moov file can reference data stored in other MooV files. This saves disk space and can happen when movies are created by cutting and pasting from other movies. In order to make a Mac file portable, it is necessary to replace all references to data in external files with an actual copy of that data. This process is referred to as "Self-containment" and is required not only when moving Quicktime files to the PC but also when moving movies from one Mac to another.

A MooV file on the Mac contains the actual video and audio streams in the data fork and all of the organizing information (headers, indices, sizes, media information) in the resource fork. For portability, Apple defined a single-fork form of the MooV format in which the resource information is stored immediately after the audio and video data in the data fork. There is no playback penalty associated with a single-fork MooV format file. This process is called "single-forking" or "making files playable on non-Apple computers."

Gamma Correction

Gamma controls the mid-tones of a gray-scale image without affecting the luminance levels for the brightest or darkest parts of the image. In effect, gamma is a contrast control, with a setting of 1.0 being the default. Macintosh monitors have a gamma filter built into them; PC monitors do not. This means that a movie that looks fine on a Mac monitor, may appear exceptionally dark when viewed on a PC. This most often occurs when a movie has been converted from QuickTime to a VfW file format. If this is the case, it will be necessary to make a gamma correction when the movie is compressed. Premiere 4.2 for the Mac offers this as both a filter and an output setting. Other programs offer gamma control as well. A setting of 0.7 or 0.8 is usually sufficient to compensate for cross-platform gamma differences.

Palettes

In 8-bit color environments, video colors must be converted to 256 colors for playback. Choosing which 256 to use is determined by the asserted color palette. Palettes can be created to contain 256 colors from a choice of 65535 or 16 million colors for 16-bit and 24-bit display modes, respectively.

There are three common approaches to palette management.

1.   The application always asserts a palette.

2.   The application never asserts a palette (uses the current palette).

3.   The application asserts a palette associated with the movie. If there is not one associated with a movie file, a default palette is asserted.

A single video Quicktime file that plays back in a QTM 8-bit color display environment may not necessarily look as good when played back under a QTW 8-bit color environment. To improve playback quality under QTW, the MooV file can be optimized using Quicktime tools on the Mac.

SetMovieColorTable and MakeMovieColorTable are two tools available with the Quicktime 2.1 developer's kit. Debabelizer is a popular application for creating palettes. To optimize a MooV file for playback under QTW, an optimized palette should be created. Both QTM and QTW offer the ability for applications to assert specific palettes.

QTM dithers the video file during playback, by default, to the currently asserted palette. This is referred to as Active Palette under VfW. Dithering the video to the system palette offers the fastest playback performance. It is possible to associate a specific palette with the movie file using either MakeMovieColorTable or SetMovieColorTable. Any improvement in performance or image quality is highly dependent on the video content. This requires that you experiment to determine if this does in fact improve playback under QTM.

Under QTW, it is the responsibility of the playback application playing the video file to assert the palette you want used. This can be a default system or codec palette or one optimized for the application. Optimized palettes are typically created in third party applications like Debabilizer. These palettes should be created with no more than 236 colors. The first and last ten entries must be left unused. This takes into account the 20 Windows-reserved palette entries.

Palettes are not retained after converting a movie. A new palette can be created for the converted movie on its target platform. For instance, if an AVI file is converted to the MooV format, it can be brought to the Mac and processed with an application like Debabilzer to create and attach an optimized palette. Similarly, a resultant AVI file (with its palette removed) can be loaded into VidEdit and a custom palette created for it under Video for Windows.

File Duplication

Finally, strategies to avoid file duplications should be developed as soon as possible in the development cycle for a hybrid CD-ROM's directory structure. Placing QuickTime movie files in two locations, one for DOS and another for the Mac, reduces the space on a CD-ROM by half. To avoid this file duplication, make file aliases to reference movie files on the Mac side of a QuickTime cross-platform CD-ROM, since Windows does not support file aliases. In this scenario, there is only one set of QuickTime files and they exist in the Windows folder. Double clicking on a file alias causes the real file to be referenced by the operating system.

A slightly different strategy is needed for creating cross-platform Video for Windows files. QTM can create files with dependencies, that is a small "stub" file that contains pointers to another source. These files are larger than Mac aliases, but certainly much smaller than the original source file. The size of the stub QuickTime file is 10K to 30K in size. This is so small that it is almost a single file solution, sometimes called "file and a quarter." When an AVI file is converted to QuickTime, the new file should be saved as a non-self contained file. This small QuickTime file will then reference the AVI file for audio and video data during playback.

Converting QuickTime to Video for Windows

The easiest way to convert MooV movie files into AVI formatted files is with the VfW Converter utility from Microsoft. It is available only on the Mac. This program allows for a variety of options for doing the conversion. Files may be uncompressed, compressed, or directly transferred without any additional compression. For example, a compressed Cinepak MooV file can be converted frame-by-frame into a compressible Cinepak AVI file without any loss in quality. There are also controls for audio conversion and batch processing of many movies at once. Once converted, the audio interleave must be corrected. VidEdit or Premiere for Windows can perform this step. Be aware, however, that this utility does not support all compression formats, for example, Intel Indeo 3.2 and Intel Raw. For those you'll need to use the following steps.

1. Start the conversion process on the Mac by flattening the MooV format files. This means making them self-contained and single-forked. This conversion capability is part of most video editing applications (e.g. VideoFusion, Premiere). Playback utilities such as MoviePlayer 2.0 and MovieConverter 1.0, also allow for self-containment and single-forking. This is achieved by opening the movie file, selecting Save As from the File menu, and selecting the "Make movie self-contained" and "Playable on non-Apple computers" options. If the movie is already self-contained, a simple utility like flattenMooV, will do the trick.

2. Complete the conversion process on the PC by changing the file format from MooV to AVI. Following are two utilities that will perform this conversion without recompression.

   TrMooV: To convert a MooV format file, start TrMoov from within Windows.

1. Select the source file using the Browse button.

2. Select the target AVI formatted file by using the other browse button. Make sure the new file name you select has an .AVI extension.

3. After having selected the source and target filenames, select the Start button to perform the conversion.

   Conversion is accomplished without recompression, and interleaving of audio and video is correctly converted as well. TrMooV will not convert the audio sampling rate from Mac to VfW, however. Nor will version 1.20 convert a palette that is attached to a MooV formatted file. A subsequent version of this utility should correctly translate palette information for optimal 8-bit color playback. There are also certain compression formats, like Intel Raw, that are not supported at this time.

   SmartVid: To convert a MooV format file, start SmartVid from the DOS command line.

1. Type "Smartvid.exe" and the Return key on the keyboard.

2. From the File Menu, choose Open Source. An Open File dialog box will appear. Select the source file you wish to convert and then click on the OK button.

3. From the Convert Menu, choose Start. A dialog box will appear. You may enter a destination file name by typing one in the File Name section or use the default name. Be sure to use the proper extension (AVI or MOV) to which the file should be converted.

4. When ready, click on the OK button. Conversion will now begin and status messages will be displayed in the SmartVid window.

5. After the conversion is completed, close the source file by choosing Close from the File Menu.

SmartVid does not convert the audio interleaving. The interleaving can be converted by opening the converted file with VidEdit and selecting File Save As. The resulting new file will have proper VfW interleaving. SmartVid will not convert the audio sampling rate from Mac to VfW. If a custom palette is attached to the MooV format file it will be removed from the converted output AVI format file.

Converting Video for Windows to QuickTime

Because PC files are single forked by definition, self-containment and single forking files issues are not relevant when converting from PC file structures to Mac. Converting AVI format files to MooV format requires both file and audio transformation.

On the Macintosh, there are many tools for doing this conversion. Microsoft's AVI to QT utility can convert without recompression. It is essentially a copy process and does not take into account the differences in audio interleaving and sampling rates.

1. From the File Menu, choose Open. A dialog box will appear.

2. On the left hand side is a source file window. By using standard folder search commands, select the AVI file to be converted.

3. Click on the Add button. The file will appear in the right hand batch list window. Continue adding files as needed.

4. Click on the Convert button. Conversion will now begin.

QTM and QTW perform best when playing movies that have QuickTime audio interleaving. When converting AVI format files to MooV format, it is a good idea to check resultant audio interleaving. The Mac-based tool MovieAnalyzer can be used to check if a movie has proper QTM/QTW audio interleaving. Select MovieAnalyzer's Info Graph Playability menu item to check audio interleaving. A message window will contain messages about potential playback problems. Audio interleave may be among these messages.

MoviePlayer 2.0 provides the means to resample to optimized Mac audio rates. The steps are as follows.

1. Open the movie file.

2. Select File Export.

3. Select options to choose the desired sample rate, 8/16 bit, and stereo or mono settings.

4. Enter a file name.

5. Select Sound to AIFF.

6. Select Save.

7. Select Edit Delete Tracks.

8. Select Sound Track.

9. Select Delete.

10. Select File Import.

11. Enter the file saved in step 4 above.

12. Select Convert.

13. Select the window associated with the imported audio track.

14. Select Edit Select All.

15. Select Edit Copy.

16. Select the window associated with the movie file.

17. Select Edit Select All.

18. Press the Option key for the next step.

19. Select Edit Add.

20. Select File Save As.

21. Enter a new file name.

22. Select Make Movie Self-Contained.

23. Select Playable on non-Apple computers.

24. Select Save.

On the PC side, TrMooV will convert the audio interleaving, but audio sampling differences are not addressed and should be converted on the Mac as stated above. SmartVid addresses neither audio interleaving or audio sample rates. Therefore, these conversion issues need to be dealt with on the Mac as described above.

Conclusion

The technology of digital video and computer and Internet video playback is rapidly changing. The need to keep up to date and to utilize the latest information and manuals from each publisher is important. It is also important to use the latest development and compression tools and carefully consider the ultimate target computer platform and audience when selecting them.

Chapter 17
Internet Video

Introduction

The first kind of videos to be delivered over the Internet were small AVI and Quictime movies and MPEG files. These offer the same quality as those delivered on CD-ROMs but must be completely downloaded before viewing. Over slow modems this could mean minutes or even hours before even the most basic video could be viewed. This is clearly not an acceptable solution for an interactive website or application. The solution to this problem is streaming video and audio. Because of it's smaller file size requirement, the first streaming media was audio but that was followed quickly by streaming video. With the proper plug-in or player streaming audio and/or video begins playing to the computer screen almost immediately after selection. The quality of both audio and video is improving very quickly. In less than two years audio has improved from less than telephone quality to FM radio quality, depending on modem speed. Video has made the same kind of rapid improvement. We can soon expect the same kind of video and audio quality over the Internet that can be delivered on CD-ROM.

Video and audio for Internet delivery can be either preprocessed or can be streamed in real time. Real time delivery can be of equal quality but the equipment required is much more expensive.

There are currently seven major technology providers of streaming audio and video tools. They are: RealAudio and RealVideo by RealNetworks, Netshow, VDOlive from VDO, Vivo, Xing from Xing Technologies, Vxtreme and Vosaic. RealNetworks has dominated the market in both technological advances and in the number of sites and users. RealNetworks conducted a market survey with the following results. Search engines Hotbot and AltaVista reveal that about 88–94% of Internetstreaming media URLs use RealAudio and RealVideo.

Results of Altavista link extension searches on 11/5/97 under "advanced search". www.altavista.com (search using "link:*.XXX", advanced search, precise count):

MEDIA TYPE	URLs	MARKETSHARE
RealNetworks	512,856	93.8%
Netshow	9,570	1.7%
VDO	10,341	1.9%
Vivo	3,736	.7%
Xing	4,148	.8%
Vxtreme	6,321	1.2%
Vosaic	2,804	.5%

SEACH CRITERIA USED:
RealNetworks: (link:*.ra OR link:*.ram OR link:*.rm OR link:*.rpm)
Netshow: (link:*.asx OR link:*.asf)
VDO: link:*.vdo
Vivo: link:*.viv
Xing: link:*.xdm
Vxtreme: (link:*.ivy OR link:*.ivx)
Vosaic: link:*.vos

Results of Hotbot link extension searches on 11/5/97 using Boolean Search. www.hotbot.com :(search using "linkext:XXX", boolean search):

MEDIA TYPE	URLs	MARKETSHARE
RealNetworks	156,586	88.1%
Netshow	758	.4%
VDO	6,222	3.5%
Vivo	11,651	6.6%
Xing	1,357	.8%
Vxtreme	1,234	.7%
Vosaic	218	.1%

SEARCH CRITERIA USED
RealNetworks: (linkext:ra OR linkext:ram OR linkext:rm OR linkext:rpm)
Netshow: (linkext:asx OR linkext:asf)
VDO: linkext:vdo
Vivo: linkext:viv
Xing: linkext:xdm
Vxtreme: (linkext:ivy OR linkext:ivx)
Vosaic: linkext:vos

NOTE: RealNetwork's URLs include RealAudio, RealVideo, and RealFlash. Netshow and Xing URLs include audio and video. Different data types from each company are authored in the same way. Search engines cannot differentiate between the different types.

Because of their dominance, this chapter will give an overview of the RealAudio and RealVideo schemes that were available at the time of writing. It is important that the reader visit the RealNetworks web site or the web sites of any other streaming audio or video providers to review their latest products and technical documentation.

RealVideo Overview

RealVideo 1.0 provides full motion video with existing RealAudio technology. RealVideo, anticipating the delivery of the new 56.6-Kbps modems, is optimized to deliver maximum performance at 45-Kbps, resulting in a reliable, high-quality video experience with over 56-Kbps dial-up connections, across ordinary phone lines. However, the most prevalent connection rate on the Internet will continue to be 28.8-Kbps for some time. In conjunction with the RealVideo 1.0 release, Progressive Networks is introducing four new low bit-rate audio codecs to maximize available bandwidth for video, resulting in high quality, high frame rate video for news broadcast, and high quality, low frame-rate for music video and high action content.

For corporate intranets and high speed connections, RealVideo delivers broadcast-quality digital video at lower bit-rates than current non-streaming solutions, such as compressed Quicktime or AVI. This technology allows intranets to deliver video training, corporate communications, and presentations without significant degradation to the network's performance.

Beyond the quality of the codecs, many other features contribute to making RealVideo 1.0 a very practical solution for streaming video on the Internet. Reliability of transmission over real-life conditions has the greatest impact on the quality of an Internet video experience. Progressive Networks developed UDP protocol enhancements for the RealAudio Server, which will allow for reliable video transmission with the RealVideo Server. These new servers also offer the same ability to be scaled up to 500–1000 28-Kbps streams on a single CPU, Pentium-based system. This is 10 to 20 times the number of streams available with other systems. This architecture is also suited to perform live broadcasts with a software only live solution.

New features, such as interactive Video Maps and Synchronized Multimedia, allow content creators to move beyond simply providing television on the Internet. Interactivity and video on demand create an experience that moves beyond passive viewing to an enhanced, user-controlled experience.

The RealVideo file format is supported by Adobe Premiere, in:sync Kohesion and Speed Razor, and Terran Interactive's Movie Cleaner Pro. Progressive Networks is also releasing the RealVideo Sequencer for assembly of multimedia video presentations, and V-Active for RealVideo, a tool for the authoring of advanced interactive Video Maps.

The Codecs

RealVideo 1.0 incorporates the audio codecs (compression, decompression algorithms) released with RealAudio 3.0, plus two new low bit-rate voice codecs and two new low bit-rate music codecs with wide frequency response. Frequency response measures the range of sound frequencies accurately rendered. The bit-rate is the bandwidth required for the audio stream.

The RealVideo codecs represent two different technologies in video compression. The RealVideo Standard codec is suited for low bit-rate natural setting content while the RealVideo Fractal (ClearVideo) is more suited for the creation of video at higher bandwidth or video requiring sharper contrasts and lines. Each codec is scaleable from 0 to 500-Kbps and beyond (500 represents near pixel perfect images at high frame rates).

The RealVideo Standard codec provides a high quality solution for motion video over the Internet. At 28.8-kbps, content providers can create newscast-quality video. At 56-Kbps, compelling content moves into the realm of high action, high frame rate delivery. The standard codec delivers the best performance over the Internet by incorporating FEC (Forward Error Correction) and intelligent image recovery of lost packets. The video will continue to be displayed at its original frame rate, regardless of the loss encountered. RealVideo Fractal can be used at low frame rates, but does not have the same level of resistance to packet loss. RealVideo Fractal employs a method in which it will hold for the next key frame when packet loss occurs. This codec is suited for corporate intranet applications. At higher bit-rates, this codec delivers broadcast quality digital video which can be decoded in real time with standard Pentium-based PCs. RealVideo Standard can produce live "broadcast" content and RealVideo Fractal can also produce live "broadcast" content with hardware assist from a capture card (Clearly Live).

The Player

The latest RealPlayer is a superset of the RealAudio 3.0 Player. This player will continue Progressive Networks' model of distributing players worldwide at no cost to the end user. In addition to adding video, the RealPlayer now supports many new features and capabilities.

The Player has the ability to switch into Buffered Play when a clip is selected which exceeds the available bandwidth. This allows 28.8-Kbps connections to experience content encoded for higher bandwidths. The Player also has a status bar to provide a much greater level of information on what is happening within the player, or with the network connection. It recognizes new interactive functions such as embedded interactive Video Maps and time Synchronized Multimedia. It can send URLs to your Web browser, seek to another point in the video stream, or launch a new video stream, all controlled by the user's interaction with the video screen or by imbedding commands in the time line. It also incorporates all the traditional levels of functionality such as network protocol control, bookmarking, connection control, and playback controls such as play, pause, seek, fast forward, rewind, double screen, volume control and nudge buttons.

The Player is designed to operate on Pentium 75 and greater CPUs. CPU requirements are dependent on content playback frame rate and streaming bit-rate. Low frame rate video can be viewed on high-end 486 machines as well.

The Server

The Servers enable broad-scale distribution of content. A single RealVideo Server can scale to over 500 streams on a standard Pentium-based system and up to 1000 streams on a higher end machine. On a multi-processor machine, a single server can scale up to several thousand streams. When this level of single server scalability is combined with Clustering and Slitting, functions introduced in RealAudio 3.0, RealVideo enables truly wide-scale distribution, limited only by the speed of the content provider's connection to the Internet.

On corporate intranets, IP Multicast capabilities allow hundreds to thousands of users to simultaneously experience one content stream, with no noticeable degradation to the server or network performance.

RealVideo also delivers an out-of-the-box live solution. This means the RealVideo Server is capable of live broadcasting using standard off-the-shelf software. Traditional RealAudio live broadcast technology has enabled hundreds of radio stations to broadcast their signal worldwide. A dual-processor machine can encode live video, serve several hundred streams, and run a Web server all from the same box.

The Tools

RealVideo authoring can be performed with several Progressive Networks and third-party tools. These tools allow for the capture, creation, compression, and enhancement of video content. Capture and creation can be accomplished with standard video capture card software, or by using in-sync Kohesion, In-Sync Speed Razor or Adobe Premier, Terran Interactive's Movie Cleaner Pro. These three editing packages can also transform the video content with advanced features and then compress the file to the RealVideo format.

Progressive Networks' Video Encoder can also be used to compress standard AVI and Quicktime files down to the RealVideo format. The RealVideo content can then be enhanced by adding interactive Video Maps and Synchronized Multimedia. Ephyx Technologies' V-Active for RealVideo can author time-based, arbitrary "hot spots" into the video stream which, when clicked, will launch an event. This tool allows the creation of static maps, image tracking maps, or maps which can morph to another shape over time. There are also several tools which use a time-line-based metaphor. These tools allow the author to lay out the various tracks on a time line and edit their timing and interaction with each other. With the release of video, these tracks are video, audio, time-based events (Synchronized Multimedia), and interactive Video Maps. These tracks will increase with roll-out of other data types in the RealMedia Architecture. Tools in this category include: in:sync Konvergence and Digital Renaissance's TAG.

Streaming Video On the Internet

The Internet is rapidly evolving into a mass medium. The explosive user-based growth in both the home and business environments is matched by an emerging wealth of content sources. This process has been made possible in part by rapid technical evolution enabling the creation of more compelling, more useful sites. RealAudio from Progressive Networks has played a leading role in making streaming media an important part of this medium.

In contrast, streaming video has, to date, not been broadly fielded, primarily because quality issues and technical limitations have hobbled its ability to meet the goals of the content provider. Consequently, video on the Net has largely remained in formats designed for CD-ROM delivery such as AVI and QuickTime. Because these formats were not designed for Internet bandwidths, download times are more than 10 times the length of the clip, and the clips are short (frequently only 20–30 seconds) and rarely more than an optional accent.

This chapter answers the technical questions of organizations evaluating whether 1998 is the time to make streaming video a meaningful part of Internet or Intranet offerings. To make this decision, a content provider must answer three main questions:

- Can I create compelling, high-quality content at existing bandwidth levels?

- Will the delivery architecture reach my intended audience under real-world conditions?

- As I proceed with my growth plan, does the technology scale in a cost-effective manner?

Until now, the answer to these questions has been, "No." First-generation streaming video codecs were not sophisticated enough to create a quality experience over dial-up bandwidth, nor were they flexible enough to adapt to high-motion content or to media requiring quality audio. Delivery systems worked in idealized environments but failed to adapt to the lossy nature of the busy Internet. Poor back-end performance mandated a high per-viewer hardware investment, and the architecture did not scale for larger sites and audiences.

RealVideo is the first real-time video technology sophisticated enough to answer "Yes" to all three criteria. This guide describes the technical innovations behind RealVideo and explains how they apply to the real-world problems of deploying rich video on the Internet and intranets. It is the first full featured, cross platform video solution supported by leading industry tools companies and content providers and built on the industry standard protocol for streaming media, RTSP. The availability of these technologies breaks through the barriers that have prevented widespread use of video on the Internet and intranets.

Bandwidth

Visual and audio quality at low bitrates has been the principal factor limiting the adoption of streaming video. RealVideo introduces new compression technologies for video and audio that offer a higher quality experience than previously available. The full-motion video codecs are scaleable for all bitrates and optimized for the two most prevalent Internet connection speeds of 28.8-Kbps and 56-Kbps. The sound quality formerly associated with streaming video is dramatically improved by RealAudio's 3.0 audio compression technology, plus three new low-bitrate codecs for voice and music.

For video to become a true Web data type, site designers must be able to integrate it fully into interactive experiences. RealVideo enables this interactivity through innovations such as clickable video maps, synchronized multimedia, and scriptable plug-ins.

The lack of a tool set supporting the range of needs from simple, template-based authoring to advanced editing has kept the body of available video content small. A full range of RealVideo tools from Progressive Networks and leading third-party companies now supports the productivity and creativity needed to create the most compelling on-demand or live video content.

A streaming video solution must perform well under less than ideal conditions. The RealPlayer client and RealVideo Server jointly provide a high level of flexibility and reliability. Advanced features such as bandwidth negotiation, dynamic connection management, sophisticated error mitigation, and buffered play help assure that the video reaches the content provider's intended audience as a compelling experience.

Scaleable Architecture

Low cost per viewer and a scaleable architecture capable of serving large audiences are essential in order for streaming video to be widely implemented. RealVideo's highly efficient server supports 500–1000 simultaneous streams on a standard PC—several times the capacity of first-generation video solutions.

As an organization's needs grow, it can take advantage of scaleable technologies such as:

IP-Multicasting to save bandwidth on Intranets and where available on the Internet, including MBONE broadcasts

- Creating hierarchical distribution of live content using Splitters

- Clustering to load-balance and maximize performance

- Creating Compelling, High-Quality Content

Uncompressed NTSC (television) video has a basic data rate of roughly 100 Megabits per second. Coding this signal for modem-based network connections implies a compression ratio of 5000:1. By comparison, audio is typically compressed at a rate of roughly 70:1 or less. Clearly, the process of compressing video is challenging.

Video Compression

Attaining subjective visual quality is a key technical hurdle for practical digital video. RealVideo's codecs offer new enhancements that deliver superior image quality at bandwidths that scale from 10-Kbps to over 500-Kbps and are highly tuned for the bandwidth "sweet spots" of 28.8 modems (20-Kbps data rate) and 56K modems/ ISDN (45-Kbps data rate). Without sacrificing clarity, these codecs are able to default size that is 30–40% larger than first-generation video systems.

Real Video's codec-independent architecture supports installable compression algorithms. RealVideo 1.0 provides two codecs, RealVideo Standard (developed by Progressive Networks) and RealVideo Fractal using Clear Video technology from Iterated Systems, Inc. (www.iterated.com). Although both codecs are general purpose, producers can choose the optimal compression for the content and delivery environment.

Requirements and features:

- Recommended for most low bandwidth and Internet uses.

- Performance is good for high action and very low bitrate encoding.

- Decoding processor requirements are higher than for RealVideo Fractal.

- Encoding is faster than RealVideo Fractal, and live encoding is possible on high-end Pentium PCs.

- Performance under packet loss is highly optimized, making RealVideo Standard a good choice for environments such as the Internet where packet losses are expected to be high.

- Recommended for high bandwidth and frame rate applications where packet losses are expected to be low, such as corporate intranets. Artifacts are primarily blocking, with very little ringing. Performance on high action scenes with very rapid motion and cuts is lower than RealVideo Standard, but subjective quality on medium and low action scenes is typically better. Decode performance is excellent, allowing high frame rate (typically 15fps) playback on lower end Pentiums. Encoding is slower than RealVideo Standard, and software live encoding is not available.

Audio Compression

Think of watching a television program with the volume all the way down, or of seeing *Star Wars* without its soundtrack. Obviously, sound carries much of the information and emotional content of a video presentation; however, audio quality has been overlooked in many attempts at streaming video.

To meet the needs of video, two new voice codecs and lower bitrate versions of the RealAudio 3.0 music codec have been introduced. This range of options insures a compelling listening as well as viewing experience. These new voice codecs offer superior voice quality at low bitrates. Use the 6.5-Kbps codec for excellent performance with voice-only content. The 8.5-Kbps codec has slightly better voice quality and better handling of background noises or music.

8- and 12-Kbps Music Codecs

These two music codecs offer quality reproduction of music at low bitrates. Use the 8-Kbps codec for excellent performance on symphonic, background, or other music with little vocal content. Use the 12-Kbps codec for general musical content where vocals are present.

Higher bitrate Music Codecs

Use for music content targeted at 40-Kbps total bandwidth and above. RealAudio's 20-Kbps Stereo codec is an excellent choice for music videos targeting 56-Kbps modems and ISDN.

- Interactivity: Clickable Video Maps and Synchronized Multimedia

- V-Active for RealVideo authoring tool by Ephyx Technologies

Click-able Video Maps are a powerful new feature that allow the user to interact with a video presentation. A mouse click on a region within the video image can cause a new clip to be played, initiate a seek within the current clip, or send a URL to the Web browser through Synchronized Multimedia. Regions are made interactive using an extension of the image-map standard with the added dimension of time creating a rich, interactive content creation opportunity.

The RealPlayer also supports interactivity through embeddable ActiveX and Netscape plug-in controls that support JavaScript and VBScript.

Tools

People creating video content range from Web Masters encoding preproduced files to video professionals designing and producing media optimized specifically for Web. Meeting this range of needs requires a set of tools from simplified template-based authoring to full professional editing suites.

RealVideo's software-only Encoder tools simplify the content creation process by allowing users to select from descriptive option templates such as "High Action 28.8-Kbps with Music". These templates provide reliable default settings and require little knowledge of the compression process. However, users still have the level of control necessary to make adjustments and trade-offs through the Advanced settings dialog. These custom settings can be saved as new templates to guarantee consistent application throughout a site.

To get the best results, content creators need the freedom to enhance and edit video material. Would cleaning up a transition sequence make the clip more compelling? Would a letter box format eliminate wasted background area? Would this content work better with a larger frame size? What if I zoomed in a little more?

Leading third party tools that support RealVideo include:

- Adobe Premiere plug-ins on both Macintosh and Windows

- in:sync Speed Razor

- Terran Interactive's Movie Cleaner Pro

- Ephyx's V-Active for RealVideo

- Automating the Encoding Process

Creating large amounts of timely media for the Web requires that the process of content creation be automated to the greatest extent possible. Regular news broadcasts and the archiving of large amounts of historical content are two examples of content that has been largely automated. To handle this type of automation, the standard RealVideo encoder offers a comprehensive command line mode. Batch processing of large amounts of content is straightforward, and log files are written which can be later parsed to verify completion of encoding and identify any errors that may have occurred.

Delivery Protocols

The Internet presents a variable and sometimes unfriendly environment for delivering streaming media. Throughput and latency can vary greatly due to high loads or poor physical conditions on devices such as dial-up modems. Neither of the two basic Internet protocols offer a turn-key for real-time media delivery. The UDP protocol is efficient but not naturally robust, and the TCP protocol is robust, but not designed for real-time efficiency.

RealVideo solves the problems of efficient and robust streaming through a client/server architecture. The RealPlayer client works with the Server to dynamically adjust the connection for latency, jitter, lost packets, and narrow bandwidth in real time. This approach is similar to a modern computer-controlled automobile that is able to deliver superior performance and mileage by monitoring the engine and dynamically making adjustments for peak efficiency.

The RealPlayer supports both UDP- and TCP-based protocols as well as IP Multicasting. Under some circumstances, such as behind a firewall or on a LAN-based intranet, TCP provides the best starting point. However, in many cases, the added efficiency of UDP-based delivery is required to avoid gapping or pauses in the audio. It also automatically selects the appropriate protocol.

Buffered Play

RealVideo's Buffered Play mode allows users to view clips that will not stream over their connection in real time. This not only provides a fall back when a connection has dropped far below the minimal real-time data rate, but also gives content providers the flexibility to offer media encoded at bit rates that meet their quality standards but might exceed the real-time bandwidth of some viewers. Buffered Play is inclusive in that it allows anyone to experience the content, regardless of bandwidth.

Error-hardened Codecs and Transport

Unlike audio, packet losses to a video stream can cause errors in the image which are persistent over many frames. RealVideo leverages the Robust UDP technology introduced with RealAudio 3.0 to reduce typical Internet packet losses to a level that can be handled by error mitigation without reducing image quality. RealVideo applies to techniques to minimize the impact of bad connections.

Damage-resistant Coding

RealVideo's codecs are tuned to minimize the damage to a video stream caused by lost packets. Subjective quality is kept high by continuing to render images whenever possible, relying on coding methods tuned to confine and dissipate any image damage. High image quality is maintained under typical levels of loss.

Forward Error Correction

When frame rates are low, the longer visual persistence of images requires a greater level of protection to ensure that no visible frame damage occurs. In these cases, RealVideo uses forward error correction (FEC) techniques to allow complete reconstruction of image packets that may be lost. The likelihood of frame damage occurring is reduced, making video frames impervious to all but extremely high levels of packet loss.

Cost Effective Architecture

Enabling the Internet as a mass medium requires a low cost per viewer and technology that continues to perform under the high demands of large audiences. For video over the Internet to be widely adopted requires a solution that scales to meet increasing popularity and the content provider's plans for growth.

Server Software

RealVideo's high-performance design supports 500–1,000 simultaneous 28.8-Kbps streams from a single Pentium-based Server. This compares to first-generation systems that may only be capable of supporting up to 100. Efficient Servers reduce both the hardware cost and maintenance effort. Also, because RealVideo is a cross-platform solution available for all popular versions of Unix and Windows NT, content providers can chose the version that matches their technology base and plan for hardware investment.

RealVideo Servers support live and on-demand streams of both RealVideo and RealAudio. Site managers can more easily balance loads and manage their media assets with this single solution.

Scalable Architecture

As an organization's needs grow beyond a single Server, the technology must be available to scale delivery in a cost-effective, maintainable manner. RealVideo provides a number of key features to enable larger audience reach.

Support for IP Multicasting

RealVideo supports IP Multicasting, a network protocol allowing multiple clients to share a single stream from a server. This uses less bandwidth than sending an individual stream to each client. While multicasting provides excellent efficiency in an intranet environment, few routers on the Internet are configured to support multicast data. In an Internet environment, splitters provide similar benefits.

The RealPlayer automatically senses multicast support and selects that mode if available. As multicast becomes more broadly available, RealVideo content providers can reach this audience without extra configuration or technical knowledge on the part of viewers.

Distributed Serving Using Splitters

In addition to content from live encoders or on-demand files, RealVideo servers can stream live video supplied by another server. This gives greater flexibility and efficiency in delivering live broadcasts to users. Additionally, splitters provide a net-friendly and reliable way to stream media across the Internet backbone.

Load Balancing Using Clustering

Clustering severs together gives large sites an efficient mechanism to balance the load of incoming requests so that viewers receive good performance. This allows sites to exceed the capacity of a single machine and enables the option of fielding an array of less expensive computers as an alternative to a single high-capacity computer.

Creating Video Image Maps

Video image maps are fully customizable—actions can be connected to content regions that are rectangles, polygons, or circles and can be varied over specific user-defined time intervals.

Encoding Content

This section is designed to outline the basic hardware and software requirements to create RealVideo content as well as provide suggestions on style and techniques for achieving optimal results. It contains information for creating on-demand content as well as real-time live broadcasting

Computer Hardware

When encoding video, the rule to be applied is, "more is better." The base machine for production level video creation is a Pentium 200Mhz Windows '95 machine. In general, the faster the machine the faster the video encoding.

Minimum Recommended Hardware—On Demand

Operating System	Windows '95
Video Source	VHS Player
Computer	Pentium 120Mhz
Memory	32MB RAM
Capture Card	Any quality video capture card
Audio Card	Any quality audio card
Video Input	Composite
Hard Drive	1Gb

Recommended Hardware—On Demand

Operating System	Windows '95
Video Source Device	Betacam SP player
Computer	Pentium 166Mhz
Memory	48MB
Capture Card	Any quality video capture card
Video Input	S-Video
Audio Card	Any quality audio card
Hard Drive	3Gb

Video Source

To create the best possible streaming video, you must start with the best possible source material. Different video formats yield different qualities when digitized. The common video formats in order of quality are:

- Betacam-SP also known simply as Beta. This format is common among video production professionals.
- Laserdisc
- S-VHS or Super-VHS
- VHS
  Video playback devices commonly have two types of video outputs, S-video and composite. S-video produces better results.

Capturing or Video Digitizing

Before you can encode RealVideo you must capture (digitize) your source material to your computer. To digitize video you will need a video capture card. To date, the capture cards listed below have been tested. In general, any card that supports Video for Windows can be used.

Video Capture Card	Manufacturer	Live broadcast
Intel Smart Video Recorder	Intel	No
Wakeboard Multimedia Pro	Digital Video Arts	No
DC30	miro	No
DC20	miro	No
Bravado 1000	Truevision	No
Osprey 100	MMAC	Yes
Osprey 1000	MMAC	Yes
Videum AV	Winnov	Yes

Each board has its strengths and weaknesses. RealVideo supports any frame size with a height and width that are multiples of 16. The RealVideo encoder will also accept a 160 x 120 image size. Typically, when creating content for the Internet, use a frame size of 176 x 144. None of these video capture cards support this size natively. The Intel Smart Video Recorder will capture 240 x 180 and 160 x 120, while the DC30, and the Bravado 1000 support 320 x 240 as the smallest capture size. Consequently, you will have to scale and crop your video before encoding it.

While the miro DC30 and Bravado 1000 produce excellent results they capture using the Zoran chip. This chip creates an AVI file that consists of a series of JPEG images, sometimes called Motion-JPEG. With these cards not only do you have to scale the image, you will also have to convert your AVI to a Video for Windows format. Therefore, RealVideo currently recommends the Intel Smart Video Recorder or Osprey 100,1000 which can capture directly to 24-bit RGB uncompressed video.

Editing

To edit video once captured, you will need video editing software. At this time the following are recommended:

- Adobe Premiere
- in:sync Kohesion

The RealVideo Encoder will install an Adobe Premiere plug-in allowing you to encode directly from Premiere.

RealVideo Encoding

AVI Requirements:

- Standard video frame size is 176 x 144, for best results

- Height and Width must both be divisible by 16

- Indeo drivers must be installed on your machine for the encoder to be able to open the AVI. Typically, if you captured the AVI on the same machine as the encoder, the encoder will have no problem opening it. Otherwise, the Indeo drivers are available at the following URL: ftp://ftp.intel.com/pub/.

There are three parameters that can be adjusted to produce RealVideo: Audio codec, video bit rate, and frame rate. The quality of the RealVideo encoding will be affected by these settings and the actual content. Below are content elements that can affect the quality of the encoding at 19-Kbps:

Content Type	**Expected Encoding Results**
Fixed camera shot, low	Good clean frames, with high frame rates
Fixed camera shot, some motion	Clean frames, somewhat slower frame rates
Multiple camera shots, low	Clean frames with 1 fps or greater
Zoom with low motion	Clean frames with moderate frame rate
Fixed camera shot, high motion	Clean frames with moderate frame rate
Multiple shots, high	Clean frames with less than 1 fps

As soon as you consider bandwidth higher than 28.8, the RealVideo encoder will produce significantly better frames with higher frame rates.

When deciding which parameters to set, the total bit rate must be considered. The total bit rate is the actual bit rate at which the AVI will be encoded. If the target bit rate is 28.8, then the total bit rate should be 19-Kbps. Here are the recommended total bit rates for popular bandwidths:

Targeted Modem Rate	**Total Bit Rate**
28.8 kbps	19
56.0 kbps	44
64.0 kbps	56
128.0 kbps	105

The first step is to choose the total bit rate according to the table above. Next choose an audio codec. Since the RealAudio codecs have discreet bandwidths, the video bit rate will be the difference between the total bit rate and the bit rate used by the chosen audio codec:

Video Bit Rate = (Total Bit Rate) - (Bandwidth of Audio Codec).

In the actual interface for the RealVideo encoder the video bit rate will be calculated automatically.

Next the frame rate should be chosen. Not all content types will support high frame rates for a given bandwidth. The highest frame rate that can be achieved at 19-Kbps, will be 7.5 to 10 frames per second (Fps) for talking head type content with decent quality. Different content types will require different frame rates. For example, while talking heads at 19-Kbps might support 7.5-Fps, music videos may support only 1-Fps or less.

NOTE: If you are getting high levels of latency or bit-rates, you are exceeding the bounds of your content type. To solve high latency:

- Choose optimize frame rate to let the encoder adjust the frame rate

- Reduce the screen size (176 x 144 recommended)

- Lower the frame rate (if not using optimize)

How to Broadcast Live in RealVideo

Computer Hardware

Recommended Hardware for Real-Time Live Encoding of 176 x 144 screen sizes

	High frame rate >2 frames per second	Low frame rate <2 frames per second
Operating System	Windows NT	Windows '95
Computer	Dual</B> CPU Pentium 200Mhz or <B>Single</B> CPU Pentium 2, 266Mhz or greater	Pentium 166 Mhz
Memory	64MB	32MB
Capture Card	Osprey 100, Osprey 1000, Videum AV	Osprey 100, Osprey 1000, ISVR III, Videum AV
Audio Card	Any quality audio card	Any quality audio card
Hard Drive	1Gb	1Gb

Computer Software

- RealVideo Encoder
- A minimum of a 60 stream RV RealServer
- RealPlayer

Configuration 1: Low frame rate (.>2 frames per second)

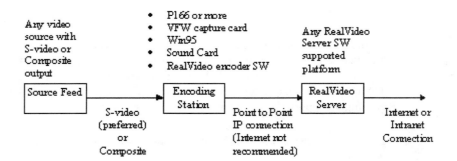

Configuration 2: High frame rate (Up to 10 frames per second*, >;200 streams)

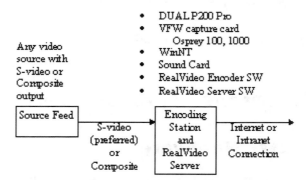

*Actual maximum frame rate is dependent on bit rate and content

Configuration 3: High frame rate (Up to 10 frames per second)

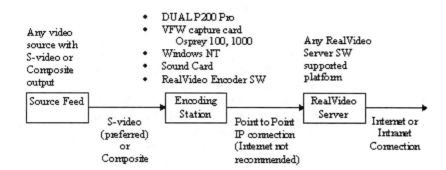

Encoding, Testing and Serving the Live Feed

Start the RealVideo Encoder
   Open session
      Source - Check capture device
         Select Video Capture and Audio Capture Destination
         Check RealMedia File to archive event
         Click on Select and specify a file name
         Check RealServer to broadcast event
         Host—enter Full host name and directory of RealServer
         Password—enter if access is protected
         Resource—enter the name for the live link (i.e. live.rm)
         Port—Enter server port for stream to be sent through
      Options
         Show filtered output (off save CPU cycles—minimize the
         encoder saves even more)
         Set video format
         Display - 24bit RGB
         Source - specify composite or
         Color - RGB24 <=important
            (second best is YVU9 or RGB-555)
         Camera
         NTSC for US standards
         PAL for European
      View
         Statistics—if you want to see result of encoding processes
      Properties
         Check selective record to allow users to record your content
         Enter Author, Title, Copyright

Templates
> Click on advanced and set parameters (see Suggested settings tables)
> Enter a template name for your new settings, click save, click close

Click start—You are now live!
Test your feed
Start the RealPlayer on a separate machine
Select File => Open Location
i.e. pnm://www.testserver.com:7070/live.rm
Create a .ram metafile to point to the live feed
i.e. file name => live.ram
text contents => pnm://www.testserver.com:7070/live.rm
Author an HTML page with reference to the .ram file

NOTE: See "content creation guide" for details on authoring RealVideo as a helper application or imbedded in the HTML

Real-time Live Capture to File

One very efficient way of producing on-demand RealVideo content is using a live, real-time capture station. Instead of only using this for live broadcast, it can be used to capture and compress directly into RealVideo format. This can be accomplished by using your live feed or the output of a video player (Beta, S-VHS, Laser Disc, etc.) and setting the encoder to capture to file instead of capturing to a live server feed. This has the advantage of eliminating the need to create and store the intermediate AVI files which are very large and take considerable disk space. It is also the fastest way to capture if time-to-post is important, such as with breaking news clips.

Broadcasting Live From a Pre-encoded File

A batch utility is included with the encoder which will allow you to create a simulated live event. That is, you can encode a file following the on-demand instructions, then broadcast the file. Users connecting to the link late will get the event "in progress" as though it was a live feed. The utility is called rvslta.exe and comes with the encoder. You can run this from the command line or from a program. The syntax is as follows:

> rvslta /i (nput file name) /o (output file name) /s (server name)
> With optional flags of /p (port number) /w (password).

Example:

> rvslta /i c:/livefile.rm /o livenow.rm /s www.testserver.com

Source Files

To create the best possible streaming video, you must start with the best possible source material. Different video formats yield different qualities when digitized. Because the RealVideo compression algorithms are lossy, some of the information contained in your original input is not included in the reconstructed signal sent to RealPlayer.

The common video formats in order of quality are:

- Betacam-sp also known simply as Beta. This format is common among video productionprofessionals.

- Laserdisc

- S-VHS or Super-VHS

- VHS

Satellite television services (e.g. Direct TV) have extremely high quality video. Their feed quality typically exceeds that of Laserdisc.

Computer Hardware

When encoding video, the faster the computer, the faster the video. Capturing video puts a burden on your computer's ability to write the captured video to your hard drive. Seagate manufactures special hard drives for capturing video called AV drives. If you do not use one of these special drives, frames may be dropped during the capture process when the hard drive recalibrates itself periodically. If you experience dropped frames with a standard drive, you can recapture the video.

Video Capture Cards

Before you can encode RealVideo, you must capture (digitize) your source material to your computer. To digitize video you need a video capture card. In general, any card that supports Video for Windows can be used.

Live Encoding

The quality of live encoding depends on the power of your computer system. Encoding at higher quality takes longer and requires more computing resources than encoding at a lower quality. Slower machines are capable of a good result in Slide Show mode, at 1 fps or less.

Encoding Files to RealVideo

Source Files

RealVideo content may be created either from previously recorded digital video files or from an external video source. The Encoder does not support compressed input files. Use a third-party editing utility to convert non-supported formats to a supported format.

The following inputs are supported. Currently RealVideo supports AVI and QuickTime (or .mov) input files. For best quality, we recommend using uncompressed files with a 24-bit color depth. RealVideo Encoder does support compressed AVI files.

Image Size

RealVideo Encoder 1.0 beta supports any size image. The most standard size is 176 pixels by 144 pixels.

Encoding Templates

RealVideo Encoder has several templates for creating RealVideo files depending on your source file and desired result. You can also create customized templates by adjusting the audio codec, video bitrate, total bitrate quality, and frame speed to meet your particular needs.

Conclusion

This is a rapidly changing technology in which the last word is far from spoken. We can look forward to exciting opportunities for distribution of commercial and amateur video over the Internet and subsequently experiencing the emergence of an entirely new distrubution medium and interactive video art form hunary for original programming. Keep up with both the technologies and the opportunities!

Chapter 18
Digital Versatile Disk (DVD)

Introduction

Since the introduction of the audio compact disc in 1982 and the CD-ROM in 1985, the CD has become a universal carrier for music, data, and multimedia entertainment. It has become the most popular consumer media format ever, yet it soon may be overshadowed by DVD.

Since the CD format first appeared on shelves, consumer electronics and CD manufacturing companies have been working on new techniques to increase the density of the standard 74-minute/650 megabyte optical media format. In 1993, Nimbus Technology and Engineering debuted the first double-density CD format with two hours of MPEG-1 video playback. This was the first demonstration that CD technology could carry high-quality video as well as audio and that a new format might be on the horizon.

After several years of intense development and cross-industry cooperation among consumer electronics companies, computer manufacturers, and the entertainment industry, the DVD format has arrived—and with it a new era of consumer entertainment. For the first time, high-quality digital video as well as surround sound audio can be delivered to the consumer on a single interactive compact disc. Playable on the set-top or the desktop, DVD bridges the worlds of consumer video and personal computing in a single, unified format.

While DVD promises to be a highly-successful consumer electronics format, preparingcontent (premastering) for DVD can be a very complex process. And like most new formats, DVD requires new tools and techniques to create rich and satisfying content that make the most of the medium.

Developing and Pre-mastering

Working with DVD requires an in-depth understanding of the format, production process, and tools required to bring titles to market. By understanding DVD and all that it entails, professional media developers can exploit its rich potential. This book is designed for those who are interested in the DVD format, want to create titles, and wish to understand the tools and technology required for DVD production.

Format

By 1994 cable, satellite, and video-on-demand services were making strong inroads into the home market, competing for the consumer's time and money. The home video industry, seeing increased competition for VHS sales and rentals, recognized the need for a new consumer video format which could deliver superior quality pictures and sound. A consumer format based on the compact disc, which had revitalized the recording industry years before, could provide the solution that Hollywood sought. An advisory committee was formed to create a set of requirements for such a format.

By January of 1995, two digital video disc formats were unveiled: the Super Density (SD) format by Toshiba and a consortium of partners, and the Multi Media Compact Disc (MMCD) by Philips and Sony. With the prospect of a "Beta vs. VHS" format war looming on the horizon, consumer electronics manufacturers and studios formed the DVD Consortium to agree upon a single unified specification for the next generation compact disc. In December of 1995, a general agreement was reached and the DVD was born.

In light of all the possible uses for optical media storage systems, the DVD Consortium has broken down Digital Versatile Disc into several "books" labeled A through E. These books are:

A	DVD ROM
B	DVD Video
C	DVD Audio
D	DVD Recordable
E	DVD Writeable

Figure 18.1 DVD Books

At present, Books A, DVD-ROM, and B, DVD-Video, have been completed and lay the foundation for the DVD media format. Books D, DVD Recordable, and Book E, DVD RAM, have recently been announced, and Book C, DVD-Audio, is expected to be available in 1998.

Physical Specifications

DVD is enabled by technical advances in both optical media data capacity and digital video compression algorithms. On the optical media side, DVD achieves its superior data capacity by increasing the density of the pits on the disc surface as well as by using a more efficient error correction scheme. Increased pit density means more bits are available for storage and better error correction results in more of those bits being available for program or data storage. DVD and CD optical media specifications are as follows:

	DVD	**CD**
Disc Diameter	120 mm (5 inches)	120 mm (5 inches)
Disc Thickness	1.2 mm (bonded .6 mm layers)	1.2 mm
Track Pitch	0.74 mm	1.6 mm
Laser Wave Length	650 or 635 mm red laser	790 nm red laser
Numerical Aperture	0.6	0.45
Minimum Pit Length		0.4 mm
Error Correction	Reed-Solomon Product Code (RS-PC)	CIRC
Signal Modulation	8-16 (EFM+)	8-14 (EFM)
Reference Scanning Velocity	3.49 m/s (Single Layer) 3.84 m/s (Dual Layer)	1.2 to 1.4 m/s
Data Capacity	DVD-5 Single sided, Single layer 4.7 GB DVD-9 Single sided, Dual layer 8.5 GB DVD-10 Double sided, Single layer 9.4 GB DVD-18 Double sided, Double layer 17GB	650 Megabytes
Maximum Data Rate	10.08 Mbps (mega bits per second)	1.4112 Mbps

Figure 18.2 DVD and CD Physical Specifications

Capacity

DVD ranges in capacity from 4.7 gigabytes up to 17 gigabytes. Two sizes for the DVD media are available: 12 cm compact disc size, or 8 cm CD-single size. A DVD can be manufactured four ways: single-sided, double-sided, single-sided with dual layers, double-sided with dual layers.

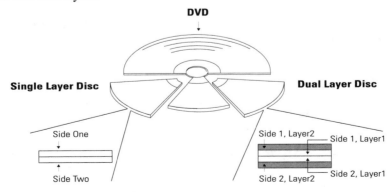

Figure 18.3 DVD Disc Layers

Even though most DVD discs manufactured today are DVD-5 (single-layer, single-sided discs), all DVD discs, regardless of capacity, are made up of two platters bonded back-to-back. This double-sided manufacturing technique increases the rigidity of the media and minimizes warpage.

All compact disc media exhibit some type of warpage. When the plastic used to make a CD cools, it takes on a slight curvature as one side typically cools more quickly than the other. Slight warpage does not present a problem for the laser beam in reading the pits. However, if the warpage is extreme, the laser will not be able to read the disc at all. Due to the increased pit density of the DVD format, the discs are more sensitive to warp and must, therefore, be as flat as possible. One easy way of solving this problem is to bond two separate discs back to back. This results in improved rigidity and the slight curvature induced in manufacturing is offset by the bonding.

All DVD players have the ability to read all of the DVD capacities, from DVD-5 to DVD-18. However, DVD players are not required to read both sides without removing the disc. This means that a single movie can seamlessly extend across an entire side of a disc, and even across dual layers, but seamless playback of a movie that extends across two sides is not possible. In order to play back a second side, the disc must be ejected and flipped over. Some DVD player manufacturers have indicated that they will create players with two lasers, one for the top and another for the bottom, so that a double-sided disc can be read without removing it from the player.

DVD-video Features and Functionality

Following the recommendations of the Hollywood advisory committee, the DVD Consortium included specific audio and video formats as well as interactive functionality into the DVD 1.0 specification. This is a major advantage that DVD maintains over CD-ROM. In CD-ROM, there is no single specification for audio, video, or a file system. This has led many multimedia developers to invent their own audio/video formats for delivering interactive content. Unfortunately, there is no guarantee that content authored and developed for one configuration of a CD-ROM-equipped computer will work with other models. Since DVD has specific audio formats, video formats, and a file system, content authored for DVD has the advantage of cross-platform compatibility. The specific features and requirements for DVD follow.

MPEG Video

MPEG-2 and MPEG-1 are defined as the video formats for DVD. Depending on the country in which a DVD title is released, it will be in either 525/60 (NTSC) format or 625/50 (PAL) format. Player manufacturers are not required to support both NTSC and PAL DVD discs in a single player, so either separate DVD discs must be created for each format, or a disc can be created with PAL on one side and NTSC on the other (assuming that the content fits on one side of a disc). Some manufacturers, however, are introducing combination NTSC and PAL players in the European market.

	NTSC	PAL
Picture Resolution	720 x 480	720 x 576
	704 x 480	704 x 576
	352 x 480	352 x 576
	352 x 240	352 x 288
Number of Picts in GOP	Less than 36 fields	Less than 30 fields
Aspect Ratio	4:3 or 16:9	4:3 or 16:9
Bit Rate (maximum)	9.8 Mbps	9.8 Mbps

* Maximum bit rate for audio, video, and subpicture program data

Figure 18.4 MPEG and Video Formats for DVD

For movie playback on DVD, the MPEG-2 format will typically be used, allowing over two hours of high-quality video to be stored on a single-sided, single-layer DVD. MPEG-1 video may also be used for DVD. Because MPEG-1 video is defined as one-quarter the resolution of a full CCIR-601 video stream, its bit-rate requirements are far less than MPEG-2 (1.856 Mbps is the maximum MPEG-1 bit rate). This enables up to four times as much video, roughly eight hours, to be stored on a single-sided, single-layer DVD. Due to the lower quality, the primary applications for MPEG-1 video on DVD would be long training or informational DVD titles, and in most cases, MPEG-2 is expected to be the preferred format.

Aspect Ratios

In the early film era, a 4:3 aspect ratio was used for filming content. This is the same aspect ratio as 35mm film. When television was invented, the same aspect ratio was used. As film technology improved, wider aspect ratios such as Cinemascope became popular as a means of differentiating film from television. Meanwhile, television has retained its 4:3 aspect ratio, forcing movie makers to change the aspect ratio of their film for display on television. One way to do this is a pan/scan process where the wide aspect ratio film is tracked across the narrow 4:3 display area of the video. This results in a video image which is cropped but tracks the most important elements of the program.

The other approach is to "letterbox" the movie by scaling down the film aspect ratio to fit within the confines of the 4:3 aspect ratio. This results in black bars at the top and bottom of the television screen. In an effort to support the aspect ratio standards of film, a 16:9 aspect ratio was developed for DVD. This is not an aspect ratio actually used in film, but is a close compromise and is the same used in the HDTV format. With 16:9 wide-screen televisions and projection systems becoming more popular in home theaters and with the objective to deliver a cinema-like experience, the architects of the DVD format included 16:9 support.

If the source video used for the disc is anamorphic (vertically expanded to fit a 16:9 aspect ratio onto a 4:3 video source) it may be viewed as a full-screen image (not letterboxed) on a wide-screen television. If the same content is played back on a standard 4:3 television, the user can select between vertically expanded (everyone looks tall and narrow), letterboxed (black bars appear at the top and bottom of the screen), or pan/scan (the image is full screen but the sides are cropped and the viewable area pans and scans the action). In order for the player to correctly pan/scan the MPEG-2 anamorphic image across the screen, the pan/scan vectors must be encoded into the data stream. Pan/scan vectors can either be created by a producer or imported with a source file, and are encoded into the data stream during authoring.

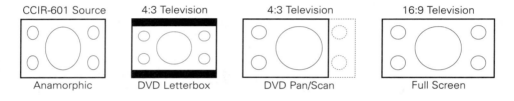

Figure 18.5 DVD Aspect Ratios

Angles

One of the unique aspects of the DVD format is the ability to place multi-angle video streams on a disc. Up to nine angles may be present within a video program. This feature provides multiple points of view for sporting events, music videos, and movies. For example, with a single click, the viewer can instantly change angle without any break in video or audio continuity. From a production standpoint, the maximum bit-rate of each of the video streams must drop slightly to accommodate the data interleaving required, but the overall quality of each angle still remains very high.

Audio

While the initial emphasis on DVD has been video, the industry has been quick to understand that high-quality, multi-channel audio* dramatically differentiates DVD from all other video formats. No other media allows for switching between languages or enables such a range of compressed and non-compressed audio delivery formats.

The three primary audio formats for DVD are PCM (pulse code modulated), Dolby Digital, and MPEG. For NTSC countries and discs, PCM and Dolby Digital may be used with MPEG audio as an option. In PAL countries, PCM and MPEG audio may be used with Dolby Digital as an option. Additionally, the DVD specification includes both DTS (Digital Theater Systems) and SDDS (Sony Dynamic Digital Sound) as options as long as a stream of PCM, Dolby Digital or MPEG audio is present.

* Up to 8 channels of 48 kHz; up to 4 channels of 96 kHz

	PCM	Dolby Digital	MPEG-1	MPEG-2
Bit rate	6.144 Mbps max.	448 kbps max.	384 kbps max.	912 kbps max.
Frequency	48/96 kHz	48 kHZ	48 kHz	48 kHz
Channels	1 to 8	1 to 5.1	2	8

Figure 18.6 Audio Formats for DVD

The DVD format supports up to eight independent audio streams on a single disc. Each stream may be stored in any of the available DVD audio formats (with the regional PAL/NTSC caveats noted above). The viewer can use the DVD remote control to switch between audio streams, which may contain different language versions of a soundtrack, a different mix, or a different format.

Still Images

To deliver high-quality still images, as well as enable the menus that are required to navigate through interactive elements, the DVD specification allows single frames of video to be encoded in full-color and full-resolution. Although primarily used for menu backgrounds, still images can also be used for still shows and slide shows. A still show is a sequence of video images that can be advanced manually by the user while a slide show is fully automated. In both cases, still images may have audio, even full surround sound, associated with them.

Subpicture Overlays

To enable the multi-language subtitling capabilities required by the entertainment industry, the DVD specification includes subpicture overlays—images which are generated by the DVD player on playback and can be keyed over background video or still images. To increase flexibility, subpictures are not limited to text information but may be any bitmap graphic up to the 720 x 480 (NTSC) or 720 x 576 (PAL) resolution. Uses for subpictures include subtitles, karaoke lyrics, buttons, animations, instructions, etc.

Subpicture overlays can be changed on a frame by frame basis and may fade in or fade out, wipe in color or transparency, or scroll up and down the screen. There is a limitation in the number of colors that can be represented, however—only four single-bit color layers are available. Each of these colors is mapped based on a 16-color palette chosen for each program chain (more on program chains later).

Parental Control

DVD is the first video format that can actively change the content based on movie rating. Using the same mechanisms that enable the format to switch between a director's cut of a movie and the theatrical release, the DVD format allows a rating to be assigned to a particular movie clip. When a DVD is placed into a player, the rating level of the movie is mapped against the rating levels set in the player; a DVD player set to play only PG movies will automatically switch to a PG version of the movie. If an R-rated DVD does not have a PG variation of the movie, the player will refuse to play the disc.

Copy Protection

One of the entertainment industry's most important requirements for DVD was copy protection. With both VHS piracy and CD bootlegging threatening worldwide entertainment media sales, major movie studios were unwilling to release near-master quality video and audio on a digital format which could be easily copied with no generation loss.

With the contribution of the cross-industry Copy Protection Technical Working Group (CPTWG), several methods of asset protection were included in the DVD format. The protection is both analog and digital. Macrovision is used to prevent copying the high-quality analog video output from the DVD player onto a VHS deck, and an encryption scheme is used to scramble the digital data streams. Encrypted data can only be decrypted with a hardware chip in the DVD player or through specially designed software for PC-based DVD decoding.

Regional Coding

The movie industry often selects different release dates for theatrical films and videos for different areas of the world. This may be done so that the VHS version of a film doesn't debut before the theater version or to allow time for the feature to be re-edited or dubbed into a new language for the target country.

In order to ensure that entertainment companies have control over the international distribution and timing of high-quality DVD title releases, the DVD specification divides the world into six regions:

Region 1	North America
Region 2	Japan and Europe
Region 3	Southern Asia
Region 4	Central and South America and South Pacific
Region 5	Asia and Africa
Region 6	China

Figure 18.7 Regional Coding

Each DVD player is hardware-coded for a single region and every DVD title is coded for one or more regions. For a DVD disc to play back, the regions of the title and the player must match; for example, DVD titles encoded as region 2 for Japan will not play back in U.S. players, which would only play discs encoded for region 1.

Compatibility

All DVD-Video players will play CD-Audio discs. Additionally, all DVD-ROM readers will play CD-ROM discs. Depending on the manufacturer, DVD-Video players may also include support for VideoCD and LaserDisc, but this is not a required element of the DVD specification.

For DVD-Video discs to play back in a DVD-ROM-equipped personal computer, the PC must contain both a DVD-ROM reader and hardware or software to decode the audio and video formats in the DVD specification. Due to the complexity of MPEG-2 video decoding and the audio output requirements for Dolby Digital audio, most PC manufacturers have elected to use hardware-based DVD decoding technology. It is possible for DVD content to be decoded in software but it requires an extremely fast CPU optimized for multimedia. While this may be an option for DVD-equipped PCs in the future, those who wish to upgrade their existing PCs will need to rely on DVD-specific hardware in the form of an add-in card.

The Structure of DVD-Video

The File System

The DVD format cleverly defines a specific file system for all types of DVD applications. To overcome the problems of multiple file systems in the CD format, DVD specifies a single file format across DVD Books A through D. This file system is the UDF/ISO-9660 Bridge Format. UDF (Universal Disc Format) was designed specifically for optical media and is an evolution of the ISO-9660 format. The benefit of this single file system is the ability for DVD media to be compatible across set-top players and personal computers with DVD-ROM readers.

The Volume Structure

The top level of organization on a DVD disc is the volume. The volume is made up of the UDF Bridge file system, a single DVD-Video Zone which contains all of the data elements for the set-top video title, and a DVD Others Zone which can be used for non-DVD-Video data elements like desktop computer applications.

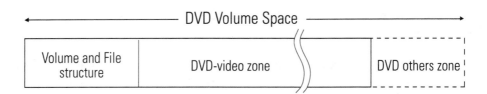

Figure 18.8 DVD Volume structure

The DVD-Video Zone begins with a Video Manager, which is a master directory for the data elements on the disc, followed by 1 to 99 Video Title Sets which include the video and audio elements. The Video Manager usually contains an introductory clip of video and audio, such as an opening logo, and a title menu which allows for navigation to the Video Title Sets. When the Title button on a DVD remote control is pressed, it will take the user back to this Title menu.

Video Title Sets and Video Objects

Following the Video Manager are the Video Title Sets; these usually comprise the bulk of the DVD disc. A DVD can contain multiple title sets, but most feature films would include only one, for the movie. A Video Title Set (VTS) is made up of a VTS Menu and one or more Video Titles. Titles, in turn, can be broken down into Part of Titles (PTT), which are akin to chapters in LaserDisc.

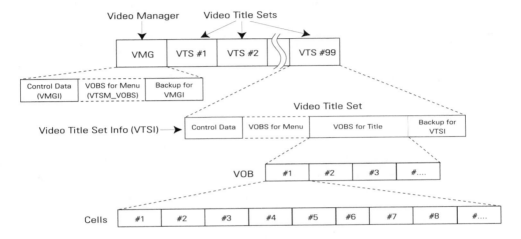

Figure 18.9 DVD-Video Zone structure

The data within the Video Title is made up of Video Object Sets (VOBS), which are themselves made up of one or more Video Objects (VOB). A video object is made up of the video, audio, subpictures, and navigation data for a program. It is the VOB which is the fundamental media file element of the DVD disc.

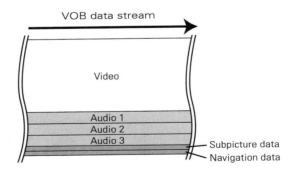

Figure 18.10 VOB Data Stream

The lowest branch of the DVD structure is the Cell. Each VOB can be broken down into one or more Cells. A Cell may be as large as the entire movie or as small as an MPEG GOP (more on MPEG GOPs later). This is the smallest unit that can be addressed by interactive playback.

As an example of the above structures, let's consider a simple movie with twelve chapters. The movie would have one Video Manager, one Video Title Set, one Title, one VOBS made up of one VOB, and twelve Cells.

The reason for having multiple Title Sets and VOBS becomes apparent when highly-interactive titles are created. For example, a DVD might include an interactive music video program with fifteen artists, each with five music videos, artist bios, and slideshows containing album covers with surround-sound music in the background. In this case the disc would have: one Video Manager, fifteen Video Title Sets, multiple Titles for each music video, as well as the artist bio and slideshow. The reason for this division is that the DVD remote control has both Title and Menu buttons. The user would click the Title button to return to the main DVD menu to select a title, or click on the Menu button to go to the menus for the particular title being viewed.

Interactivity

As evidenced by the data structures described above, DVD can be a highly interactive format. It is interactive both in the range of controls the user has in selecting the data presented and in the way the format has been structured to enable multiple story lines and interactive games. As a descendant of the Video-CD format, DVD has inherited much of the VCD hierarchical branching-menu style of interactivity allowing a user to navigate through a disc by jumping from menu to menu or video to video. Most LaserDisc-style DVD movies will have basic interactivity, limiting the user to menu choices such as language, biographies of the actors, or a chapter menu to jump into the disc at various points.

On a deeper level, DVDs can be authored for extensive user interaction during the course of a disc's play. A good example would be an interactive movie requiring the user to choose the outcome of each scene.

By selecting a direction on the remote control, the user can tell the DVD player to move up, down, left, or right. The player then branches to the appropriate video scene and continues to play.

User Interface

The user interface to the DVD player is a remote control. All DVD player manufacturers are required to have similar buttons and functionality on their remotes, including play, stop, pause, next program, previous program, title menu, root menu, up, down, left, right, enter, and return. Additionally, remotes must include a numeric keypad for number entry, although this may be hidden in an access panel within the remote control.

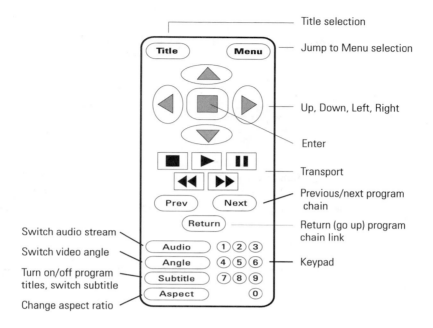

Figure 18.11 DVD Player Remote Control

Presentation and Playback

Program Chains

The way in which a DVD plays back video is directed by program chains (PGCs). While the VOBs represent the multiplexed audio, video, and subpicture overlay, the PGC instructs the DVD player on how those VOBs should be played back, under what conditions they should play, and in what order. Program chains are the maps used by the DVD player to navigate through the data on the disc.

Each program Chain in made up of a pre-command, a group of programs, and a post-command. The pre-command sets the condition for the VOBs which follow, such as which audio stream will be played, or whether a program has recently been viewed. This is followed by a list of cells within the VOB to be played back. Lists of cells are similar to Edit Decision Lists (EDLs) in that two different programs may reference the same Video Objects, but include different subsets of cells, such as an R-rated program and a PG-rated program. In the example in Figure 8, PGC-1 shows a video clip with rain and lightning while PGC-2 shows only rain, even though both program chains are playing back the same video and audio streams.

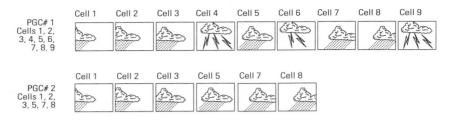

Figure 18.12 Program Chain composition

After the programs have been presented, a post-command can be used to set a link to another program chain, return to a main menu, or any one of up to 128 possible commands from the DVD command set which make up the the navigation control for DVD presentation.

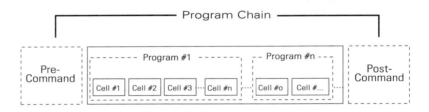

Figure 18.13 Program Chain structure

Navigation Commands

The 128 navigation commands which can be used in the program chain are broken down into a few basic categories: Jump and Link, Calculation, Comparison, Parameter Setting, and Program Flow. Through the use and combination of these commands, complex functions can be performed, such as keeping a game score, randomizing title playback, or ensuring that a unique ending is chosen for a movie. To group multiple commands or move between Video Title sets, Dummy Program Chains can be used. These dummy PGCs do not hold any VOBs and are only used for their pre- and post-command areas.

Menus

Virtually all DVD titles will use menus as a way for users to interact with the program content. Menus are comprised of a background image (either motion video or still frames), a subpicture overlay, a button highlight area, and sometimes even audio. If the DVD is set up for a 16:9 aspect ratio, three different sets of buttons and highlights must be created, one set for each possible display mode; wide-screen, letterbox, and pan/scan.

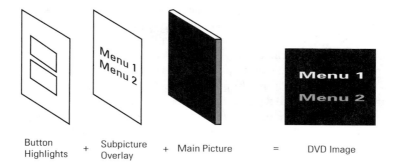

Button Highlights + Subpicture Overlay + Main Picture = DVD Image

Figure 18.14 DVD Menu composition

Menus can be designed in many different ways. A background image can be a motion video or a 24-bit color still. Choices displayed on-screen can be created as part of the background image to take advantage of the 24-bit color depth or they can be created as subpicture overlays using the four possible colors. In either case, a button highlight is superimposed on top and can represent the selection and action of a button. Using subpicture overlays provides the fastest navigation; however, background images can be changed if greater color depth or image variety is desired.

A button highlight is defined as a rectangular region of the screen which can have a color and transparency for both a selection and an action. The highlight region can also key a highlight color over a predetermined color in a background image or subpicture. For example, a text selection may be in black, but when it is selected, the letters turn green. This allows the highlight region to color complex shapes, even though the highlight area is limited to x and y coordinates that define a box.

The DVD specification defines a certain number of menus available to the user through the press of a button on the remote control. These are known as systems menus and are defined as Title, Root, Part-of-Title, Audio, Angle, and Subpicture.

- The Title menu resides in the Video Manager and is used to access Titles on the disc. It may be accessed with the Title DVD remote button.
- The Root menu resides in each Video Title Set and can be accessed with the Menu DVD remote button.
- Audio, Angle, and Subpictures menus reside within each VTS and can be used to change audio stream, video angle, and subpicture stream.

Whenever a system menu is accessed, the DVD player remembers where in the video stream it was playing and can then return to the same location after the viewer is finished looking at the menu or making a selection, such as a language or subpicture stream.

Although there is an area in the Video Title Set and Video Manager for menus to be placed, all of the interactivity, subpictures, and highlights are also available within the course of VOB playback. In this sense, there is no conceptual difference between a movie and a menu. The main difference is that by placing menus in the Video Manager and Video Title Set, the user can quickly jump to them using the remote control. By thinking of a movie as a menu, one can conceptualize the rich set of user interactions that are possible. For example, a movie may be playing back when a subpicture appears, indicating a choice the user can make in the direction of the story. By clicking the left or right button on the remote, a highlight command indicates the selection, while pressing Enter links to a new program chain. These types of in-play menus can have a specific time associated with them and continually change as the movie plays on.

System and General Parameters

DVD players are equipped with two kinds of memory parameters, System and General. The System parameters are used by the DVD player to remember default settings such as language, aspect ratio, and parental rating level. These parameters can be set by the user or by the DVD title in play.

In order to increase the interactivity of a DVD title, the DVD specification requires players to have sixteen 16-bit memory locations that can be used for basic computations or value storage. These are known as General parameters and can only be addressed by the DVD disc in play. One example of the use of general parameters is the storage of values, such as the number of game lives or the previous direction of a story for interactive titles and games.

Title Examples

Given the flexibility of the DVD format, a wide range of possibilities exists for title design. The following example shows a simple DVD title with a Title menu, a PTT (Chapter) menu branching to multiple chapter points, a Language menu stemming to an Audio menu and a Subtitle menu, and a still image for the actor's biography. Many of the Hollywood-style DVD movies are using templates similar to this.

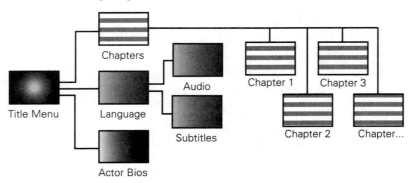

Figure 18.15 Basic movie DVD

An example of a slightly more complex title would be a DVD of music videos featuring different artists. In the template below, the title begins with a Title menu which branches into a list of titles, an audio menu, and a Subtitle menu. The menu listing each title is used to branch to individual Title sets (VTS) on the DVD, one for each artist. Within each VTS, there is a choice of videos or artist biography. By laying out a title in the manner below, a user can select the DVD remote control's Title button to return to a list of all artists on the disc while selecting the Menu button will return to information about the artist currently being viewed.

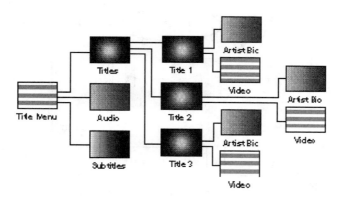

Figure 18.16 Music video DVD

DVD titles can quickly become quite complex. Once motion video menus are included, general parameters are used, and multiple storylines are devised, the template for a highly interactive title can fill a blackboard. Other possible DVD titles include interactive training manuals, multi-language education, archival video and audio storage, interactive movies, games, and hybrid DVD-ROM and DVD-Video titles.

DVD-ROM and DVD-Video

There are several ways to approach DVD-ROM. It can be thought of as a way to store general information, as a platform for reissuing older CD-ROM titles with MPEG-2 video and surround audio, or as a whole new medium for title development leveraging off of the flexibility of the DVD-Video format.

As was discussed earlier, DVD-Video includes a DVD Others Zone. This area of the DVD disc may be used to store standard computer data files, creating a hybrid DVD disc which can be played back on both DVD set-top players as well as PCs equipped with DVD-ROM readers. This type of hybrid disc can have both set-top interactivity and video while sharing files with an application written especially for a personal computer. An example of

DVD hybrid title would be a feature film which, when placed in a set-top DVD player, has simple interactivity but when placed in a DVD-ROM equipped PC, has additional games and links to the movie studio's web site. These types of Hybrid DVD discs are already in production and will undoubtedly bring additional value to the format.

DVD PreMastering

The process of taking video and audio assets and turning them into a final DVD disc image is called DVD premastering. In this segment, we will explore the tools and techniques required to premaster a DVD.

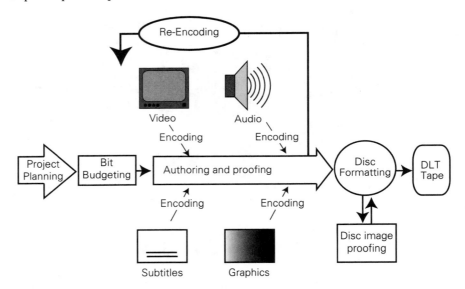

Figure 18.17 DVD Production workflow

The DVD premastering process can be broken down into several key steps: project planning, bit budgeting, asset capture, authoring, proofing, and formatting. Each of these steps relies on the others for complete title production. While some of the different processes involved are not required to be in the same physical location, the more tightly they can be integrated and controlled, the more efficient the title production process becomes.

Project Planning

The first step in DVD production is to define the scope and basic structure of the project. This may range from a simple movie with limited interactivity to a multi-angle, multi-story adventure game. By determining the level of interactivity required, the premastering facility can begin to create a DVD flowchart or project template which will be used to guide the premastering process. Building a project template begins by asking the right questions.

How Interactive Is the Project?

If a DVD project is a straightforward, linear-play title, interactivity is not a major concern in the project planning stage. A simple flowchart can be designed to represent the Title and Root menus. If, however, a title such as a video game requires intense interactivity, an elaborate project template must be created. The more interactive a title, the more time and resources it will take. If multiple video angles and general parameters are used, additional time must also be spent on video preparation and authoring.

How Many Languages Are Required?

Multi-language discs may be handled in several ways. First, multiple soundtracks may be placed along with the video. Second, subtitles may be used to represent languages other than those used for the soundtrack. Third, different menu structures may be generated for each language to correspond to the default language programmed into the System Parameters of the DVD player. Depending on the level of language support, more or fewer resources will be required.

What Is the Look and Feel of the Project?

A DVD title's look and feel is most often determined by the art direction taken in menu design and remote control interaction. The more elaborate the title design, the longer it can take in production. For example, motion menus with surround sound are much more exciting than static still frames, yet they require more disc space and greater authoring skills.

On the other hand, using few still menus might not make a title intriguing from an interactive standpoint, but it can make title production faster. Once there is a clear idea of the scope of the DVD title, the bit budgeting process can begin.

Managing Assets

From the Project Template, a list of required source assets can be derived. Assets will include video sources, audio sources, graphic files and subtitle files. For a basic 120-minute movie with English, Spanish, and French audio tracks, subtitles, and graphical menus, one would need the following source assets:

Video	Digital video source tapes for the movie and any associated trailers
Audio	English surround source
	Spanish stereo source
	French stereo source
Graphics	TIFF graphic files for every menu in each language (average of about 20 files)
Subtitles	Bitmap files for each subtitle graphic (approximately 1500 subtitles per movie per language)

Figure 18.18 Asset List for DVD production

Once the general project plan is complete, the next step is to allocate the 4.7 GB of data (on a DVD-5) to audio, video, subpicture, etc. We call this process "bit budgeting."

Bit Budgeting

Although DVD storage capacity is significantly greater than that of CD-ROM, it is still limited to 4.7, 8.5, 9.4, or 17 GB of data storage depending on the number of sides and layers of the disc. Because space is not unlimited, the capacity of the DVD disc and the length and type of title dictate how much audio and video can be stored and the relative bits that can be allocated to each. A standard DVD player has a maximum data delivery rate of 10.00 Megabits per second (Mbps) for video, audio, and subpictures. Given the length of the program, the audio configuration, and the size of the disc, one can calculate how the bits will be delegated for video, audio, subpictures, and interactivity.

The Bit Budgeting Process

Since one of the original goals of DVD was to store an entire movie on one side of a disc, we will use DVD-5 (4.7 GB) in the following example. Let's imagine that you had a 120-minute movie with three audio soundtracks, four subtitle tracks, and some limited interactivity. With some simple calculations we can determine what our bit budget is going to be for the program.

Total Delivery Capability

While the DVD specification uses Gigabytes to describe the storage capacity of a disc, it does so differently than the computer industry. Gigabyte in the DVD specification refers to 1.0 billion bytes (1000^3). while in computer terminology, a Gigabyte is defined as 1.073

billion bytes (10243). Thus when the DVD specification defines a DVD-5 as having 4.7 Gigabytes of capacity it means 4.7 billion bytes, which in computer industry terms is actually 4.37 Gigabytes. To remain consistent with DVD convention, we will use DVD specification terminology.

To continue with our calculation of a bit budget for a DVD-5:

Step 1

4.7 GB (DVD-5) x 10003 (bytes/GB) x 8 (bit/bytes)/1,000,000 (bits/megabit) = 37,600 megabits per disc
To be safe, we should allow some room for overhead; let's say in this case, we reserve four percent of the disc for menu graphics, navigation information, and an extra cushion.

37,600 megabits per disc x .96 = 39,167 megabits per disc

Step 2

To determine what our average data rate should be for a 120-minute movie, we divide the total capacity (net of our reserve for overhead) by the number of seconds of our program material.

39,167 megabits/(120 mins. x 60 sec/min) = 5.44 megabits per second

So, to fit our 120-minute movie onto a DVD-5 which holds 4.7 GB, the average data rate for our program material must be 5.44 Mbps or less.

Step 3

Now that we've determined our average bit rate per second across the entire program, we must decide how to allocate this capacity between video, audio, and subpicture overlays.

In our example, we chose to have three language soundtracks. Let's assume that the first is in English in Dolby Digital surround, the second in Spanish in Dolby Digital stereo, and the third in French in MPEG stereo. With this configuration, the following bits would typically be allocated to audio:

Audio Stream	Bit rate
English - Dolby Digital surround	.384 Mbps
Spanish - Dolby Digital stereo	.192 Mbps
French - MPEG - 1 layer II	.192 Mbps
Total	.768 Mbps

Figure 18.19 Audio bit rates

Step 4

Subpictures (or subtitles) don't consume much space, but we still have to factor them into the equation. For subtitles, we would reserve .040 Mbps per track. With four subtitles, an average bit-rate of .16 Mbps must be allocated.

Step 5

Note that audio and subpicture tracks are encoded at a constant bit rate across the entire program (though there is some discussion about variable bit rate audio encoding for the future). Let's combine them and figure out the allocation for video.

	Bit Rate (Mbps)
Average total bite rate for 120 minute program	5.38
Less:	
•All audio tracks (English, Spanish, French):	.768
•Subpicture	0.16
Average bit rate for video	4.45

Table 18.20 Video bit rate

After deducting the bit rates for audio and subpicture overlays, we have determined that we can encode our video at an average of 4.51 Megabits per second.

To determine the maximum bit rate, subtract the audio and subtitle overhead from the maximum DVD bit rate of 9.8 Mbps. In this case, the maximum bit rate would be 9.8 - 0.93 = 8.87 Mbps.

To ensure the highest quality, it's always advisable to use as much of the space on a DVD disc as possible, because in DVD, the average data rate for video affects the quality of the picture—encoding at a higher bit rate will give you a higher quality picture.

Now that we have allocated our bits among overhead, graphics, audio, subpicture and video, we can begin capturing our assets. For long programs such as the 120-minute movie in this example, most publishers would use variable bit rate encoding (more on this below) to achieve the highest quality video across the entire program.

One important thing to note about the DVD format is that the average bit rate allocated to the video stream will vary depending on the length of the program. For a DVD-5 disc, this means that the shorter the program, the higher the possible bit rate allowed for encoding (up to the maximum of 9.8 Mbps).

Assuming that we kept the same audio and subpicture configuration (three language tracks and four subtitle streams), the table below shows how the average bit rate for video would vary depending on the length of the program.

Length of program (minutes)	Audio/Subpicture (Mbps)	Video	Average bit rate across total program
30	.928	8.87	9.80
60	.928	8.87	9.80
90	.928	6.24	7.17
120	.928	4.45	5.38
150	.928	3.37	4.30

Figure 18.21 Average bit rate variance

Since a DVD set-top player can play a maximum of 9.8 Mbps, short programs (60 minutes or less) could be encoded at a constant bit rate of 8.8 Mbps. As the program increases in length, the overall average bit rate declines, and hence variable bit rate encoding should be used to yield higher overall image quality.

Note that these bit budgeting examples are based on the capabilities of standard DVD set-top players. Though many PCs will have DVD cards, for PC playback you may need to lower the average bit rates further to accommodate the limitations of software decoding. For hybrid discs, you would need to reserve space for the "DVD other" files before allocating the remainder to audio, video, and subpicture.

Without an accurate bit budget, premastering can be a little like shooting in the dark—you just hope you come in at or below your maximum size when you create your disc image. If you go over, you throw away the disc image (and the hours it took to create it), re-encode one or more assets at a lower bit rate and hope that on the second (or later) try you get it right.

You can also manually calculate your bit budget, then check and add all the pieces up as you encode them to make sure that you don't go over, but this is tedious and time-consuming, if it gets done at all. In order to facilitate the bit budget calculation process, a built-in bit budget display that tracks the project as you assemble your assets to help you stay within the budget can be a valuable tool.

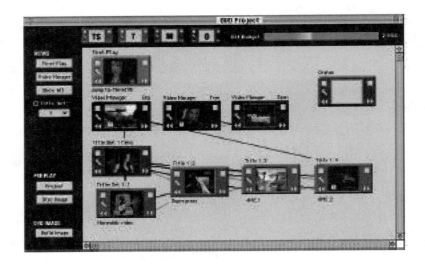

Figure 18.22 Sonic DVD Producer with bit budget display

Multi-angle Considerations

In order to enable multi-angle video streams in DVD, the Video Objects must be interleaved. This process allows up to nine video angles to co-exist, with the viewer able to switch seamlessly between them. One might imagine that multiple video angles in a data stream would drastically cut into the maximum bit rate for the Video Object. This, however, is not the case. To play back multiple angles, the DVD player skips over blocks of data which contain information that is not being viewed. This skipping process allows the bit rate for each of the angles to remain relatively high. The restrictions for multi-angle video are a maximum bit rate of 7.0, 7.5, or 8.0 Mbps for video, audio, and subpictures combined. The difference in maximum bit rate is determined by the location of the VOBs on the DVD disc and the maximum jump distance.

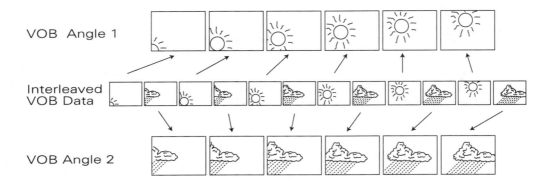

Figure 18.23 Interleaved video angles

Asset Capture

MPEG-2 and Video Compression

High quality video compression is the enabling technology for DVD. To illustrate the level of compression required for two hours of high quality video, consider this: the raw data rate for uncompressed CCIR-601 resolution 4:2:2 serial digital video is roughly 20 MB per second. For a 120-minute movie, this would require 144 GB of storage space, before accounting for audio. With DVD capable of storing 4.7 GB of data, compression ratios of roughly 32:1 are required in order to fit the video for a feature film along with audio and subtitles on a single-sided DVD-5 disc.

To address this compression problem, the Motion Picture Experts Group developed MPEG-2 video compression. This data compression scheme is based on the principle that temporal and spatial redundancy in motion pictures makes up the majority of the visual information that humans perceive. By comparing changes from frame to frame and removing as much of the information as possible, data storage and transfer requirements are reduced.

GOP Structures

An MPEG-2 stream is made up of three types of frames, defined as I-frames, B-frames, and P-frames, Of the three frame types, only I-frames contain the complete pixel information of a video frame, thus providing the backbone of the MPEG-2 video stream. A standard sequence of I-B-B-P-B-B-P-B-B-P-B-B-P-B-B-I would have a Group of Picture (GOP) of 15, with 15 representing the interval at which I-frames repeat.

I-frames   Intra-frames are single compressed frames which contain all of the spatial information of a video frame.

P-frames   Predictive frames are computed based on the nearest previous I or P-frame. P-frames are more highly compressed than I-frames and provide a reference for the calculation of B-frames.

B-frames   Bi-directional frames use both a past and a subsequent frame as a reference to calculate the compressed frame data.

Figure 18.24 MPEG picture definitions

I-frames are the building block of the MPEG-2 sequence. B- and P-frames are based on the notion that the video sequence will not change drastically between I-frames, which would impair the B- and P-frames from accurately representing the motion of pixel information from one I-frame to the next. In video production, however, rapid scene changes and excessive motion can have negative impacts on the quality of the compressed video.

Thus, the sequence of I-B-P frames must often be modified. This is usually done by adding or "forcing" I-frames, usually on scene cuts. In this way, each new scene can start with a fresh I-frame which is then used for the calculation of subsequent

B and P Frames

By definition, I-frames contain much more information than B- and P-frames. As I-frames are inserted into the picture sequence to accommodate scene changes, the data requirements and the bit rate for MPEG videos increase.

DVD requirements for PTT (chapter points) and Cell boundaries also make demands on the GOP structure of the MPEG video. Any time an entry point for a chapter designation is needed in an MPEG-2 stream, a GOP header must be present. A GOP header exists at the beginning of each group of pictures and contains information about the MPEG structure which follows. This may require that the GOP structure be changed so that an exact entry point can be made. For example, a chapter entry may need to start at the first video frame following a scene change. If the MPEG GOP sequence places a B- or P-frame at that same location, it will force the entry point to move to the nearest GOP sequence header, which would be wrong. To avoid the situation, the GOP structure must be changed for that area of the video stream and re-encoded.

VBR Encoding

Video source material can vary dramatically in its complexity. As the video information changes throughout the course of a movie or video, so will the demands on the MPEG encoding process. As the difficulty of the source material increases, the quality of the resulting MPEG video decreases for a given bit rate. Difficult material includes grainy or noisy source footage, rapid scene changes, and areas of high detail. Because MPEG compression is based on spatial and temporal redundancy, any video content that is highly non-redundant can be difficult to compress.

There are two solutions to the problem of varying video complexity; increase the bits allocated to the video or decrease the complexity of the source. By raising the bit rate, more bits are allocated per frame and the picture quality is maintained. Alternatively, the video may be preprocessed to reduce redundancy and image complexity. For optimum MPEG picture quality, a combination of both is often required.

MPEG-2 video running at a bit rate of 4.0 Mbps is required to place a 120-minute movie onto DVD-5. Depending on the source material, this bit rate may not be high enough to maintain a constant quality. This limitation may be overcome, however, by maintaining an average bit rate of 4.0 Mbps and raising or lowering the bit rate over time to suit the complexity of the source material. By allowing the bit rate to vary up to a maximum of 9.8 Mbps in difficult areas, the DVD specification takes into account the need for short bursts in the data rate to accommodate complex scenes where additional I-frames or higher overall bit allocation are necessary to prevent visible compression artifacts. This is compensated for by lowering the bit rate in other, less complex source areas. This technique is known as Variable Bit Rate (VBR) MPEG-2 encoding, and is critical for optimal picture quality.

Figure 18.25 shows how changes in source video complexity can affect quality and bit-rate demands of MPEG-2 video encoding.

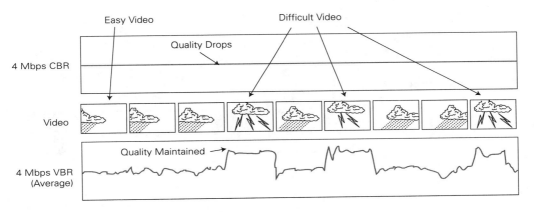

Figure 18.25 Variable bit rate encoding

Preprocessing

Video noise and frame redundancy are two areas in which the source video may be improved or modified to make compression more successful. Noise in a video stream is the equivalent of random information. Since MPEG-2 is based on detecting similar information between frames, noise represents a problem because it can be totally random on a frame by frame basis. Noise can come in the form of grainy film, dust, snow, or extremely detailed textures such as a white stucco wall or a waterfall. By applying a digital noise reducer or low-pass filter prior to encoding, high-energy noise may be reduced, resulting in a video stream which has less random information and is thus "easier" to encode by a temporal compression algorithm like MPEG .

Inverse Telecine

Frame redundancy is another area in which preparation prior to encoding can improve MPEG-2 video. Redundancy of video information is built into every video stream that originates on film. The telecine process, in which film is transferred to video, creates additional redundancy. During telecine, individual frames of film are duplicated at regular intervals during the 3:2 pull-down process which converts 24 frame-per-second film into

30 (29.97) frame-per-second, 60 (59.97) field-per-second NTSC video.

For example, in Figure 18.26 two fields derived from film frame A are followed by three fields from film frame B, etc. Two video fields are derived from each frame of film. The ordering of fields is alternated, resulting in a unique pattern that repeats every five video frames.

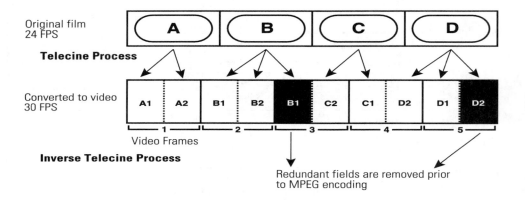

Figure 18.26 Telecine/inverse telecine

MPEG-2 decoders, such as those on DVD players, can have the ability to read 24 fps MPEG video streams, and turn them back into 29.97 fps video on output. This unique property of converting 24 fps MPEG-2 video back into 29.97 fps video means that prior to encoding, 29.97 fps video may be turned back into the original 24 fps film frame sequence. This removal of redundant frames from a video source which had originated on film is called inverse telecine. Inverse telecine has several benefits: it eliminates redundant fields, allowing the compression system to allocate more bits to the remaining unique frames, and it eliminates any motion artifacts, such as jerky, hesitant pans, that might otherwise occur between fields if the duplicate fields in the 3:2 sequence are left intact.

The Encoding Process

Encoding high quality video for DVD requires powerful MPEG-2 compression tools. These tools must be able to handle multiple aspect ratio video, variable bit rate encoding, inverse telecine, video pre filtering, and make the compression process easy and intuitive for the operator. The quality of the source material directly affects the quality of the final MPEG-2 stream, and the best results will be from CCIR-601 digital video on a D1, Digital Betacam, or DCT tape. A higher quality source, such as an HDTV master is even better.

Although VBR encoding can be done in a single pass, the window of optimization is too small for significant improvements over constant bit rate video. In theory, the more passes that are made, the more carefully the MPEG-2 algorithm can match video content and the better the overall quality. Professional VBR encoders will allow for two- or three-pass encoding, depending on the quality desired and time available for encoding. Optimum MPEG-2 VBR encoding is done via a multi-pass analysis and compression process.

- Pass 1: A preprocessing pass is made through the source video during which the encoding system previews the program material, detects scene changes, and determines the optimum GOP structure. After this initial pass, the operator can make additional adjustments to the GOP structure to force sequence headers at DVD entry points. The result is an Encoder Control List (ECL).

- Pass 2 (optional): The ECL containing the optimized GOP structures is used as the encoder makes another analysis pass through the video. During this pass, the encoder analyzes the entire program and fluctuates the bit rate depending on the complexity of the source material. The result of this pass is a bit rate profile for the video with more bits allocated to difficult areas and fewer bits allocated to easy passages.

Note that passes 1 and 2 can sometimes be combined, but this assumes I-frame placement and program analysis are done simultaneously during Pass 1.

- Pass 3: Finally, the target average and maximum bit rates dictated by the initial DVD bit budget are mapped against the GOP and bit rate parameters from the ECL, and a third pass is made. This time, rather than dictating the exact bit rates for the MPEG-2 bit-stream, a high quality MPEG-2 encoder will instead regulate the quantization scale and carefully throttle it to maintain the bit rate profile for the target numbers. This results in a field by field VBR encoding, rather than a GOP by GOP encoding, improving picture quality.

Each pass in the VBR process is done in real time, allowing the operator to view the results of the compression process as it takes place. In a real time networked production environment with guaranteed bandwidth, the MPEG-2 video stream can be recorded directly to a shared hard disk so that an encoded stream may be accessed across the network by other DVD premastering systems while it is still being encoded.

Segment-based Re-encoding

Although an MPEG-2 VBR encoder can be designed to use the best encoding parameters for a given video source tape, invariably small segments of MPEG-2 video will have to be modified manually for maximum quality. Additionally, the DVD premastering process may dictate changes to the project's bit budget after the movie has been encoded, necessitating bit rate changes to the MPEG-2 video source.

If it is determined that an area of the MPEG-2 video stream needs to be re-encoded, it is critical that the MPEG-2 VBR encoder has the ability to select specific segments of video and re-encode them. Unsophisticated MPEG-2 encoders will often force a user to re-analyze and re-encode the entire movie just so a small change can be made to a GOP structure or a bit rate level. This is too time consuming for professional production work. The best systems employ a segment-based approach which allows many small regions to be re-encoded and then spliced into the original MPEG-2 video stream. The streams can be selected, re-encoded in a single pass, and seamlessly reinserted into the encoded stream. This segment re-encoding eliminates the need to re-encode an entire stream for a few small changes and dramatically speeds up the encoding process when changes are required.

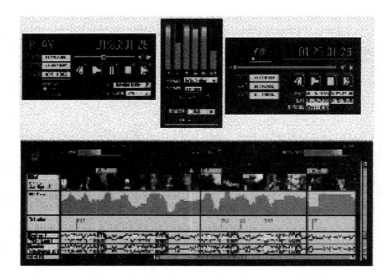

Figure 18.27 Sonic DVD Studio, showing a segment-based re-encode

Still Images and Subpictures

The static graphical images that make up subpicture overlays and still images begin as bitmap graphics. In the case of subtitles, these subpicture graphics begin as a text script which is then converted to bitmap graphic files with the associated timecode of the source movie.

Subpicture overlays and still images are often created with image editing applications, such as Adobe Photoshop. Subpictures, with a maximum of four colors allowed, are run-length coded for DVD in the authoring application. Still images, which are full color, are compressed as MPEG-2 I-frames. Once all of the still images and subpictures are created, they must be imported into the authoring program.

Audio Preparation and Compression

Some producers may assume that all of DVD's premastering complexity and "magic" is in the video encoding. However, when they delve into the myriad of audio options for DVD, they are surprised to find that preparing audio for DVD can be even more complex and time consuming than video. This complexity stems not just from the compression processes used, but from the variety and number of simultaneous streams of audio that may be placed on a single disc. This also means that the production tools for DVD audio must be capable of capturing PCM, MPEG, and Dolby Digital audio.

Editing Soundtracks

With Dolby Digital designated as the compressed audio format for NTSC DVD players (with MPEG-2 as an option) content providers must be able to prepare multiple language mixes, either in stereo or in combination with surround. A typical mix might include a single 5.1 surround sound track with two or three Dolby Digital stereo language-dubbed versions and perhaps a single stereo PCM version.

Prior to encoding, the separate language versions must be compared for level, mix, and equalization to ensure that radically different audio is not heard when switching from English to French to Spanish. If audio has been prepped prior to encoding (typically this would be done on full-resolution audio data), Dolby Digital compression can be performed directly on the stored audio data. This streamlines the production process as final mix tracks can be transferred directly to the DVD authoring system.

Dolby Digital

The primary audio format for DVD in NTSC countries is Dolby Digital, both stereo and 5.1 surround. The 5.1 configuration includes three speakers across the front, a stereo pair in the rear, and a low frequency effects channel. This is often abbreviated LCRSS.

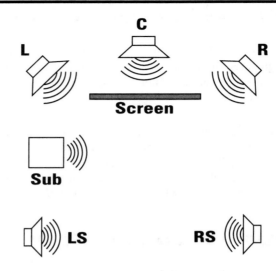

Figure 18.28 5.1 Surround listening environment

Dolby Digital is an algorithm which compresses audio by removing sound from frequency bands which, over time, contain limited signal energy. In addition, a noise shaping scheme is used to remove audio information in frequency areas where humans are less apt to hear missing sound. Dolby Digital also uses a scheme of cross-correlation in which the various channels of a surround or stereo mix are compared, and the difference between the channels is stored while the redundant information is eliminated. The result is a six channel (5.1 surround) audio mix with a lower bit rate and storage requirement than the standard compact disc format of 44.1 kHz, 16-bit stereo audio. By using Dolby Digital compression, the new DVD format has enough space to allow several different Dolby Digital streams to be placed onto the disc.

Dolby Digital audio can run at various bit rates and with different coding schemes based on the source content. In laying out the DVD title, the producer has to decide how many bits to allocate to each audio stream. Once the audio bit allocation has been made, the data rate for a given audio stream is constant (unlike the variable bit rate encoding for video). By utilizing Dolby-certified encoding tools, the DVD premastering system can convert source audio into Dolby Digital, either in real time or in software based on the application.

PCM Capture

From mono to eight channels of sound, DVD is the first consumer format to allow more than four channels of uncompressed audio. Even more impressive, it can have double the frequency range and much greater bit resolution than audio CD. The PCM audio that is available for the DVD format ranges from mono to eight channels and can be 48 kHz (24-bit up to four channels, 20-bit to six and 16-bit to eight) or 96 kHz (24-bit for stereo, 20-bit for three, and 16-bit for four).

With more than double the sampling rate of CD, 96 kHz audio is able to deliver pristine sound unobscured by the low-pass filter-induced artifacts that traditionally distort the high-frequencies in 44.1 kHz audio. The addition of 24-bit resolution also goes a long way toward improving low level signal clarity and definition. In order to take advantage of the 96 kHz 24-bit format, DVD premastering systems must be able to encode and format High Density Audio™.

MPEG-2 Audio

The audio standard for 625/60 (PAL) DVD players, MPEG-2 audio is an extension of MPEG-1 Layer II audio popularized as the audio component of MPEG-1 video. MPEG-2 audio can extend from stereo up to eight channels (7.1 surround). It is also able to run at higher compression ratios than Dolby Digital.

Encoding Audio

Because of the flexibility and the complexity of the DVD audio formats, sophisticated production tools are required. Ideally, audio production for DVD should be streamlined, with encoders able to edit and modify soundtracks if need be and automatically process the resulting audio into Dolby Digital, MPEG, or PCM formats.

Source audio for DVD typically comes in on an MDM (Modular Digital Multitrack) format, such as Tascam DA-88. This is the source format most often used for Dolby Digital encoding, and it can hold eight tracks of 48 kHz, 16-bit audio. Professional audio encoding systems enable the source to be transferred in real time in PCM, Dolby Digital, or MPEG audio formats. If the audio needs to be edited—for level, panning, EQ, phase adjustment, or time compression or expansion—it would be captured as PCM, and then processed using integrated audio mixing capabilities or a digital audio workstation. Once the editing is complete, the audio would then be batch-processed into Dolby Digital or MPEG.

Source audio for DVD has usually been carefully mixed for surround, but the level balancing process doesn't end there. Dolby Digital specifies several different home listening compression levels that can be assigned during the compression process. This allows a viewer to set a listening level where the dialog maintains its volume while louder and softer audio is balanced to match it. This feature of Dolby Digital is convenient for the consumer, but requires that the audio production tools be able to simulate this compression level to ensure the audio system operator that the correct settings have been made. The same is true for channel downmix.

Every 5.1 surround mix for Dolby Digital can fold down to a stereo output. This enables consumers who do not have a 5.1 decoder to hear the audio soundtrack as a stereo mix. While this frees DVD premastering operators from having to place both a stereo and 5.1 mix on the DVD disc, it requires that the operator be able to listen to the 5.1 downmix to ensure that no artifacts or other problems arise in the stereo version.

Once audio encoding is complete, the resulting files must be played back with the captured MPEG-2 video to ensure proper synchronization. This process can be done on either an audio system (if it has an MPEG-2 decoder) or a video system (if it has audio decoding). A separate workstation, called a proofing station, may also be used for final quality assurance.

DVD Authoring

Much of the excitement around DVD has centered on its application as a new, superior medium for viewing movies at home. As a standardized ROM-type format, DVD has universal applications in audio and computer software as well. Even in "linear" video DVDs, interactivity is involved when pressing Play or hitting Fast-Forward, or Reverse. This is because, unlike consumer VCRs, the navigation command structures are programmed in the authoring stage and embedded in the disc. As a result, compressing audio and video files does not by itself create a DVD; the compression merely provides video and audio files for the authoring process. A sophisticated tool is required to assemble the content and create the interactivity for a title. This is where the real DVD premastering work begins.

Authoring represents the most complex and least understood of the DVD premastering tasks. The term authoring includes the processes that are performed after video and audio encoding and before disc replication. It is the process in which all the encoded audio and video are linked together, multiple language tracks are laid out, subtitles are imported or generated, chapter points and transport control functions are introduced, multi-story or multi-angle program chains are created, menus and buttons are designed, and any final MPEG video or audio editing is done. It is also where parental block features, language codes, region codes, and copy protection are introduced.

The authoring process can be broken down into several steps: storyboarding, asset assembly, interactivity editing, proofing, multiplexing, and disc image creation. Each of these steps is highly iterative and requires close integration of the authoring system with the video and audio encoding stations and the emulation station.

Storyboarding

The first authoring step is to lay out the title in a storyboard that shows all of the assets (even if they have not yet been captured or assembled) plus all of the menus and navigation steps that will join the assets together into a seamless title. Storyboarding a title can begin even before asset capture, and serves three main purposes: to provide a roadmap for multiple operators working on the same project, to avoid errors in asset assembly and menu creation; as a checklist for the producer to ensure that production resources are allocated appropriately and to minimize rework; and finally, as a "preflight check" of the title's navigation to avoid dead ends, confusing or overly complicated menus, or inconsistent and user-unfriendly disc navigation. The end result of the storyboarding process is a complete roadmap of the DVD title, as well as a bit budget and asset capture list.

DVD Title Layout

Storyboarding can either be done manually, or, preferably, in the authoring software using storyboarding templates or project planning assistants that help define the parameters of a project. These can include the size of the disc (DVD-5, DVD-9, DVD-10, DVD-18), number of audio streams and video angles, the regions it will be encoded for, and parental levels, and should take place before the project gets started, rather than as the last step in the premastering process.

To facilitate storyboarding, it is useful to lay out projects before asset capture using placeholder icons that can later be assigned to audio, video, or menus. As assets are imported, you will want to carefully track of the total number of bits used, so that you can make sure that the size of your project will not exceed the capacity of the disc.

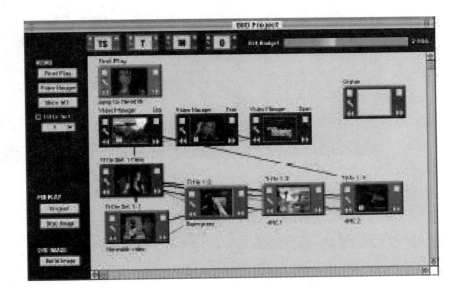

Figure 18.29 Sonic DVD Producer layout window

Assembly of Assets

The next step is to assemble all of the source assets that have been captured: MPEG video, audio, graphics, subtitles, and subpictures. These elementary files are linked together into objects with one or more video angle files associated with one or more audio clips and subpicture clips. The objects are not multiplexed (interleaved) until the project is complete, however.

During the assembly process, information about Part of Title entry points must be created as well as all of the information for displaying the subpictures: time location, wipe, fade-in, scroll, color, and duration.

377

Subpicture Assembly and Import

Importing stills for menus and creating highlight areas, colors, and "hot spots" for buttons can be one of the most labor-intensive aspects of authoring. It is essential to have a graphical interface for subpicture assembly that allows you to control features like fades, wipes, button activation times, and highlights quickly and easily,

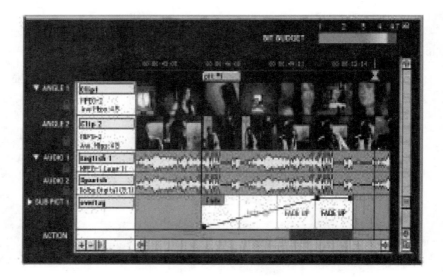

Figure 18.30 Sonic DVD Producer presentation window

Interactivity Editing

Once all of the objects have been assembled, you are ready to create program chains to give the title interactivity. In this process, the pre- and post-commands are set and links are made between the various program chains and video title sets. This is also the time to bring in still or motion video to use as menus. During the authoring process, it is important to be able to simulate the project that you are working on in order to see the project as it progresses and proof it in real time. You will want to play back VOBs in full resolution during authoring, so that quality control can begin in parallel with authoring and asset capture. This will save you time throughout title production.

Multiplexing

With the navigation data and presentation data complete, you can lay out the final project. In this process, all of the presentation data (video, audio, subpictures) are multiplexed together into the VOBs that are used by the DVD format. The PGCs that have been created for interactivity are placed into the VTSI (Video Title Set Information) area at the beginning of each VTS and any volume information about the DVD is generated. The end result of this process is a new set of files which comply with the DVD 1.0 format.

Creating the Disc Image

The last step in DVD authoring is to create the disc image. This is the process by which the DVD 1.0 files are formatted for the UDF-Bridge file system. This disc image is created on hard disk and then written out to Digital Linear Tape (DLT). It is also at this stage that analog and digital copy protection flags are set, so that data can be encrypted by the manufacturing plant as it is fed in. A 20-Gigabyte DLT tape is the standard premastering format which is sent to DVD manufacturers today, although With DVD-R and DVD-ROM becoming available, these formats will also soon be used to store the final DVD disc image.

Creating the disc image can be processor-intensive and time consuming, but should not require supervision once the process has been started. In order to minimize operator and workstation time, it is desirable for disc image creation to be able to take place on a data transfer station, so that both the operator and the authoring workstation can continue on to the next project.

Final QC

Once a DVD disc image has been generated, it should be played back prior to replication to proof it for audio and video sync, menu navigation, and video quality. Playback of disc images gives the producer a preview of what the title will look like when it is played on a set-top DVD player, allowing final quality checking to take place on the desktop rather than by manufacturing a one-off test disc.

DVD Manufacturing

After proofing, the final step in the DVD creation process is manufacturing. The DLT premastering tape is sent to the manufacturing facility, where the disc image is loaded onto the hard disk of the mastering system. It is at this stage that data encryption is added to the DVD disc image. The copy protection scheme, regulated by the DVD Forum, looks at the encryption flags set in the authoring process and encrypts the program data accordingly.

Premastering Work Flow

Traditionally, audio production work has always been done separately from video production work. The two crafts have developed in parallel but independently, with integration of products at the final edit stage (i.e., soundtracks produced for films) but with little sharing of resources, standards, operating procedures, or personnel.

As a result, the hardware and software tools for audio and video production in first-generation premastering systems can be inflexible—"black box" systems that don't allow much user control – and rarely integrated. A video encoder may not be capable of simultaneous Dolby Digital or MPEG audio capture during encoding. An audio encoder may not allow all versions of encoding, from MPEG-2 to PCM. Assets may need to be physically carried from station to station ("sneakernet") because different systems cannot be tied together over a network. This lack of flexibility and control leads to bottlenecks and inefficiencies in the premastering process.

The Evolution of Premastering Systems

Today's DVD production requires an entirely different approach to premastering than first-generation systems provided. A DVD producer needs to be able to integrate production of video and audio assets, manage a bit budget, control quality during production with proofing, schedule encodes and re-encodes to ensure the highest quality, and process multiple premastering projects at the same time to ensure the highest productivity and efficiency.

The traditional dual-system approach in post production, where audio post and video post are done separately, breaks down when confronted with the interdependencies of the media formats for DVD. Although we have discussed DVD production as a series of steps, it is not a linear process. In order to produce titles efficiently, the steps must be done in parallel on a common asset base and information passed back and forth among production systems. Commonly, DVD production will start with simultaneous video and audio encoding, move into authoring, back to encoding to re-capture or process new video, move back to authoring to incorporate, then to proofing, back to encoding, etc. Because these steps are not separate and are intensely intertwined, a workgroup environment is critical.

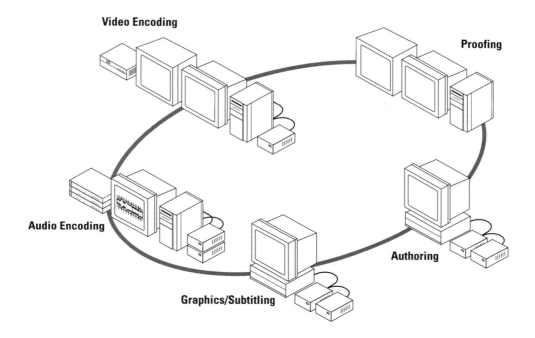

Figure 18.31 DVD premastering workgroup

The workgroup allows the various systems to work in parallel: video encoding can take place while an author is laying out a title, audio for a new project can begin while proofing takes place on the previous project, etc. This parallel production process can keep each of the systems productive while more than one DVD project is run through at a time. While a single complex project may take X hours of production time, four complex projects might take 3X hours, not 4X hours.

In a networked DVD production environment, a workstation containing both audio and video capture hardware may be located in a machine room for loading of source material while other digital audio workstations can access and process the sound files remotely. Proofing of encoded assets can take place simultaneously with production, making instant quality information available to the producer. Authoring can be started on one workstation while assets are still being assembled and encoded on others.

Conclusion

Ultimately, DVD title design is a highly creative and iterative process. It requires forethought, careful planning, a networked production environment, and the tight integration of project planning, asset capture, and authoring tools. Being successful in DVD means understanding the format and the production process while building a production environment to move titles through quickly and efficiently.

Glossary

A

A-B rolls: Two videotapes used to record a single-camera segment so that during the editing process the two can be combined alternately to create more sophisticated effects.

Absorption: A general term for the process by which incident flux is converted to another form of energy, usually and ultimately to heat. Note: All of the incident flux is accounted for by the process of reflection, transmission, and absorption.

Accent light: A source used in addition to basic light to call attention to an object or area.

Accommodation: The process by which the eye changes focus from one distance to another.

Adaptation: The process by which the retina becomes accustomed to more or less light than it was exposed to during an immediately preceding period. Thisresults in a change in the sensitivity to light.

AGC: See **automatic gain control**.

Amplifier: An electronic device to increase the intensity of an electrical signal. Amplifiers are used for both audio and video.

Analog: A signal which can accommodate any value within a range. Betacam SP video is an analog format.

Analog to Digital Conversion: The process of converting analog information to digital information.

Angle of acceptance or **angle of view:** The horizontal and vertical angle "seen" by a given lens, indicating whether the lens will have a wide or narrow field of view. Angle of acceptance is inversely related to **focal length**, that is, the greater the focal length, the narrower the angle of acceptance.

Angle of incidence: An angle perpendicular to the surface upon which a lighted ray falls.

Angle of light: The angle between the subject and the light axis and the angle between the camera and the subject. Rim light 180 degrees, Key light, 15 to 45 degrees.

Aperture: The opening (often adjustable) within a camera lens which determines the amount of light which may pass through the lens. See *f-stop.*

Aspect ratio: The proportions or ratio of an image expressed as the width divided by the height. 1:1.33 is the aspect ratio of 16 MM film. 4:3 is the aspect ratio for television.

Attributes of light: Hard or soft, intensity, direction, color and beam pattern or angle.

Audio compressor: An electronic device which can boost weak signals and limit very strong signals, thus reducing **dynamic range** but achieving a higher average level.

Audio mix: A sound track created by combining input from several sources.

Automatic gain control: An electronic circuit which automatically increases or decreases the strength of an incoming signal (audio or video) so that a predetermined level is maintained.

Auto white balance: A feature of some video cameras which automatically adjusts the relative portion of red, blue and green in order to compensate for color variations between light sources.

Available light: The light in a given location without any added lighting.

B

Background light: Lighting of a set or background behind the primary subject.

Back light: A light placed behind and above the subject, providing highlights which enhance edge contrast and add a sense of shape and separation from the background.

Baffle: A single opaque or translucent element to shield a source from direct view at certain angles, to absorb or block unwanted light, or to reflect and redirect light.

Ballast: An auxiliary device consisting of induction windings wound around a metal core that sometimes includes a capacitor for power correction. It is used with fluorescent and HID lamps to provide the necessary starting voltage and to limit the current during operation.

Bandwidth (in telecommunications): The range of frequencies required to transmit a particular type of signal, and (in digital systems) the rate at which data can stream through a particular component or system. A CD-ROM player (double speed) can transfer 150 MB of information per second. This would be referred to as its bandwidth.

Bank: A group of attached lighting instruments.

Barn doors: Movable flaps (resembling barn doors) which attach to the front of a light source and serve to control the size and area of the light beam.

Base light: The basic lighting needed to adequately illuminate a subject or scene.

Beam: The cone of light of a light source.

Beam angle: The point in a beam of light where the intensity of a source drops to 50% of maximum. It is measured in degrees of the full angle. The width of a beam of light.

Beam pattern: The beam angle, shape or any patterns that interrupt the beam.

Beam spread (in any plane): The angle between the two directions in the plane in which the intensity is equal to a stated percentage of the maximum beam intensity.

Best Boy: The first assistant of the Gaffer (chief electrician on a film crew).

Betacam: A broadcast-quality series of video recording equipment manufactured by Sony.

Black: A synchronized video signal containing no information. A blank screen.

Blocking: The planning and coordination of the positions and movements of talent, cameras and other production equipment, prior to the actual rehearsal of a scene or taping of a show.

Boom: A movable beam or pole used for supporting a camera or suspending a microphone in an elevated position. Also, to raise or lower the position of a camera mounted on a boom arm.

Bounce light: A soft light source created by reflecting light rays off light-colored panels or walls.

Breakdown sheet: An outline of the production script as to location, cast, props, equipment, etc.

Brightness: The intensity of light, usually referring to the light reflected from an object or scene, or the intensity of an image on a television tube.

Brightness range: The range in reflectance from the brightest to the darkest portions (highlights to shadows) of a scene, as measured by a light meter.

Broad: A floodlight with a large, rectangular reflector which casts a broad beam over a wide area.

Butt edit: Two segments of video placed together so that the beginning of one immediately follows the end of the other.

C

Camcorder: A video camera and videotape recorder integrated into one unit.

Cameo lighting: Lighting of a foreground subject against an unlighted, totally black background.

Camera head: The actual television camera, consisting of lens, pickup tube and viewfinder (head of a series of electronic components).

Camera mounting head: See **pan head**.

Candlepower, cp: Luminous intensity expressed in candelas.

Capture: The process of converting and storing analog video information in digital form. This applies to single frames (still) and to sequences of frames (motion).

Cassette: A cartridge containing a sealed reel of audio or video tape and an integrated take-up reel.

CCD (charge-coupled device): A microchip that is used to pick up picture information. It replaces the image tube in video cameras and camcorders.

Character generator (C.G.): An electronic device that produces text in electronic format for recording, editing or mixing with video productions. In non-linear editing most, if not all of the characters and titles are created in the computer software used for editing or effects.

Chroma or **chrominance:** The color information in a video signal, including both hue and saturation.

Chroma key: An electronic special effect technique whereby a specific color is used to identify a portion of the image (typically a background of saturated blue or green) to be cut out and replaced with material from another video source.

Chrominance channel: The color portion of a video signal. It contains hue and saturation information rather than luminance information.

Clip art, sound, music, etc.: Libraries of images, sound effects, etc. that are purchased or licensed for generic use in productions.

Close up: A view of a subject from a short distance.

Color bars: An electronically generated series of vertical bars of specific color properties used as a standard for adjusting and calibrating the performance of cameras and other components of a video system.

Color burst: The part of a composite video signal produced by a camera that serves as the reference for the receiving device.

Color Rendering Index (CRI): A scale used to evaluate the accuracy of the color of light sources. Daylight is 100.

Color temperature: A scale that expresses in measurable terms the color of a light source. It has nothing to do with the actual temperature of a light source. Daylight is usually about 5,600K (Kelvin) and a tungsten spotlight about 3,200K.

Colorimetry: The measurement of color.

Compact disc (CD): A digital audio recording and distribution medium.

Compact Disc Read Only Memory (CD-ROM): A digital multimedia recording and distribution medium.

Complementary colors: Those primary or secondary colors that are opposite each other on the color wheel. In lighting: yellow, cyan and magenta.

Component video: A video system in which information is recorded and transmitted in three separate channels—luminance (Y), red difference (R–Y), and blue difference (B–Y)—resulting in a higher quality than available from either composite or S-video systems.

Composite video: A video system in which a combination of luminance and chrominance information is recorded and transmitted together.

Compression: A variety of techniques, technologies and algorithms used to reduce the amount of data space needed to store digital information. In video, this includes both inter- and intra-frame compression.

Compression frame rate: The number of frames per second contained in a compressed video file. This is in contrast to the playback or display rate which refers to the actual number of frames per second displayed when played back.

Condenser microphone: A high quality microphone based on the principal of electrical capacitance. Used for all recording purposes.

Console: The audio control or mixer board.

Contrast: The difference between the darkest and lightest parts of an object or scene.

Controller (edit controller): A dedicated electronic device to control recording and editing video decks and sources.

Cool: The blue part of the spectrum. A blue light or filter.

CPU: Central processor unit. The main processor chip in a computer. Also refers to the entire main computer itself.

Cropping: Cutting or trimming the edges or border of an image.

Cross fade: An audio or video transition that fades out one signal while fading up another.

Cross light: Lighting a subject from both sides.

Cue: (1) A signal to talent to start. (2) Setting up an audio source or recording device in anticipation of recording or playing back.

Cut: (1) The end of a rehearsal or take. (2) To eliminate something from a clip or script. (3) A type of edit that moves, without any effects transition, from one shot or clip to another.

Cutaway: A reaction shot from a third party inserted in a video edit to cover a transition or emphasize a point.

Cyc, cyclorama: A cloth or hard surface background on a set or stage that can be lit to represent the sky. It is usually curved on the sides and bottom to eliminate seams in the frame. It is an important tool when painted blue or green and used in Chroma key video.

D

D1: An international standard for component digital video systems and information.

D2: An international standard for composite digital video systems and information.

Data rate: The rate at which data must be supplied in order to support video playback. An uncompressed stream of video captured at 320 x 240 at 24 bits and 30 frames per second will require a data rate of 6.9 MB per second.

Daylight: Direct and/or diffuse light from the sun.

DCC, Digital compact cassette: A digital audio tape format developed by Philips for the consumer market.

DCI (Display Control Interface): A specification used to make more efficient video decompression and display. Developed jointly by Microsoft and Intel.

Decibel (db): A unit of measurement of sound comparing the relative intensity of sound signal or sources.

Delta frame: A digital video frame which contains only information about how that frame differs from the key frame. See **Interframe compression**.

Depth of field: The range between the minimum distance and the maximum distance at which objects appear sharp or in focus.

Diffuse reflectance: The ratio of the flux leaving a surface or medium by diffuse reflection to the incident flux. Note: Provision for the exclusion of regularly reflected flux, which is nearly always present, must be clearly described.

Diffuse transmission: That process by which the incident flux passing through a surface or medium is scattered.

Diffuser: A device to redirect or scatter the light from a source, primarily by the process of diffuse transmission.

Diffusing surfaces and media: Those surfaces and media that redistribute at least some of the incident flux by scattering.

Digital: Any information stored in binary form (i.e.: a series of zeros and ones).

Digital Video: Video information converted to, and stored in, digital form.

Digitize: The process of converting analog information (e.g.: Video, audio, text, etc.) to digital form.

Dimmer board: A lighting control unit or console.

Direct Glare: Glare resulting from high luminances or insufficiently shielded light sources in the field of view. It usually is associated with bright areas, such as luminaires, ceilings, and windows that are outside the visual task or region being viewed. A direct glare source may also affect performance by distracting attention.

Director of Photography, DP, Videographer: The person with primary responsibility for lighting on film and video crews.

Display rate: The number of frames per second of displayed video. This represents the quality of a video codec's performance.

Dissolve: A video transition where one signal is faded out while the next is faded up. This transition superimposes part of image A onto image B during the process.

Dolly: A camera mount secured to a platform with wheels so that the camera may be operated while in motion. Also, to move a camera on its mount nearer to (dolly in) or away from (dolly out) a subject.

Dubbing: Duplicating video or audio tapes.

Dynamic microphone: A standard microphone based on a moving coil. This is the rugged mainstay of audio and video production.

E

Edit: To assemble pieces of program material into an organized sequence (either by physically cutting and splicing film or tape, or by electronic transfer to a new tape). Also, any point in a film or tape where editing has occurred.

Edit decision list (EDL): A paper or electronic list of all the video or audio segments and their times and locations to be assembled into a final production.

Edit deck: A video tape machine designed to receive the edited program being assembled, and which can be very accurately controlled by computers or edit controllers.

Editing: The process of selecting and assembling a final audio or video production from the raw pieces.

Ellipsoidal spotlight: A focusing spotlight which produces a sharply defined beam of light.

Establishing shot: A wide shot which establishes for the audience the locale and the relationship between elements of a scene.

F

Fade: The gradual bringing in or taking out of an audio or video source. The gradual transition of an image from black to the image itself, and vice versa.

Fall-off: The size of the area on a surface where light and shadows merge.

Far-side key: The main light which is set on the far side of a subject's face, leaving his/her face in partial shadow.

Feedback: In audio, the reintroduction of output signal to input signal. This causes over-amplification and disruption of the signal.

Fill light: A light used to lighten shadows and control lighting ratios and contrast.

Film chain: (1) A device for converting film or still slides into electronic images. (2) A device for converting video information to film. Also referred to as a telecine.

Filter: A transmitting medium that absorbs, diffuses or in some other way modifies light coming (a) from a light source (placed on the front of the light source) or (b) into a camera lens (placed on the front of the lens).

Fish pole: A pole, onto which a microphone is attached, which is held by a sound technician during recording. This provides instant control of the position of the microphone in relationship to the talent and the camera.

Fluorescent lamp: A low pressure mercury electric-discharge lamp in which a fluorescing coating (phosphor) transforms some of the ultraviolet energy generated by the discharge into light.

Focal length: The distance from the optical center of a lens (focused at infinity) to the plane where the image is in focus. The longer the focal length, the greater the ability of the lens to magnify distant objects. The shorter the focal length, the greater the field of view of the lens.

Foot-candle: A standard (non-metric) unit for light measurement equivalent to the illumination provided by one candle at a distance of one foot, equal to one lumen per square foot.

Fps: Frames per second.

Frame: One of a series of images that make up an animation, clip of video or movie film.

Frame grabber: A computer board use to digitize video.

Frame rate: The speed the image moves before the camera gate (film) or image gate (video). Film standard in the USA is 24 FPS. Video is 30 FPS in NTSC and 25 FPS in PAL.

f-stop: A measure of lens aperture, which is calculated by dividing the focal length of a lens by the diameter of its aperture. The lower the resulting number, the larger the aperture and thus the greater the amount of light which the lens is able to transmit.

G

Gaffer: The chief electrician on a film or video crew.

Gain: The strength or amplification of an audio or video signal.

Gel, Media: A filter used primarily for lighting.

Glare: The sensation produced by luminances within the visual field that are sufficiently greater than the luminance to which the eyes are adapted which causes annoyance, discomfort, or loss in visual performance or visibility. Note: The magnitude of the sensation of glare depends upon such factors as the size, position and luminance of a source, the number of sources and the luminance to which the eyes are adapted.

Graphics: Two-dimensional visual material prepared for film or video presentation, e.g., titles, maps, slides and computer-generated art.

Gray scale: A theoretical scale of the shades of gray ranging from white to black. Also, a test card containing patches of gray from white to black and used as a reference for adjusting cameras and other equipment

H

Hardware codecs: Video codecs that require hardware to decompress. Examples are MPEG and motion JPEG .

Helical scan: A video signal recorded at a slight angle along the horizontal dimension of video tape.

Hertz (HZ): A unit of measure of frequency of electromagnetic waves. Most often expressed in Kilohertz (kHz) or Megahertz (MHz)

Hi-8: A consumer and prosumer video tape format based on 8mm tape cassettes.

High-definition television (HDTV): Most commonly used to refer to the aspect ratio of emerging video standards. Most systems also have 1,100 or more scan lines. It is used for both analog and digital schemes.

High Intensity Discharge (HID) lamp: An electric discharge lamp in which the light producing arc is stabilized by wall temperature and the arc tube has a bulb wall loading in excess of 3 W/cm2. HID lamps include groups of lamps known as mercury, metal halide, and high pressure sodium.

Highlights: The bright areas of a subject or scene.

Horizontal sync pulse: The portion of a video synchronizing pulse that controls the horizontal sweep of the scanning beam.

Hue: Color. Used to refer to a specific color or group of colors, red, orange, magenta, etc., without reference to other characteristics such as saturation or brightness.

I

Insert editing: Electronically inserting a new program element into a previously recorded segment.

Intensity (candlepower) distribution curve: A curve, often polar, that represents the variation of luminous intensity of a lamp or luminaire in a plane through the light center. Note: A vertical candlepower distribution curve is obtained by taking measurements at various angles of elevation about a source in a vertical plane through the light center; unless the plane is specified, the vertical curve is assumed to represent an average such as would be obtained by rotating the lamp or luminaire about its vertical axis. A horizontal intensity distribution curve represents measurements made at various angles of azimuth in a horizontal plane through the light center.

Interframe compression: Compression of digital video data achieved by eliminating information about pixels which do not change from frame to frame. For example, the background of a scene may remain constant for many frames, and thus information about that portion of the picture need not be stored in every frame. See **Key frame** and **Delta frame**.

Interleave: To combine both the audio and video portions of a data stream into a single file for more efficient retrieval, as in the AVI (audio/video interleave) file format of Video for Windows.

Intraframe compression: Compression of digital video data achieved entirely within a given frame and without reference to any other.

Inverse-square law: A law stating that the illuminance E at a point on a surface varies directly with the intensity I of a point source, and inversely as the square of the distance d between the source and the point. If the surface at the point is normal to the direction of the incident light, the law is express *by* $E = I/d^2$. Note: For sources of finite size having uniform luminance this gives results that are accurate within one percent when d is at least five times the maximum dimension of the source as viewed from the point on the surface. Even though practical interior luminaires do not have uniform luminance, this distance *d* is frequently used as the minimum for photometry of such luminaires, when the magnitude of the measurement error is not critical.

J

Joystick: A cursor control device used in place of a mouse.

Jump cut: (1) A take between two cameras. (2) A bad edit without proper continuity between the two shots.

K

Key: A term that covers a variety of visual effects, usually an electronic effect in which a video source is electronically inserted into background video.

Key frame: A digital video frame which is complete without reference to any other frame (may contain intraframe but not interframe compression). Also known as reference frame. Contrast with delta frame.

Key light, main light: The primary lighting instrument used to light a scene or subject.

L

Lamp: A generic term for an artificial source of light. By extension, the term is also used to denote sources that radiate in regions of the spectrum adjacent to the visible. Note: Through popular usage, a portable luminaire consisting of a lamp with shake, reflector, enclosing globe, housing or other accessories is also called a lamp. In such cases, in order to distinguish between the assembled unit and the light source within it, the latter is often called a bulb or tube, if it is electrically powered. The bulb is only the glass envelope of the lamp.

Laser disc: An analog video disc base recording and distribution system.

Level: Sound volume or intensity. Also light intensity.

Light: Radiant energy that is capable of exciting the retina and producing a visual sensation. The visible portion of the electromagnetic spectrum extends from about 380 to 770 nanometers. Note: The subjective impression produced by stimulating the retina is sometimes designated as light. Visual sensations are sometimes arbitrarily defined as sensations of light, and in line with this concept it is sometimes said that light cannot exist until an eye has been stimulated. Electrical stimulation of the retina or the visual cortex is described as producing flashes of light. In illuminating engineering, however, light is a physical entity—radiant energy weighted by the luminous efficiency function. It is a physical stimulus that can be applied to the retina.

Light fixture, luminaire, instrument: The part of a lighting device that surrounds the lamp.

Light meter: A common name for an illuminance meter.

Lighting ratio: The ratio of key light plus fill versus fill light only. Measured with incident light meter.

Line monitor: The master program monitor.

Looping: (1) A continuous clip of audio, video or film that plays endlessly. (2) The process of re-recording dialog track on a film production.

Lossless: Compression schemes that return the compressed data as an exact representation of the data before compression. These usually don't exceed two to one compression.

Lossy: Compression schemes that are used primarily on video and audio that, when decompressed, loose some of the data in comparison with the original uncompressed data. Some loss is generally acceptable in AV data. Current schemes can produce up to 200:1 compression.

Louver (or louver grid): A series of baffles used to shield a source from view at certain angles, to absorb or block unwanted light, or to reflect and redirect light. The baffles are usually arranged in a geometric pattern.

Lumen: Measurement of the quantity of light.

Luminance: The black and white component of a color video signal, serving both to provide a correct picture on a black and white receiver and proper contrast in a color image.

Luminance channel: A black and white signal in color video cameras used to provide correct contrast and color balance, and to provide correct information for monochrome monitors.

Luminance key: A technique or process used to overlay a foreground image onto another background.

Lux: The metric unit of light intensity. 1 foot candle = 10.74 lux.

M

Matte: An electronic effect where two signals are keyed together with one signal providing the foreground image and the other the background. Related to chroma key and luminance key processing.

Matte surface: A surface from which the reflection is predominantly diffuse, with or without a negligible specular component.

MCI, Media Control Interface: A multimedia API or applications programmers interface. Created by Microsoft and IBM in 1991.

Microphone: An audio pickup or transducer.

MIDI (musical instrument digital interface): A standard for storing, retrieving and interfacing musical instrument control information within electronic musical instruments or with computers.

Mix-down: The audio editing process of combining all the intermediate audio tracks into a final set of audio tracks.

Mix track: The final edit audio track.

Moiré effect: Visual vibration caused by the interaction of a narrow striped pattern and the video scan lines.

Monitor: An audio speaker or video display device used to check the actual sound or video being produced.

Motivated lighting or **light source:** Light that appears to come from actual sources that are part of a scene. For example, table lamps, windows, etc.

Multiple camera production: A video production in which more than one camera is used simultaneously to record the scene.

N

NTSC: National Television System Committee. The standards organization that promulgated the current technical video specification used in North and South America and Japan.

O

Off-camera: A sound or action that takes place during a production but is not recorded by the camera.

Off-line editing: The electronic editing process during which an intermediate video is edited into a submaster and then an edit list is created for a final on-line edit session.

Omnidirectional microphone: A microphone that picks up sound from all sides equally well.

On-line editing: The final electronic editing stage where the final master is created.

Optical radiation: Electromagnetic radiation having wavelengths between approximately 100 nanometers and one millimeter.

Over-the-shoulder shot: A camera position that places one person with his/her back to the camera, with the camera focused over his/her shoulder at the principal subject.

P

Pad: Extra material added to a script to lengthen it. An audio attenuation device.

Palette: The specific assortment of colors from which all screen images must be created (which for 8-bit displays is limited to 256 at one time).

Pan: To move a light or camera horizontally.

Pan head: The device which connects a camera to the camera mount, allowing the camera to tilt vertically and pan horizontally

Panning: Rotating the camera (on the pan head) left and right.

Patch bay: A board or box that contains a series of input and output terminals that facilitate the interconnection of audio, video or lighting signals. It may be a physical wiring device or a virtual one on the computer screen that controls a remote electronic switching device.

Pedestal: A heavy duty camera mount.

Picture continuity: The relationship of one shot to the next.

Pixel: A single digital picture element. The smallest addressable nexus of phosphor dots on a picture tube that can be illuminated by a scan gun.

Playback: The processing and retrieving of audio or video signals.

Pop filter: A shield placed over or in front of a microphone to prevent plosive bursts of air from consonants.

Preamplifier: An electronic device to increase the gain of a signal prior to its reaching the main amplifier.

Pre-roll: The time that a source and edit deck need to get up to full speed in tape motion.

Primary colors: Additive (e.g., paint) primary colors are red, blue and green. Subtractive (e.g., light) primary colors are yellow, magenta and cyan.

Primary target system: The system and medium for which video is optimized.

Producer: The Primary project manager of a video or audio production.

PZM (pressure zone microphone): An omnidirectional flat microphone used on table tops or floors for general ambient pickup.

R

Raster: The display of scanning lines on a cathode ray tube.

Real-time capture: The process of digitizing video at 30 frames per second.

Reference white: A large piece of white material used in white-balancing a video camera.

Reflected Glare: Glare resulting from reflections of high luminance in polished or glossy surfaces in the field of view. It usually is associated with reflections from within a visual task or areas in close proximity to the region being viewed.

Reflection: A general term for the process by which the incident flux leaves a (stationary) surface or medium from the incident side, without change in frequency. Note: Reflection is usually a combination of regular and diffuse reflection.

Reflectors: Devices used to redirect sun light or artificial light.

Refractor: A device used to redirect the flux from a source, primarily by the process of refraction.

Regular transmission: That process by which incident flux passes through a surface or medium without scattering.

Resolution: The sharpness of a picture or the ability of a system to reproduce detail within an image. On a video screen, refers to the actual number of pixels comprising the display. In digital video, refers to a series of three numbers (e.g., 640 x 480 x 256), the first representing the number of pixels along the horizontal axis, the second the number along the vertical axis, and the third the number of bytes providing color information.

Reverberation: Electronic echo added to audio tracks.

RGB: Red, green and blue, the primary colors used to produce a color TV image.

S

Saturation: The purity (freedom from neutral gray), and intensity of a hue. See **Chroma**.

Saturation of a perceived color: The attribute according to which it appears to exhibit more or less chromatic color judged in proportion to its brightness. In a given set of viewing conditions, and at luminance levels that result in photopic vision, a stimulus of a given chromaticity exhibits approximately constant saturation for all luminances.

Scale: To reduce the resolution of digital video in order to reduce the amount of data required for playback.

Seamless editing: A video editing technique that overlaps audio and video elements to avoid abrupt transitions.

Segue: An audio transition in which one sound is completely faded out then a second is faded in.

Set: A construction of scenery and props for photographing a scene.

Shoot: To record information on video or film. The entire process of recording program information.

Shooting schedule: A written plan of the entire shoot.

Short lens: A wide angle lens.

Shotgun microphone: A highly directional microphone used for recording at a distance.

Shot sheet: A list of shots to be acquired by the camera person.

Show card: A large sheet of cardboard used as a reflector or to block light.

Shutter (light): A venetian blind-like device attached to the front of a light source to adjust the intensity without changing the color temperature (as would occur if an electrical dimmer were used).

Single camera production: A shoot that uses only one camera. This is similar to film production. The content is acquired in series rather than in parallel.

Skewing: A video picture that bends or turns in at the corners.

SMPTE time code: A frame-location accurate system developed by the Society of Motion Picture and Television Engineers that can be used to synchronize multiple sources of audio and video during the recording or editing process.

Soft light: Subtle shadows, diffuse light.

Source deck: The playback video deck used to feed video information to the computer, editor or edit deck.

Specular surface: A surface from which the reflection is predominantly regular. A highly reflective surface.

Split screen: A special effect that divides the screen into multiple sections and simultaneously displays signals.

Spot light: A hard light that focuses down to create a brightly lighted area, generally used to emphasize an area or subject. It creates crisp shadows unless filtered.

Spread: The width of a light beam. To widen a light beam.

Step-frame capture: Digitization of video in non-real time. This system uses frame accurate video recorders or laser discs and digitizes one frame at a time using a frame grabber board.

Storyboard: A series of thumbnail drawings used to design and organize a shoot or edit plan.

Stretch: To slow down a voice or camera talent to fill out a segment of time.

Super (superimposition): The display of one image over another simultaneously.

S-VHS (Super-VHS): A high-resolution consumer and prosumer video tape format.

Sweetening: The augmentation of an audio track with effects such as reverberation, equalization or compression. The addition of ambient sound such as laughter or audience reactions to a production.

Switcher: An electronic device to mix video signals during editing. A person who uses a switcher.

Sync generator: A device which produces a synchronization signal for video.

Sync pulse: A signal added to picture information used by the electronic devices to keep all the video components synchronized.

T

Talent: The actor, announcer, voice artist or on-camera performer.

Tally lights: The red indicator lights on the front of video camera used to signal the active camera.

Telecine: See **Film chain**.

Teleprompter: A mechanical or electronic device that projects a moving script onto a mirror in front of the camera lens. A trademark of the Teleprompter Corporation.

Three point lighting: The traditional arrangement of key, fill and back lights.

Time-base corrector (TBC): An electronic device used to compensate for slight time variation in video signals during editing or playback.

Tone: An audio signal used to calibrate audio equipment. A tone is often placed at the beginning of master tapes and is used to calibrate or set the audio level before it comes on-line.

Top light: A light placed directly over and focused down on a subject.

Tracking: The VTR control that adjusts the video head for optimum position during playback.

Transfer edit: The re-recording of master tape information to intermediate tape prior to final edit assembly.

Transmission: A general term for the process by which incident flux leaves a surface or medium on a side other than the incident side, without change in frequency. Note: Transmission through a medium is often a combination of regular and diffuse transmission.

Trim: The adjustment of lighting instruments. To eliminate head and/or tail information from a video segment prior to final editing.

Tripod: A three-legged device to support a camera or light source.

Tungsten-Halogen Lamp: A gas-filled tungsten filament incandescent lamp containing a certain proportion of halogens in an inert gas whose pressure exceeds three atmospheres. Note; The tungsten-iodine lamp (UK) and quartz-iodine lamp (USA) belong to this category.

U

U-matic: A standard 3/4-inch videocassette format.

Unidirectional microphone: A microphone that picks up in a limited direction. Usually with a cardioid (heart shaped) pickup pattern.

V

Vectorscope: An electronic test instrument used to monitor graphically the saturation levels for each of the three primary colors and complementary colors.

Video Co-processor: A chip on graphics boards used to assist in the scaling and filtering of video so that larger resolutions may be achieved.

Video for Windows: A multimedia video specification developed by Microsoft and introduced in 1991 with Windows 3.1.

Visual field: The locus of objects or points in space that can be perceived when the head and eyes are kept fixed.

Vertical interval time code (VITC): A frame-location system similar to SMPTE.

VHS (Video Home System): A consumer 1/2-inch video cassette system developed by JVC.

Voice-over: An audio track of narration by an off-camera narrator played back over a video segment.

VU meter (volume unit meter): A meter that displays the relative volume level of an audio signal in decibels.

W

Waveform monitor: A specialized oscilloscope that displays the brightness of all the picture elements of a video signal. It is used to optimize the capabilities of video equipment.

Wavelength: The measurement of the length of an electromagnetic base from one crest to the next. The longer the wavelength (expressed in meters) the lower the frequency (expressed in Hertz).

White balance: The process of adjusting a video camera's red, blue and green gain controls in order to compensate for differences is light sources. See **Auto white balance**.

Wild track: A non-synchronized audio track made on location to record ambient sound to mix with the final edit.

Wipe: A video transition where one image gradually pushes another off the screen. A wipe may move horizontally, vertically or diagonally.

Wireless microphone: A miniature FM radio transmitter attached to a microphone. The receiver is patched into the console or the camera.

Y

Y signal: The luminance portion of a video signal.

Z

Zoom in; zoom out: To increase (zoom in) or decrease (zoom out) the focal length of a zoom lens so that the field of view is made narrower or wider respectively.

Zoom lens: A lens with focal length (and thus angle of acceptance) continuously variable throughout a limited range.

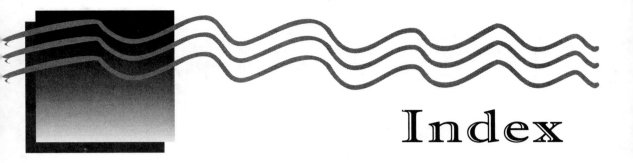

Index

ADOBE SYSTEMS INCORPORATED
MINIMUM TERMS OF END USER AGREEMENTS

(1)   Licensor grants Licensee a non-exclusive sublicense to use the Adobe software ("Software") and the related written material ("Documentation") provided by Adobe Systems Incorporated ("Adobe") to Licensor as set forth below. Licensee may install and use the Software on one computer.

(2)   The Software is owned by Adobe and its suppliers and its structure, organization and code are the valuable trade secrets of Adobe and its suppliers. Licensee agrees not to modify, adapt, translate, reverse engineer, decompile, disassemble or otherwise attempt to discover the source code of the Software. Licensee agrees not to attempt to increase the functionality of the Software in any manner. Licensee agrees that any permitted copies of the Software shall contain the same copyright and other proprietary notices which appear on and in the Software.

(3)   Except as stated above, this Agreement does not grant Licensee any right (whether by license, ownership or otherwise) in or to intellectual property with respect to the Software.

(4)   Licensee will not export or re-export the Software Programs with the appropriate United States or foreign government licenses.

(5)   Trademarks, if used by Licensee shall be used in accordance with accepted trademark practice, including identification of the trademark owner's name. Trademarks can only be used to identify printed output produced by the Software. The use of any trademark as herein authorized does not give Licensee rights of ownership in that trademark.

(6)   LICENSEE ACKNOWLEDGES THAT THE SOFTWARE IS A 'TRY-OUT" VERSION OF AN ADOBE PRODUCT, CONTAINING LIMITED FUNCTIONALITY. ADOBE IS LICENSING THE SOFTWARE ON AN "AS-IS" BASIS, AND ADOBE AND ITS SUPPLIERS MAKE NO WARRANTIES EXPRESS OR IMPLIED, INCLUDING, WITHOUT LIMITATION, AS TO NON-INFRINGEMENT OF THIRD PARTY RIGHTS, MERCHANTABILITY, OR FITNESS FOR ANY PARTICULAR PURPOSE. IN NO EVENT WILL ADOBE OR ITS SUPPLIERS BE LIABLE TO LICENSEE FOR ANY CONSEQUENTIAL, INCIDENTAL OR SPECIAL DAMAGES, INCLUDING ANY LOST PROFITS OR LOST SAVINGS, EVEN IF REPRESENTATIVES OF SUCH PARTIES HAVE BEEN ADVISED OF THE POSSIBILITY OF SUCH DAMAGES, OR FOR ANY CLAIM BY ANY THIRD PARTY.

IF A SHRINKWRAP LICENSEE IS USED [Some states or jurisdictions do not allow the exclusion or limitation of incidental, consequential or special damages, so the above limitation or exclusion may not apply to Licensee. Also some states or jurisdictions do not allow the exclusion of implied warranties or limitation on how long an implied warranty may last, so the above limitations may not apply to Licensee. To the extent permissible, any implied warranties are limited to ninety (90) days. This warranty gives Licensee specific legal rights. Licensee may have other rights which vary from state to state or jurisdiction to jurisdiction.]

(7)   Notice to Government End Users: The Software and Documentation are "Commercial Items," as that term is defined at 48 C.F.R. §2.101, consisting of "Commercial Computer Software" and "Commercial Computer Software Documentation," as such terms are used in 48 C.F.R. §12.212 or 48 C.F.R. §227.7202, as applicable. Consistent with 48 C.F.R. §12.212 or 48 C.F.R. §§2277202-1 through 227.7202-4, as applicable, the Commercial Computer Software and Commercial Computer Software Documentation are being licensed to U.S. Government end users (A) only as Commercial Items and (B) with only those rights as are granted to all other end users pursuant to the terms and conditions herein. Unpublished-rights reserved under copyright laws of the United States.

(8)   Licensee is hereby notified that Adobe Systems Incorporated, a Delaware corporation located at 345 Park Avenue, San Jose, CA 95110-2704 ("Adobe") is a third-party beneficiary to this Agreement to the extent that this Agreement contains provisions which relate to Licensee's use of the Software, the Documentation and the trademarks licenses hereby. Such provisions are made expressly for the benefit of Adobe and are enforceable by Adobe in addition to Licensor.

Adobe is a trademark of Adobe Systems Incorporated which may be registered in certain jurisdictions.

EQUILIBRIUM DEBABELIZER PRO DEMO END USER LICENSE AGREEMENT

Equilibrium grants you a non-exclusive license to use this demonstration version of Equilibrium DeBabelizer Pro for Windows95/NT (the "Software") free of charge for the sole purpose of evaluating whether to purchase an ongoing license to the Software. The evaluation period is limited to 90 days. Under this license, you may use the Software on a single computer only. Hard-copy documentation, support, and telephone assistance are not available to users of this demo version.

Under this license, you may not:

- use the Software in actual production;
- use the Software over a network or on multiple computers;
- copy or reproduce the Software; or
- modify, translate, reverse engineer, decompile, disassemble or create derivative works based on the Software.

The Software is Equilibrium's property and title thereto remains in Equilibrium. All applicable rights in copyrights, trademarks, and trade secrets in the Software are retained by Equilibrium.

EQUILIBRIUM PROVIDES THIS SOFTWARE ON AN "AS-IS" BASIS, AND MAKES NO REPRESENTATIONS OR WARRANTIES OF ANY KIND, INCLUDING WITHOUT LIMITATION THE WARRANTIES OF MERCHANTABILITY, FITNESS FOR A PARTICULAR PURPOSE AND NON-INFRINGEMENT. The entire risk as to the quality, performance, and use of this demonstration version is borne by you.

This license terminates 90 days from the installation of the Software on your computer, and will automatically terminate earlier if you fail to comply with the limitations described herein. On termination, you must destroy all copies of the Software.

This agreement represents the complete agreement concerning this license and may be amended only by a written agreement signed by both parties. If any provision of this agreement is held to be unenforceable, such provision shall be reformed only to the extent necessary to make it enforceable. This agreement shall be governed by California law (except for conflict of law provisions).

LICENSE AGREEMENT AND LIMITED WARRANTY

READ THE FOLLOWING TERMS AND CONDITIONS CAREFULLY BEFORE OPENING THIS SOFTWARE MEDIA PACKAGE. THIS LEGAL DOCUMENT IS AN AGREEMENT BETWEEN YOU AND PRENTICE-HALL, INC. (THE "COMPANY"). BY OPENING THIS SEALED SOFTWARE MEDIA PACKAGE, YOU ARE AGREEING TO BE BOUND BY THESE TERMS AND CONDITIONS. IF YOU DO NOT AGREE WITH THESE TERMS AND CONDITIONS, DO NOT OPEN THE SOFTWARE MEDIA PACKAGE. PROMPTLY RETURN THE UNOPENED SOFTWARE MEDIA PACKAGE AND ALL ACCOMPANYING ITEMS TO THE PLACE YOU OBTAINED THEM FOR A FULL REFUND OF ANY SUMS YOU HAVE PAID.

1.   **GRANT OF LICENSE:** In consideration of your payment of the license fee, which is part of the price you paid for this product, and your agreement to abide by the terms and conditions of this Agreement, the Company grants to you a nonexclusive right to use and display the copy of the enclosed software program (hereinafter the "SOFTWARE") on a single computer (i.e., with a single CPU) at a single location so long as you comply with the terms of this Agreement. The Company reserves all rights not expressly granted to you under this Agreement.

2.   **OWNERSHIP OF SOFTWARE:** You own only the magnetic or physical media (the enclosed software media) on which the SOFTWARE is recorded or fixed, but the Company retains all the rights, title, and ownership to the SOFTWARE recorded on the original software media copy(ies) and all subsequent copies of the SOFTWARE, regardless of the form or media on which the original or other copies may exist. This license is not a sale of the original SOFTWARE or any copy to you.

3.   **COPY RESTRICTIONS:** This SOFTWARE and the accompanying printed materials and user manual (the "Documentation") are the subject of copyright. You may not copy the Documentation or the SOFTWARE, except that you may make a single copy of the SOFTWARE for backup or archival purposes only. You may be held legally responsible for any copying or copyright infringement which is caused or encouraged by your failure to abide by the terms of this restriction.

4.   **USE RESTRICTIONS:** You may not network the SOFTWARE or otherwise use it on more than one computer or computer terminal at the same time. You may physically transfer the SOFTWARE from one computer to another provided that the SOFTWARE is used on only one computer at a time. You may not distribute copies of the SOFTWARE or Documentation to others. You may not reverse engineer, disassemble, decompile, modify, adapt, translate, or create derivative works based on the SOFTWARE or the Documentation without the prior written consent of the Company.

5.   **TRANSFER RESTRICTIONS:** The enclosed SOFTWARE is licensed only to you and may not be transferred to any one else without the prior written consent of the Company. Any unauthorized transfer of the SOFTWARE shall result in the immediate termination of this Agreement.

6.   **TERMINATION:** This license is effective until terminated. This license will terminate automatically without notice from the Company and become null and void if you fail to comply with any provisions or limitations of this license. Upon termination, you shall destroy the Documentation and all copies of the SOFTWARE. All provisions of this Agreement as to warranties, limitation of liability, remedies or damages, and our ownership rights shall survive termination.

7.   **MISCELLANEOUS:** This Agreement shall be construed in accordance with the laws of the United States of America and the State of New York and shall benefit the Company, its affiliates, and assignees.

8.   **LIMITED WARRANTY AND DISCLAIMER OF WARRANTY:** The Company warrants that the SOFTWARE, when properly used in accordance with the Documentation, will operate in substantial conformity with the description of the SOFTWARE set forth in the Documentation. The Company does not warrant that the SOFTWARE will meet your requirements or that the operation of the SOFTWARE will be uninterrupted or error-free. The Company warrants that the media on which the SOFTWARE is delivered shall be free from defects in materials and workmanship under normal use for a period of thirty (30) days from the date of your purchase. Your only remedy and the Company's only obligation under these limited warranties is, at the Company's option, return of the warranted item for a refund of any amounts paid by you or replacement of the item. Any replacement of SOFTWARE or media under the warranties shall not extend the original warranty period. The limited warranty set forth above shall not apply to any SOFTWARE which

the Company determines in good faith has been subject to misuse, neglect, improper installation, repair, alteration, or damage by you. EXCEPT FOR THE EXPRESSED WARRANTIES SET FORTH ABOVE, THE COMPANY DISCLAIMS ALL WARRANTIES, EXPRESS OR IMPLIED, INCLUDING WITHOUT LIMITATION, THE IMPLIED WARRANTIES OF MERCHANTABILITY AND FITNESS FOR A PARTICULAR PURPOSE. EXCEPT FOR THE EXPRESS WARRANTY SET FORTH ABOVE, THE COMPANY DOES NOT WARRANT, GUARANTEE, OR MAKE ANY REPRESENTATION REGARDING THE USE OR THE RESULTS OF THE USE OF THE SOFTWARE IN TERMS OF ITS CORRECTNESS, ACCURACY, RELIABILITY, CURRENTNESS, OR OTHERWISE.

IN NO EVENT, SHALL THE COMPANY OR ITS EMPLOYEES, AGENTS, SUPPLIERS, OR CONTRACTORS BE LIABLE FOR ANY INCIDENTAL, INDIRECT, SPECIAL, OR CONSEQUENTIAL DAMAGES ARISING OUT OF OR IN CONNECTION WITH THE LICENSE GRANTED UNDER THIS AGREEMENT, OR FOR LOSS OF USE, LOSS OF DATA, LOSS OF INCOME OR PROFIT, OR OTHER LOSSES, SUSTAINED AS A RESULT OF INJURY TO ANY PERSON, OR LOSS OF OR DAMAGE TO PROPERTY, OR CLAIMS OF THIRD PARTIES, EVEN IF THE COMPANY OR AN AUTHORIZED REPRESENTATIVE OF THE COMPANY HAS BEEN ADVISED OF THE POSSIBILITY OF SUCH DAMAGES. IN NO EVENT SHALL LIABILITY OF THE COMPANY FOR DAMAGES WITH RESPECT TO THE SOFTWARE EXCEED THE AMOUNTS ACTUALLY PAID BY YOU, IF ANY, FOR THE SOFTWARE.

SOME JURISDICTIONS DO NOT ALLOW THE LIMITATION OF IMPLIED WARRANTIES OR LIABILITY FOR INCIDENTAL, INDIRECT, SPECIAL, OR CONSEQUENTIAL DAMAGES, SO THE ABOVE LIMITATIONS MAY NOT ALWAYS APPLY. THE WARRANTIES IN THIS AGREEMENT GIVE YOU SPECIFIC LEGAL RIGHTS AND YOU MAY ALSO HAVE OTHER RIGHTS WHICH VARY IN ACCORDANCE WITH LOCAL LAW.

ACKNOWLEDGMENT

YOU ACKNOWLEDGE THAT YOU HAVE READ THIS AGREEMENT, UNDERSTAND IT, AND AGREE TO BE BOUND BY ITS TERMS AND CONDITIONS. YOU ALSO AGREE THAT THIS AGREEMENT IS THE COMPLETE AND EXCLUSIVE STATEMENT OF THE AGREEMENT BETWEEN YOU AND THE COMPANY AND SUPERSEDES ALL PROPOSALS OR PRIOR AGREEMENTS, ORAL, OR WRITTEN, AND ANY OTHER COMMUNICATIONS BETWEEN YOU AND THE COMPANY OR ANY REPRESENTATIVE OF THE COMPANY RELATING TO THE SUBJECT MATTER OF THIS AGREEMENT.

Should you have any questions concerning this Agreement or if you wish to contact the Company for any reason, please contact in writing at the address below.

Robin Short
Prentice Hall PTR
One Lake Street
Upper Saddle River, New Jersey 07458

ABOUT THE CD-ROM

We have included a number of software products referred to or covered in this book on an accompanying CD-ROM. They include utilities, demonstration versions of software packages and other information. We have also included an Adobe Acrobat hypertext version of the entire book. This may prove useful as a reference or help text when learning or using your audio or video editing software. It is identical to the print book with the added advantage that many of the illustrations, in particular the screen captures, are in color. This will enable you to have a much clearer view of the effects illustrated. Please don't distribute this file to others who haven't purchased the book. We depend on royalties from these efforts to make a living and to be able to write more books. Thanks!

The software on the CD-ROM are Windows versions. The MAC version, when available, and more recent versions of the demos are also often available from the publisher's websites. You can also visit our website, www.JonesSquare.com/videosquare for links and updates. The individual requirements to run the demos are contained in the readme files in their respective directories. Generally, however, a Pentium with 16 MB or more and a good amount of disk drive space is required. Check the aboutcd.txt file on the root directory of the CD-ROM for the final table of contents and last minute details.

DISK CONTENTS

Acroread

This directory contains the Adobe Acrobat reader required to read the hypertext version of the book in the Bookfiles directory. To install select either the 16 or 32 bit versions contained in subdirectories, then click on the .exe file to install.

After_fx

This directory contains the Adobe AfterEffects demo. It only works on Windows95 or NT 4.0 or above. Click on Setup.exe in the Disk1 subdirectory.

Bookfiles

This directory contains the Adobe Acrobat hypertext files of the book. There is a file for each chapter and book section. They are indicated by the file names: ch01.pdf indicates that it is Chapter 1.

Photoshp

This directory contains an Adobe Photoshop demo version. Click on Setup.exe in the Disk1 subdirectory.

Xtras

This directory contains dependent files for some of the demos.

Root Directory

The root directory contains setup files and associate files for:

Demo versions of Kinetix 3D StudioMax. Read MaxRead.txt for more information. Click on MaxSetup.exe to install.

Technical Support

Prentice Hall does not offer technical support for this demo software; contact the software vendor directly. However, if there is a problem with the media, you may obtain a replacement copy by e-mailing us with your problem at: disc_exchange@prenhall.com